'Truly great cities,' writes Jonathan heady mix of the planned and the the irrational, the dreamlike and is this more true than in Bath, which in the eighteenth century was transformed from a small provincial spa to one of the most fashionable and architecturally dazzling cities in the world.

By the end of the eighteenth century, Bath was the tenth largest city in the country. In the early years of the following century, however, its star suddenly faded and growth came to a virtual standstill. For the past 200 years the city's residents have struggled to come to terms with that extraordinary legacy.

These fifteen walks, published to coincide with the 25th anniversary of Bath's designation as a World Heritage Site, explore the resonances of that legacy today. As well as shedding new light on familiar landmarks, they go in search of hidden treasures in out-of-the way corners, before heading out to explore old villages absorbed by the city.

Bath is one of the best cities in the world for walking. Not only is it compact enough to explore on foot, but it is surrounded by unspoilt countryside whose beauty is matched by its variety. Less than half an hour's walk in almost any direction will take you from the heart of the city to wooded hills and secluded combes that have changed little since Jane Austen walked them over two centuries ago. City and country are more inextricably linked in Bath than anywhere else in Britain and these walks do full justice to that unique inheritance.

Lavishly illustrated, with photographs, engravings and archive maps to guide you on, these walks range from gentle strolls around the city's streets to challenging climbs through woods and along country lanes to visit spectacular buildings high in the hills above. Nine of the walks are step-free or have step-free alternatives indicated, and all start and end in the heart of the city.

Andrew Swift is the author and co-author of several books on Bath and regularly contributes walk features to *The Bath Magazine* and *The Bristol Magazine*. He has also devised and led guided walks for groups and organisations including the Bath Literature Festival and the Bath International Music Festival.

A fine Sunday in Bath empties every house of its inhabitants, and all the world appears on such an occasion to walk about and tell their acquaintance what a charming day it is.

Jane Austen, *Northanger Abbey*

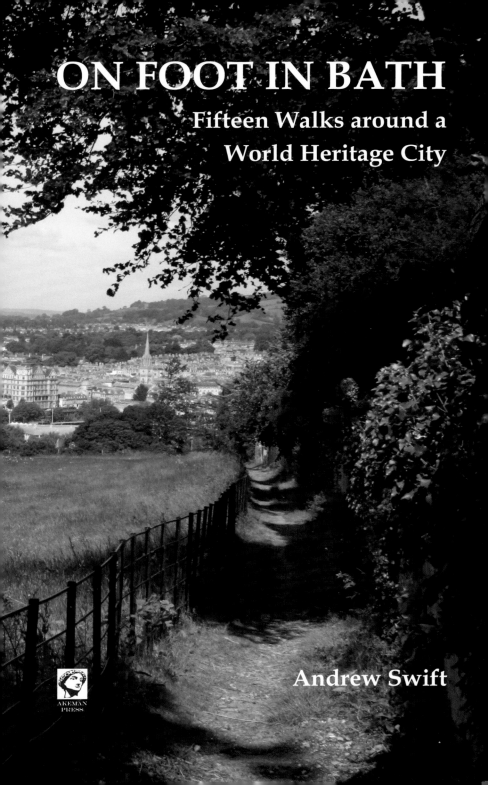

ON FOOT IN BATH

Fifteen Walks around a
World Heritage City

Andrew Swift

AKEMAN
PRESS

Published by AKEMAN PRESS
www.akemanpress.com

ISBN 978-0-9560989-4-8

Printed by Butler Tanner & Dennis, Frome, Somerset

CONTENTS

FOREWORD

There was a time, until quite recently, when I thought I had actually got to know this great city as well as any locally born Bathonian. I was happy to advise visitors that a great way to learn about Bath's nooks, crannies and out-of-the-way architectural delights was to ride on the top deck of a tour bus, because few people ever look up when walking and a seat on an open-top double-decker would fill in the gaps. I did walk the streets of Lambridge – all of them – when I first became a local councillor, because it was the only sure way of getting to know one's 'patch' but the gradual onset of osteoarthritis coupled with an extremely dodgy hip, seriously reduced my walking range and Shank's pony was replaced by a trusty 1974 Trabant motor car with a 2-stroke engine. These days the little yellow Trabbie is my preferred mode of transport but when the proof pages of *On Foot In Bath* arrived on my computer screen and I began to read about Andrew Swift's epic trundles, it struck me how much I missed walking for pleasure.

It was the ancient Chinese philosopher Lau Tzu who famously wrote, 'The journey of a thousand miles begins beneath one's feet' and the 'walks' devised and undertaken by Andrew in this incredibly detailed book must have totalled that number; if not in actual mileage, then certainly a combination of shoe leather and the range accounted for by the mind's eye. Nothing is glossed over in the author's quest for a definitive work to compare with the legendary Wainwright and as a Bath guide-book, it's just about as good as it gets and will not be bettered for years to come.

Andrew Swift has approached his subject with the mind of a scholar but left room for his strong personality and wry humour to permeate the chapters and create a thoroughly readable and hugely entertaining book. The fact that Swift loves Bath shines through in every page and he obviously deeply resents those who would tamper with its history and fabric. You can detect from Andrew Swift's gentle humour that he clearly laments the destruction of so much of old Bath in the name of 'progress'.

The reader will notice the reference on various walks to the lack of public toilets, and this must be of great concern to those who embark on frequent trips to the continent, where it is par for the course to simply pop into a café or bar for a comfort-break (as the Americans put it) but here we shrug our shoulders and press on regardless. Keep calm and carry on, as they said during World War Two!

Those of you who read the earlier *Literary Walks In Bath* by Andrew Swift & Kirsten Elliott, will want this as a companion volume, because both are inextricably linked. *On Foot In Bath* takes no prisoners when it comes to exploring every little wrinkle that makes up this amazing city's history, architecture, streetscapes, industrial heritage and, above all, its people. Bath might be a UNESCO World Heritage Site but, in the grand scheme of things it's still a small city with a village attitude – and the latter is what makes it so special. It's what prompted Andrew and Kirsten to formulate their 'walks', where people were encouraged to appreciate alternative aspects of Bath and absorb intricate details of its past at the hands of two highly experienced and popular local historians.

A fair number of buildings were destroyed or damaged during the bombing raids of 1942 but it was often said in later years that the city planners wreaked more havoc on Bath then the Luftwaffe ever did. Alan Bennett summed it up in 1994 when he wrote: 'I wish the sixties hadn't happened because that was when avarice and stupidity got to the wheel of the bulldozer. They called it enterprise and still do.' The beloved John Betjemen was equally dismissive of the modernists and wrote: 'Goodbye to old Bath. We who loved you are sorry – they've carted you off by developer's lorry.'

Fortunately for us, the destruction was halted in the nick of time and there is still much of the old city to be seen. The author has illustrated *On Foot In Bath* with an enormous cross-section of photographs and early prints, ranging from the grandeur of the famed Royal Crescent, through to faded Victorian set-pieces and details of such bygones as link-snuffers and sedan-chair ramps. Andrew Swift has an excellent eye when it comes to selecting alternative views of familiar Bath scenes and an uncanny knack of homing in on fascinating detail. I like, too, his inclusion of areas like Twerton and Lyncombe, which both played their part in the industrial past of this great city. Twerton, in particular, has much to offer the discerning walker who flinches at the heady slopes of Lyncombe, Widcombe, or Bathwick. My own ward, Lambridge, has been well researched but one feels that there is still more to come from the indominitable, indefatigable and hugely entertaining Andrew Swift.

I was personally drawn to the author's observations about various aspects of Bath's industrial past, as this has been a theme of mine as Mayor (2011-12) and currently Member Champion for Heritage & Historic Environment. The fact that Bath had breweries, coal mining, furniture manufacture, crane building, printing, book binding and milling, and many other industries, seems to have escaped the attention of so many of the city's chroniclers, but I suspect that such omissions are due more to snobbery than ignorance. Jane Austen, Charles Dickens and Richard 'Beau' Nash are still huge tourist draws but mention the name of Thomas Fuller in Canada, and you'll be greeted by sighs of adoration. Bath-born Fuller was responsible for the design of the Newark Works which, in 1856, was the headquarters of the famed Stothert & Pitt engineering firm. After moving to Canada, he designed the Parliament Buildings in Ottawa and became one of North America's most iconic architects – and yet you will find little or no mention of him in the city of his birth. If

Thomas Fuller's image was good enough for Canada's $10 bill, why airbrush him from Bath's history? It's little details like this that provide grist for Andrew Swift's literary mill. He ducks and dives, weaves and spins and you can almost hear a chortle as Andrew discovers another hitherto unsung treasure, such as a minute piece of medieval masonry or fragment of half-timbered building lurking between Bath's meandering Georgian streets. He is quick to focus on faded Victorian and Edwardian advertising signs still to be seen on buildings in Larkhall, Walcot and the City Centre – and rightly so. In drawing our attention to these period commercials, we might yet see them preserved for future generations – but then so many of us said that about the much-lamented Churchill House.

You don't have to live in the past to live with the past and that is essentially what *On Foot In Bath* is about. It records Bath as it is now and if you have Andrew Swift's stamina, or can pace yourself between any pubs left open in this age of austerity, then the book must rate as an essential read and permanent companion.

Councillor Bryan Chalker,
Member Champion for Heritage & Historic Environment,
Bath & North East Somerset Council

INTRODUCTION

Bath was accorded World Heritage status by UNESCO in 1987. Unlike most World Heritage cities, the whole of Bath, not just its major buildings, is included in the World Heritage Site. This is largely because the city's setting is as important as its buildings. One of the main attractions of the city for eighteenth-century visitors was the surrounding countryside. The hills encircling the city not only provided dramatic sites for many of its most memorable buildings but also afforded viewpoints from which the

city could be surveyed. Almost miraculously, over two centuries later the integrity of Bath's rural setting remains largely intact.

These fifteen walks explore the whole of the World Heritage Site, starting within the old walled city before venturing out to discover little-known delights in the byways, lanes and footpaths round about. By encompassing the whole of the World Heritage Site, the walks also take in much that has been overlooked or marginalised in previous explorations of Bath's heritage. Bath was an important industrial centre, and an understanding of how the city expanded and reinvented itself in the nineteenth and twentieth centuries is as crucial to an understanding of its heritage as the more familiar story of its eighteenth-century heyday.

Heritage – despite the backward-looking resonances of the term – is not something fixed and inviolable, nor is it something confined to museums and tourist honeypots. Like history, it is ever evolving. Significant components of Bath's heritage – including a large chunk of one of the world's first railway stations – disappeared as this book was being written. Many more hang in the balance. The highest-profile loss over the last decade was that of Churchill House, a 1930s neo-classical building demolished, despite mass protests, to make way for a bus station. Today, though, that bus station, whether we like it or not, is part of Bath's heritage. Most changes, though, go largely unremarked and unrecorded. Viewed in isolation, the closure of a shop, the realignment of a road, the cleaning of a grimy building may not amount to much. Taken together, over time, however, they constitute that inevitable process of change in which creation is the corollary of destruction. As TS Eliot wrote in 1940,

> In succession
> Houses rise and fall, crumble, are extended,
> Are removed, destroyed, restored, or in their place
> Is an open field, or a factory, or a by-pass.
> Old stone to new building, old timber to new fires,
> Old fires to ashes, and ashes to the earth.

Attempting to understand and engage with our heritage – in the broadest sense of the term – is our best hope for creating a sustainable vision for the future. To put it another way, the best way of working out where we go from here is to understand how we got here in the first place.

BATH: A CITY FOR WALKING

Bath is one of the best cities in the world to explore on foot. Not only is it compact, its streets seem designed to lead the walker constantly on, with new surprises round just about every corner. Although it is hilly, this means that vistas are always changing, with magnificent prospects opening up in the most unlikely places. One of the glories of Bath is the way sunlight falls on Bath stone, with shadows ever shifting, so that, however many times you see a particular building, there is always the possibility of seeing it – literally – in a new light.

Walking in Bath has an illustrious tradition. It formed part of the health cure that many came for in the eighteenth century. When it was too cold or too muddy to walk in the fields and woods around the city, visitors promenaded along specially-designed parades or strolled around pleasure gardens. In 1742, John Wood wrote that, 'when noon approaches ... some of the company appear on the Grand Parade, and other public walks, where a rotation of walking is continued for about two hours ... There are others who divert themselves with ... walking in Queen Square, and in the meadows round about the city.' One of the keenest walkers was Thomas Gainsborough. Although he came to Bath to work as a portrait painter, one of his chief delights was to head for the hills and valleys around the city, where he could indulge his passion for sketching rural scenes.

As you walk round the city's streets, you never lose sight for very long of the green hills that encircle them. Bath is surrounded by unspoilt countryside, whose beauty is matched by its variety. Much of it belongs to the National Trust, which owns around 10% of the land within the World Heritage Site. This not only preserves public access to it, but guarantees it will never be built on. Less than half an hour's walk in almost any direction will take you to the heart of the country. And, if the prospect of climbing

those hills seems a little daunting, here are a few reassuring words from John Wood:

> The difficulty of ascending our hills is not so great as is generally reported; but when surmounted, what beautiful prospects do they give? And what fine air do the invalids breathe in upon them? I will venture to say, that ... so many beautiful points of view, and matters of curiosity may be found about Bath, as conducive to the health and pleasure of mankind in general, as can be met with in ten times the space of ground in any other country.

THE PERILS OF PEDESTRIANISM

Despite Bath's unparalleled advantages as a walking centre, the needs of twenty-first century residents and visitors in what is still a busy – and remarkably compact – city inevitably create conflicts of interest. Bath's streets were not designed for cars, still less for coaches and lorries, and a combination of heritage concerns and geography has so far frustrated all efforts to divert traffic away from the city centre. Although the walks in this book take advantage of pedestrian crossings wherever possible, there are times when you will have to cross busy roads, taking extreme care and not assuming that motorists will give way to you.

One area where extreme care needs to be taken is that around the railway and bus stations. In theory, this should be one of the most pedestrian-friendly parts of the city, but Dorchester and Manvers Streets, when they are not mired in gridlock, present so many conflicting traffic movements that pedestrians are made very aware that they are second-class users of the public space and need to be mindful of potential hazards.

Another hazard, of which you need to be constantly aware, is the state of the pavements. Many paving stones are loose and uneven because they are old; many others are uneven because cars, vans and lorries park on them. The result is the same, and pedestrians – especially pedestrians wandering around looking up at buildings – need to keep a close eye on where they are walking. The pavements of Bath do not make for soft landings.

Those with mobility difficulties are faced with other problems. Given the city's history, this may seems a little odd. Bath grew rich in the eighteenth century catering for invalids, many of whom were suffering from gout or other complaints that made walking difficult. From their lodgings they made daily trips to the pump room and the baths to take the waters and bathe in the healing springs. You would think it would have been made as easy as possible for them to get around – but it wasn't. This was because they were carried in sedan chairs – glass-windowed boxes carried on poles by two strong men, for whom steps were not a problem. By the time sedan chairs disappeared in the nineteenth century, the city, with all its imperfections, had been built.

Problems of access in Bath have been recognised. A consultation draft for the World Heritage Site Management Plan identifies the 'need to address tensions between conservation and the desirability of providing physical access … for as many people as possible.' It will not be easy.

Very few old buildings in Bath have level access. Most have steps up to their entrances; the really old ones have steps down (indicating that the street level has been raised since they were built). This means that wheelchair access to most pubs, cafés, restaurants and shops is difficult. Another problem is that most of Bath's streets were laid out before the advent of dropped pavements. Although this deficiency is slowly being remedied, parking space is at such a premium that you are likely to find dropped pavements blocked by cars, vans or coaches. And, as if Bath's pavements were not narrow enough, they are cluttered up with A-boards. In April 2012, however, the council decided that enough was enough and decreed that anyone using an A-board had to leave at least 1.5m width of pavement for pedestrians.[1]

Nine of the walks in this book are either step-free or, where there are steps, have step-free alternatives.[2] However, it should be borne in mind that much of Bath is built on the slopes of the Avon valley and some of its streets are very steep.

TAKING THE AIR

Although air quality is a universal problem, it is particularly so in Bath. Not only is there a lot of traffic in the city, it spends a lot of time in queues. Bath's situation at the bottom of a valley surrounded by high hills means that pollution often cannot escape, which is especially bad news for asthmatics or those with respiratory problems.

As over 90% of pollution is caused by traffic, it follows that the worst affected areas are those with the highest concentrations of traffic.[3]

Two of the walks in this book – No 4 (Walcot Street and the Paragon) and No 5 (Larkhall and the London Road) – include some of the worst affected areas, although most of the walks include short stretches along busy roads.

PUBLIC INCONVENIENCES

The walks in this book are littered with references to closed public toilets. A century ago, public-spirited councillors established them to discourage

---

1 More information can be found at www.bathnes.gov.uk/a-boards.

2 Walks 1, 2 and 13 are step-free; in walks 3, 4, 5, 6, 7 and 14 step-free alternatives are indicated.

3 Monitoring in 2009 established that national air quality objectives were not being met in several areas. Worst affected were St James's Parade and the west end of the London Road, with an average annual concentration of nitrogen dioxide in excess of 60 $\mu g/m^3$ (the objective is 40 $\mu g/m^3$). Other black spots (with average annual concentrations in excess of 50 $\mu g/m^3$) included Bathwick Street, Broad Street, the Paragon, Manvers Street, Beckford Road, Windsor Bridge and the bottom of Wells Road. Information on current pollution levels can be found on the internet at uk-air.defra.gov.uk. Although an Air Quality Action Plan for Bath was adopted by the council in April 2011, it will obviously take some time to implement.

people from relieving themselves in the open, as had previously been the custom. That was, however, when most people did not have their own means of transport and walked everywhere. The growth of car ownership in the last 50 years means that walking is now the exception rather than the norm. Hardly surprising then that, when cuts are made, public toilets are easy targets.

All of which makes life somewhat difficult for the urban walker. There is always the option of nipping into a pub, shop or café and asking to use their facilities, but not everyone is happy with this, and you are likely, in busier spots at least, to find signs informing you that toilets are for the use of customers only.

There are, however, still a few public toilets in the city centre, along with some in the suburbs (although it is anyone's guess as to how secure their future is) and each of the walks is prefaced by information on the facilities available en route.

WALKING AT NIGHT

Bath is one of the safest cities in the country, certainly in the daytime and, in the majority of places, after dark as well. Although none of the walks in this book is designed to be undertaken at night, certain parts of the city look even better after dark. The view of Pulteney Bridge and weir, especially from the viewing platform down the steps from Argyle Street, is magical at night, as is the view along Great Pulteney Street. Other spots worth visiting at night include the Abbey Church Yard, the High Street (dominated by the floodlit Abbey), Queen Street (especially after rain), the Circus, the Royal Crescent, Abbey Green and Lilliput Alley (North Parade Passage). However, there are a few places which, although safe by day, are probably best avoided after dark – but, as they are not lit up, you are unlikely to want to go there anyway. These include the city's parks and the paths alongside the river and canal.

ON FOOT IN BATH

A FEW OTHER PRACTICALITIES

All the walks start outside the Visitor Information Centre on Kingston Parade.[1] With the Abbey to the north and the Roman Baths on the west, this is about as central as you can get. Another advantage is that – except when the Christmas Market is on – it is relatively quiet and has a large number of seats, so it is a good place for meeting up or for a spot of preliminary reading before setting off on the walks.

Each of the walks is accompanied by an old map – dating from the early nineteenth to the mid-twentieth centuries – with the route of the walk superimposed on it. Although there have inevitably been changes since the maps were published, in most cases it is surprisingly easy to find your way around using these old maps. And, as detailed instructions appear in the text, any significant changes are easily dealt with. Old maps have been used not only because they are fascinating in their own right; they also give an idea how the city has evolved and reinforce the idea that you are walking in the footsteps of those who were here before you.

For ease of navigation, directions in the text appear in **bold type**.

Spelling and punctuation in old quotations have been modernised where this has been possible without altering the meaning.

Every attempt has been made to ensure all information is accurate, but it is almost inevitable that in a book which covers so much ground some errors will creep in. Changes to road layouts, provision of pedestrian crossings and so on may also mean that directions in the text will no longer apply. Please contact the publishers (at 58 Minster Way, Bath BA2 6RL or via info@akemanpress.com) so that any errors or anomalies can be corrected in future editions.

As well as being subjective, the walks are by necessity selective. These walks are intended as an introduction to the city rather than a comprehensive survey. If they inspire you to find out more, the reading list on page 277 should set you off on the right track.

---

1 Walk 5 and 14 also have alternative starting points.

1
WITHIN THE WALLS
The Old City

Distance *1.25 miles*

Time *2-3 hours*

Accessibility *Step-free, although with a lack of dropped pavements at points indicated in the text. There are steps at the entrances to the King's Bath/Pump Room and the Guildhall, although level access to both buildings is available.*

Public toilets *Pump Room/Roman Baths Museum, Abbey Church Yard; Monmouth Street (west of Sawclose at end of alleyway past Garrick's Head)*

Starting point *Kingston Parade (outside Visitor Information Centre)*

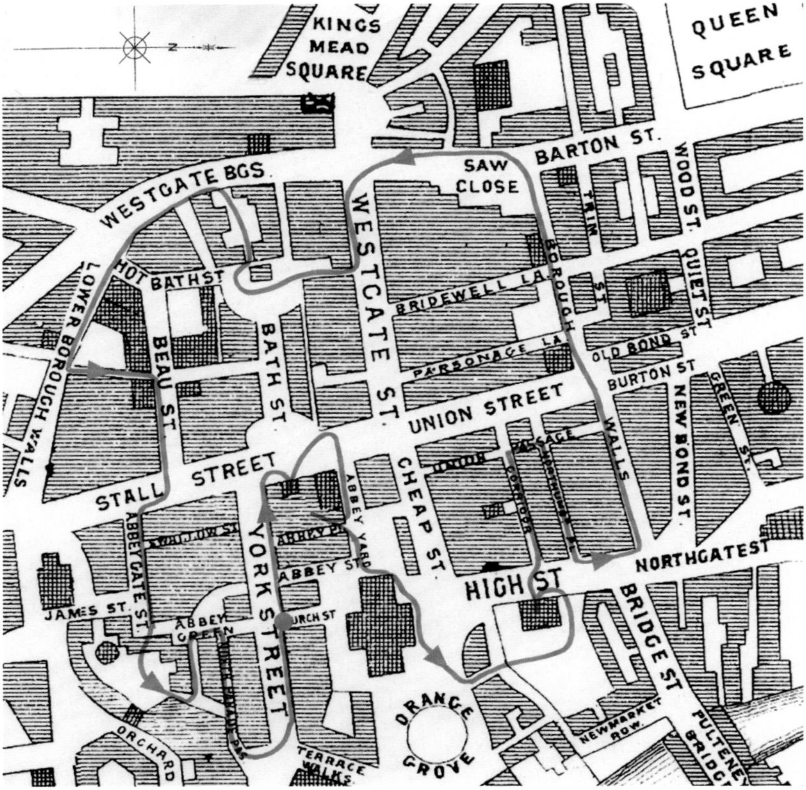

Opposite: The old East Gate, the only one of the city's medieval gates to survive

The dead were and are not. Their place knows them no more and is ours today ... The poetry of history lies in the quasi-miraculous fact that once, on this earth, once, on this familiar spot of ground, walked other men and women, as actual as we are today, thinking their own thoughts, swayed by their own passions, but now all gone, one generation vanishing into another, gone as utterly as we ourselves shall shortly be gone, like ghosts at cockcrow.

GM Trevelyan, 1949

The past is never dead. It's not even past.

William Faulkner, 1951

This walk explores the old walled city of Bath, which occupied a very small area – just 23 acres. The walls started off as a rampart built by the Romans. In the ninth century, King Alfred rebuilt the rampart as a wall, and this defined the city limits for the next 800 years. The map below, which dates from around 1600, shows that development outside the walls was confined to three streets – Walcot Street, Broad Street and Southgate Street. Within the walls, the street pattern followed that laid down in

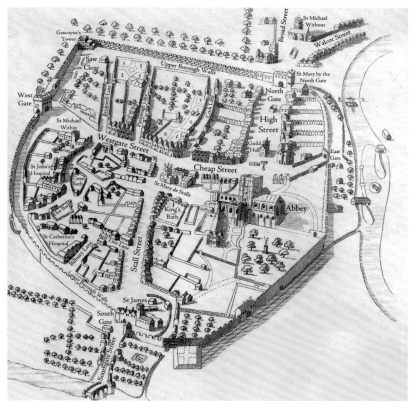

early medieval times. That pattern has survived largely intact, and, with a few modifications, it is still possible to use this 400-year-old map to find your way round Bath today.

The level of the city has risen significantly over the centuries, as buildings have been demolished and new ones built on their foundations, yet there is a real sense in which, as you walk the streets of the old city, you are treading in the footsteps of the Romans who walked here almost two thousand years ago. You can get a good idea what Roman Bath was like by visiting the Roman Baths Museum, but if you want to see what medieval Bath was like you have to search very hard. Alfred's walls, patched and repatched over the centuries, were torn down by order of the corporation in 1754. In the years that followed, the city was so comprehensively rebuilt that, apart from the Abbey, virtually nothing survives from before the seventeenth century.

More than a little imagination is required, therefore, to understand what the old city was like. Take Kingston Parade, where you are standing – or sitting – at the moment. If you have visited the Roman Baths, you will know that part of the baths lie under your feet. After the Romans left, the Saxons founded an abbey on the north side of the ruinous baths complex. It was rebuilt in the late eleventh century as a cathedral priory, and cloisters were laid out in the area where are you standing. In the late fifteenth century, the Norman cathedral was demolished and work started on a new one. In 1539, however, with the building still unfinished, the priory was dissolved by order of King Henry VIII and the cathedral was abandoned. The lead was stripped from its roof, the glass removed from its windows and houses built against its walls. In 1543, Matthew Coulthurst, MP for Bath, acquired it, largely, it seems, because he wanted to establish a tennis court on part of the site. It seemed only a matter of time before it would be as ruinous as the Roman Baths that preceded it.

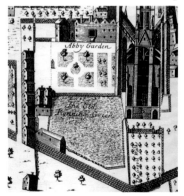

A map from around 1700 showing the 'Abby Garden' on the site of the cloisters, with a bowling green alongside it

In 1572, however, the corporation decided that the abandoned church – known henceforth as Bath Abbey – should become the city church. Matthew Coulthurst agreed to part with it and Queen Elizabeth authorised a nationwide appeal for its restoration. The cloisters and most of the outbuildings, however, were demolished, and for a time the land south of the Abbey became a garden. In the 1620s, new buildings started appearing on the southern edge of the garden. Some of them – including

Right: A map of 1852 showing the Kingston Baths and other buildings standing where Kingston Parade is today. To the west are the Pump Room and the King's and Queen's Baths. The pink-shaded buildings in between were demolished in the late nineteenth century when the Roman Baths were excavated.

Below: A late nineteenth-century photograph showing the recently-excavated Roman Baths before the colonnades and promenade were built around them.

Sally Lunn's tea room – survive, and are now among the oldest buildings in the city. In the mid-eighteenth century, a suite of private baths, fed by the hot springs, was built on the garden. They belonged to the Duke of Kingston, and when they were demolished in the early twentieth century, the open space created was called Kingston Parade.

The Roman Baths, meanwhile, lay forgotten about below all this development. Although evidence of Roman occupation survived in carvings and elaborately-crafted stonework incorporated into the city walls, it was not until archaeological investigations began in the eighteenth century that the scale of what had once existed here began to be appreciated. And not until the late nineteenth century were enough buildings cleared away for the baths to be revealed again after more than a millennium.

Having outlined the history of this corner of the old city, it is time to explore the rest of it. **Head west along York Street past Abbey Photo Service.** York Street dates from around 1796; the story goes that it was named after the Duchess of York, the first person to ride along it in a carriage. The life-size Roman centurion on the corner of Abbey Street – known as Ronnie the Roman – became a cause célèbre in 2007. Council officials ordered his removal, but backed down after hundreds of people signed a petition calling for him to stay.

On the opposite corner, the doorway of No 4 is flanked by splendid Corinthian columns. The fanlight over the door is believed to be the oldest wooden fanlight in the city. On the side wall of the building, the blocked-up archways indicate that this row of buildings originally carried on, but was cut back to make way for York Street.

The arch that spans York Street, with its splendid array of animal and human heads, was built in the late nineteenth century to carry water from the hot springs to a laundry. Although the laundry is no longer used, its tall chimney can be seen to the left along Swallow Street.

The plaque on the right-hand side of York Street was put up to mark the restoration of the Roman Baths in the nineteenth century. The Greek inscription means 'water is best'.

As you **turn right at the end of York Street**, the cold swimming bath at the west end of the Roman Baths complex lies directly beneath your feet. The grand portico on your right, beyond the Roman Baths shop, was the entrance to the King's and Queen's Baths. The pair of sphinxes in the pediment flank Hygeia, Greek goddess of health.

The entrance to the King's and Queen's Baths

Climb the steps, go through the entrance and turn left to where a viewing platform overlooks the King's Bath.[1] This was one of three medieval hot baths in the city, and the only one that still looks much as it did before Bath's eighteenth-century redevelopment. It was built in the

---

1 If you are following a step-free walk, you will have to forego a visit to the viewing platform. However, there is just as good a view over the King's Bath from the lobby of the Pump Room, which you will be visiting shortly.

twelfth century in the ruins of the buildings erected around the Sacred Spring by the Romans. In 1979, the floor of the King's Bath was removed and the water lowered to the level it was in Roman times. A rust-red stain indicates how far it once came up the walls. The statue of King Bladud on the right dates from the sixteenth century. The Queen's Bath – built in the sixteenth century and supplied with water from the King's Bath – lay behind the statue. It was demolished in 1885. To your left is the Pump Room, which you will be visiting shortly.

As you **head back out of the building**, look straight ahead to take in the prospect of Bath Street, the finest piece of urban design in the old city. Its quadrants create a semi-circular space in front of the entrance to the King's Bath, while the colonnades lead your eye to the Cross Bath at the end. No wonder, then, that the World Heritage symbol is set into the road at this point.

Bear right, crossing the street towards a colonnade of shops. This is one of the busiest parts

An early twentieth-century view of the King's Bath

Stall Street, for centuries one of the busiest parts of the city

of the city – as it has been for centuries – but if you stand by one of the columns to the right of the entrance to BHS you will be out of the way of passing crowds. Facing you is the high windowless wall of the Pump Room. It was designed, like the colonnade to the left of it, along with Bath Street and the entrance to the King's & Queen's Baths, by Thomas Baldwin and built between 1789 and 1806.

In Roman times, the spot where you are now standing was the religious and ceremonial heart of the city – the Temple of Sulis Minerva. After the Romans left, Stall Street was driven through the site and a church built – possibly as early as AD596 – where the cafés to the left of Baldwin's colonnade now stand. Known as St Mary de Stalls, it fell into disuse when the Abbey became the city church. After being used as a military prison and a hospital during the Civil War, it fell down in 1659.

Stall Street was the main north-south route through the medieval city. It got its name because of the stalls set up here by market traders; today's stallholders are upholding a long tradition. The colonnade under which you are standing dates from around 1960. One of Bath's top inns, the White Hart, once stood here. Despite featuring in Jane Austen's *Persuasion* and Charles Dickens' *Pickwick Papers*, it was demolished in 1867 and replaced by a large hotel which was itself demolished in 1959. To your left, the crossroads at the end of Stall Street was the site of the White Hart's great rival – the Bear. This was pulled down in 1805 to make way for the street you see today. It was called Union Street because it linked the old city with new developments to the north.

Cross the street and go through the colonnade into the Abbey Church Yard. On your right is the imposing façade of the Pump Room. This is the second pump room on the site. The first was built in 1705 when it was becoming fashionable not only to bathe but also to drink the waters that flowed from the hot springs. The Pump Room was the social hub of Georgian Bath and a morning visit was all but obligatory for visitors to the city. The original pump room was replaced by the present one in the 1790s because Bath's growing popularity meant that it could no longer cope with the numbers wishing to use it. If you look up to the architrave, you will see that it bears the same Greek inscription as the plaque in York Street.

The Pump Room

Go through the entrance to the Pump Room, turn left, then right and right again along a corridor with a sign directing you to 'spa water'.[1] This leads past a painting of an assembly in the original Pump Room, a portrait of Beau Nash, a panel devoted to Bladud and another window overlooking the King's Bath.

Carry on into the Pump Room, where you can take morning coffee or afternoon tea, serenaded, as you would have been in the eighteenth century, by a band of musicians. To your right is a clock by the celebrated clockmaker Thomas Tompion. Above it is a statue of Beau Nash holding plans for his pet project, the General Hospital. To your left is the portrait of someone else you will be encountering frequently in these walks – Ralph Allen. Beyond it is the pump from which spring water was served to those anxious to restore their health. They were advised to drink up to seven pints a day; should you be tempted to follow their example – and no visit to Bath is complete without taking the waters – you will probably regard

1 For step-free access, go through the entrance to the Roman Baths Museum (to the left of the entrance to the Pump Room), turn right and then left.

the meagre quantity dispensed today as more than adequate. Mr Pickwick's servant, Sam Weller, thought the taste similar to warm flat irons, a verdict which many have endorsed.

Head back out to the Abbey Church Yard and turn right. The extension to the Pump Room, which now forms the entrance to the Roman Baths, was built as a concert hall in the 1890s. To make way for it, several Georgian buildings

had to be demolished. Although unremarkable in themselves, their associations should have saved them for posterity. On the corner was Thomas Gainsborough's first home in Bath, which he continued to use as a studio and showroom throughout his time in the city. A couple of doors along from it was a building where Mary Shelley wrote part of *Frankenstein*.

On your left, the exuberant Baroque-style building with five giant pilasters was built around 1720 for General Wade, who was MP for Bath from 1722 to 1747. The shopfront was added later. The building to the right of it, although plainer, dates from the same time and is a fine example of an early eighteenth-century townhouse. Like everything else in the Abbey Church Yard, however, it is dominated by the west front of the Abbey. On the buttresses at either end you will see carvings of an olive tree encircled by a crown below a bishop's mitre. These are elaborate conceits known as rebuses: the mitre represents a bishop, the olive tree stands for the name Oliver (if you add an extra letter!) and the crown represents the king – which gives you Bishop Oliver King, who ordered the construction of the Abbey in the late fifteenth century.

Bishop King's most imaginative touch was the pair of ladders flanking the west window, with angels ascending and descending. The mason in charge of the project must have thought long and hard about how to distinguish between the two, before coming up with the rather unsatisfactory solution of showing the descending angels upturned and crawling Dracula-like down the ladder. According to legend, after being made Bishop of Bath & Wells in 1495, Oliver King had a dream in which he saw a host of angels on a ladder and heard a voice declaring, 'Let an Olive establish the Crown, and let a King restore the Church.' The bishop took this as a call for him to support King Henry VII as King and to restore – or indeed rebuild – the Abbey. A statue of King Henry VII, who supported the Abbey's rebuilding, appears above the main door.

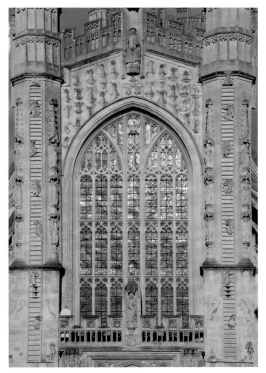

Above: The west front of Bath Abbey

Left from top: Bishop Oliver King's rebus; one of the angels climbing down the ladder; the statue of Henry VII

Below: 'The Lantern of the West' seen from the High Street

Opposite: The pump from which spa water was served to visitors, seen here in the mid-nineteenth century

The west front is a fitting introduction to this superb building. Although a tour of the interior does not feature in this walk, it should form part of every visitor's itinerary. Architecturally, it is a tour de force, with breathtaking fan vaulting and an interior flooded with light. With its 52 windows occupying around 80% of the wall space, it is no surprise that it has long been known as 'the Lantern of the West'. The memorials that line its walls not only provide a vivid record of those who lived and died in Bath during in its Georgian heyday, but are adorned with evocative – and sometimes bizarre – carvings.

Go to the left of the Abbey and head for the fountain straight ahead. This portrays Rebecca from the Book of Genesis. Temperance campaigners placed it here in 1861 on the site of a notorious inn they had persuaded the council to demolish. Around its base, 'Water is Best' is inscribed in English. Standing by the fountain, look up to see the most impressive view of the Abbey, with the tower rising above a mighty flying buttress.

The wide street to your north – as likely as not full of buses – is the High Street. It was the widest street in the old city because for centuries it was the main market place. On the right-hand side is the Guildhall, the administrative centre of the city. The central section was designed by Thomas Baldwin in 1775; the extensions on either side were added in the late nineteenth century. The previous Guildhall stood in the middle of the High Street. It was supported on pillars and provided a covered space for market traders. In front of it were stocks and a pillory, where miscreants

The Guildhall before it was extended in the late nineteenth century

were confined by order of the mayor. The stocks still survive and, after years of languishing in a council store, were returned to the Guildhall at the instigation of the then mayor, Bryan Chalker, in 2012.

To your left, with London Camera Exchange on the corner, is Cheap Street. 'Cheap' was a medieval word for market, indicating that stalls were also set up here. To the right of Cheap Street is the Christopher Hotel – now renamed All Bar One, but with the old name still above the windows on the second floor. There were once several large hotels and inns in the High Street, but this is the only one to survive. It dates from the sixteenth century and, although the present façade and much of the interior is modern, a large and very old fireplace can be seen inside.

Carry on alongside the Abbey for a few metres before crossing two sets of pedestrian lights, turning right and walking along to the archway next to Brown's Restaurant. This is the only spot from which you can stand back and get a full view of the Abbey. Most other cathedrals and large churches are surrounded by an open space, but because of the Abbey's unusual history – abandoned then readopted as the city church – it is hemmed in by buildings on virtually every side. Before the buildings up against its northern and eastern walls were cleared away in the nineteenth century, it was boxed in on this side as well.

In the middle ages the area in front of you was the 'litten' or churchyard of the Abbey. In the seventeenth century it became a fashionable place for visitors to promenade and gravel walks were laid out. At first it was known as Mitre Green, but after rows of trees were planted its name changed to the Grove. The obelisk in the centre commemorates the visit of the Prince of Orange to Bath to take the waters in 1734. It was erected by Beau Nash to remind visitors of this royal endorsement of the city's hot springs, and the Grove was known henceforth as Orange Grove.

Apart from the obelisk and the Abbey, little of eighteenth-century Orange Grove survives. The shops on the south side, to the left of the

The Orange Grove and Abbey in the mid-nineteenth century

Abbey, were built around 1705 but refronted in the 1890s by a man who did more than most to change the face of Bath. He may not be the most famous of Bath's architects, but few people had a greater impact on the city than Major Charles Davis. The Abbey aside, present-day Orange Grove is largely his creation. He not only refronted the shops; he built Browns (originally the police station) and the archway beside it (originally the entrance to the fire station). Beyond Browns, the building that dominates Orange Grove was his crowning achievement. Opened in 1901 as the Empire Hotel, it is now an apartment complex.

The Empire Hotel

Over to the east, there is a view of wooded hills. There are few places in the city without a view – or at least a glimpse – of the country, and the way in which the urban landscape interacts with its surroundings is one of the most important aspects of the World Heritage Site. If you look towards the top of the hill, you should be able to make out a castellated building with two turrets on either side of a gothic archway. This is in fact a folly called Sham Castle, which consists of a wall with nothing behind it.

So far you have followed a fairly well-trodden path, but now you are heading where only the most enterprising visitors venture. **Go through the archway beside Brown's, turn right at the back of the building and walk down towards the large locked gate on the left.** Unpromising though this may look, it leads to one of the city's most remarkable – and most neglected – treasures. If you look through the bars of the gate you will see an archway. This is the old East Gate of the city. The lane leading through it, known as Boat Stall Lane, ran down to the river, following the original lie of the land. The ground was built up on either side of it in the eighteenth century so that buildings could be

WALK 1: WITHIN THE WALLS

raised high above the floods that regularly inundated this area. The East Gate only survived because it was in an unfashionable area. This part of town was the 'shambles', where animals were slaughtered and meat sold. The other gates, much grander and guarding the main roads out of the city, were demolished because they obstructed traffic. It is extraordinary to think that this subterranean survival from the distant past once stood high above the surrounding land and was flanked by mighty walls. Today, it is one of Bath's dingiest secret places; it is regrettable that, in a city with so little of its pre-Georgian heritage left, it should be hidden away behind a locked gate, down an alley lined with dustbins.

Boatstall Lane, leading down through the East Gate, on a map of around 1700. The old North Gate can be seen at top left

The entrance to the market from the High Street

As you turn around and **walk up from the gate**, the back of the Guildhall is in front of you. Behind the high windows on the first floor is the Banqueting Room. Its central window, although glazed, is false because there is a fireplace behind it. Leaving the wall blank would have destroyed the symmetry of the building; for the Georgians symmetry was everything, especially in a building as grand as this. But, as so often in Georgian Bath, grandeur here overlooked something far less refined. As a correspondent in the *Bath Chronicle* pointed out in 1775 when it was being built, 'the dining room will have an agreeable view of the raw meat in the shambles.'

Turn right past the back of the Guildhall and go through a door into the Guildhall Market.[1] Built in the 1860s, this is a hidden gem, and if you want to get under the skin of the real Bath this is a good place to start. Resolutely non-corporate and full of local businesses, you can stock up on ingredients for an al fresco lunch from its various stalls. The 1950s-themed Espresso Bar beneath the central dome is also an excellent place to take a break

1 If the market is closed, retrace your steps through the archway into the Orange Grove, turn right and right again into the High Street and walk along to the front of the Guildhall.

and see the market in action, while the deli near the main entrance is probably the only place in the city where you still find the local delicacy known as Bath Chaps.

Head to the left, past the eighteenth-century 'nail' where deals were transacted (and where the expression 'paying on the nail' comes from), **through the double doors beside the deli and out into the High Street. Turn left and walk along to the entrance to the Guildhall.** You will see that the stone here is curiously pitted; it was carved like this to give visual weight to the central section of the ground floor. It was said to look like worm casts, and the architectural term for it – vermiculation – is derived from 'vermiculus', Latin for 'worm'.

A costume ball in the Banqueting Room

The Corridor in the early twentieth century

If it is open, **go into the Guildhall** to ask at the reception desk if you can visit the Banqueting Room on the first floor.[1] Although functions and other events are held here, especially during festivals, it is normally open to the public at other times. This, despite several strong contenders for the title, is generally reckoned to be the finest room in the city. Magnificent in green and gold, lit by spectacular chandeliers, and lined with eighteenth-century portraits of royalty and nobility, it nevertheless has a warmth and charm that many other grand rooms lack.

Cross at the pedestrian lights in front of the Guildhall and carry straight on into the Corridor, one of the earliest shopping arcades – or malls – in existence. Designed by Henry Edmund Goodridge, it opened in 1825. Customers were originally serenaded by musicians in galleries overhead. As the galleries are still there, this is one tradition that seems worth reviving.

Turn right when you reach the two marble pillars at the end to walk

---

1 The step-free access to the Guildhall is by the entrance to the market.; there is a lift to the first floor.

along one of the oldest thoroughfares in the city. Although the buildings are no earlier than the eighteenth-century, the street dates back to medieval times, if not earlier, and indicates how narrow most of Bath's streets were before they were widened in the eighteenth and nineteenth centuries. It was originally known as Cock Lane, but, after a brief spell as Charlotte Place in the late eighteenth century, was renamed Union Passage around the time Union Street was built.[1]

Take the first right into Northumberland Place, built in the early eighteenth century and home to a range of small businesses, including the Coeur de Lion, Bath's smallest pub. Its stained-glass window is often thought to be Victorian; it actually dates from the 1950s. The Duke of York's coat of arms can be seen in the gable at the end. A jewellery shop in this building was patronised by the duke in the late eighteenth century and his coat of arms was installed on the front wall, facing the High Street. In the nineteenth century, when it became a post office, the duke's coat of arms was consigned to the back. This building is, as far as can be determined, the oldest in the city, and some of its original beams can be seen as you walk through the archway. It may not look that old, having been refurbished and refronted in the eighteenth century, but the core of the building probably dates from the fourteenth century.

Inside the Coeur de Lion, Bath's smallest pub

The Duke of York's coat of arms

When you reach the High Street, turn left and walk along to the corner of Upper Borough Walls. The North Gate, where most visitors entered the city, once straddled the street here. It was demolished in 1754, but the street that led through it is still called Northgate Street. The shops on the east side of the street stand on the site of the church of St Mary by the Northgate. Like St Mary de Stalls, this was deconsecrated

---

1 The suggestive overtones of the original name were almost certainly not accidental. Many towns and cities had back streets with similar names, indicating the sort of nefarious activities that went on there. There is still a Cock Lane in Smithfield in London, which dates back to medieval times and was once lined with brothels.

when the Abbey became the city church. Its fate was even more bizarre; the nave became the grammar school and the tower became the city jail. It was eventually demolished in 1773, but to find out why you will have to wait until Walk 7.

So far you have seen the East Gate and the site of the North Gate. To see where the West and South Gates stood, **turn left along Upper Borough Walls**. This started out as a walkway or 'rampire' along the top of the walls. In the seventeenth century, it was fashionable for visitors to promenade

here, admiring the views over open countryside. In the eighteenth century, it became a street with buildings on the left-hand side. When the wall was demolished, the houses on the right took its place, their front walls built on its foundations.

The buildings on the left are modern, and, while the façades on the right date from the eighteenth-century, everything behind them is modern. Above Brad Abrahams opticians you will see the letters SMP SPPP. There are many similar sets of letters around the city, indicating parish boundaries: SMP was St Michael's Parish, SPPP was St Peter & Paul's. Boundary markers were needed because each parish collected rates for such things as poor relief, and it was essential to know which parish buildings stood in.

The Royal Mineral Water Hospital

Further along, you will see Union Passage – or Cock Lane – rising up to meet Upper Borough Walls on the left. The next street on the left is Union Street, which you saw the southern end of earlier. Barton Street and Old Bond Street on the right were built after the walls were demolished.

On the far corner of Union Street is the Royal National Hospital for Rheumatic Diseases. Originally known as the General Hospital, it was designed by John Wood

WALK 1: WITHIN THE WALLS

and built in 1738-42. An extra storey was added in 1793. This is the hospital whose plans the statue of Beau Nash holds in the Pump Room. It provided care for people who came to Bath to be cured by bathing in the hot springs, but could not afford physicians' fees. It was renamed the Mineral Water Hospital in 1887; the 'Royal' followed in 1935. It received its current name in 1993. It is generally referred to, however, as the 'Min'.

As you continue along Upper Borough Walls, you will see an archway linking the hospital to an extension built in 1860. Despite the narrowness of Upper Borough Walls, elaborate sculptures were incorporated into the pediments of both buildings. Above the original hospital is an impressive Royal crest, while the extension has a tableau depicting the Good Samaritan.

The Good Samaritan on the Royal Mineral Water Hospital extension

The last surviving stretch of the city walls

The archway spans Parsonage Lane, whose name recalls a parsonage – home to the Rector of Bath Abbey – that was demolished when the extension was built. On the opposite side of the road, you finally come face to face with the city wall. This section survives because, from 1736 to 1849, there was a burial ground on the other side, reserved for patients who died in the hospital. As the ground could not be built on, there was no incentive to demolish the wall.

Although it gives an idea what the walls were like, the six-foot drop into the courtyard on the other side pales by comparison with the 20-foot drop into a ditch filled with filth and refuse you would have encountered three centuries ago.

From here, you can also get a good idea of the size of the walled city. Looking back, you can see where the North Gate stood. Looking the other way, the buildings at the end of the street mark the old city's western boundary. That was almost the full extent of the medieval city from east to west; it was roughly the same from north to south.

A little further along Upper Borough Walls, the street on the right marks the first point at which the walls were breached, in 1707. It is called Trim Bridge, because that is what it was – a bridge spanning the ditch to give access to a new street called Trim Street outside the walls. The bridge was demolished in 1769 and replaced by the street you see today.

Opposite is Bridewell Lane – originally known as Plum Tree Lane, but renamed when a barn was converted to a bridewell or house of correction in the 1630s. This forsaken by-way was once a bustling thoroughfare. When Jane Austen came to Bath in 1801, it was home to a muffin man, a whitesmith, a brushmaker, a druggist, a bacon seller, a pipe maker, two grocers, a baker, two pubs and a perfumer.

Continue along Upper Borough Walls, past the eclectic extravagance of the old Blue Coat School, built in 1860, **to the Sawclose**.[1] The Sawclose

71 BATH. — The Blue Coat School. — LL.

was so called because there was a timber yard and a sawpit here. It was here, however, that Beau Nash chose to live. The building straight ahead, now the Strada restaurant, was his second home in the city. He moved here when new laws restricting gambling drastically reduced his income and forced him to downsize. It is nevertheless an impressive building, and would be even more so if the theatre foyer had not been built up against it, consigning its main entrance, crowned with two dubious-looking eagles, to a cramped yard.

To see Beau Nash's first house, **turn left past the entrance to the theatre** and look to the right. Part of the house has been incorporated into the theatre, part is now the Garricks' Head pub – but try to imagine it as it looked in 1720, newly-built and standing in glorious isolation outside the city walls, and you will understand why Nash's contemporaries described it as a palace. Perhaps not surprisingly given its history, the Garrick's Head claims to be the most haunted pub in Bath. It is also one of Bath's top gastropubs, with an extensive range of wines and real ales. The Theatre Royal was built in 1805, but it was only after a disastrous fire in 1862 that it was extended and the current foyer built in the Sawclose. You will see the original entrance in Walk 2.

The Garrick's Head

---

1 There is a distinct lack of dropped pavements at this point; to avoid the high kerbs, turn left at the end of the Blue Coat School and right across the car park.

WALK 1: WITHIN THE WALLS

Top: Flan O'Briens, originally the County Wine Vaults

Above: Westgate House, with the old West Gate on the left

Below: The three orders of columns above the Grapes

The course of the city wall is marked by the row of modern buildings running down the west side of the Sawclose. The grey rubble-stone building opposite – now a bar – is one of the oldest in the city, dating from around 1636. To the left of it is the ornate façade of a music hall built in 1895 on the site of the old Hay and Straw Market, and now used as a Bingo Hall.

Continue down to the corner of Westgate Street. The large pub on the corner – now Flan O'Brien's but originally the County Wine Vaults – is one of the finest Victorian buildings in the city. The old West Gate stood on the right-hand side of the street. Beside it was Westgate House, where royal visitors to the city were accommodated. Beyond it lay Kingsmead Fields, developed in the seventeenth century as pleasure grounds. In May 1728, Princess Amelia, the daughter of King George II, watched from Westgate House as celebrations in her honour – including an ox roast, morris dancing and fireworks – were held on the fields.

The city walls continued southward, their course now indicated by the curve of Westgate Buildings, with Pizza Hut on the corner. Instead of following them, **turn left along Westgate Street, keeping to the right-hand pavement.** The Grapes pub, a little way along, occupies the left-hand side of a seventeenth-century mansion which was refronted around 1720. You may glimpse, through the first-floor windows, a superb seventeenth-century plasterwork ceiling, which sadly is not open to public view. In the centre of the building, the original entrance is flanked by a pair of Doric columns, with a pair of Ionic columns above and a pair of Corinthian columns on top – the same architectural device that John Wood later used at the Circus.

Turn down the alley beside the Grapes. The building on the right, where the alley widens into St Michael's Place, stands on the site of yet another medieval church, St Michael's Within. It too was deconsecrated when the Abbey became the city church, before suffering a series of indignities, including conversion to an alehouse. The present building,

Ram's head decoration on the Cross Bath
Looking west along Bath Street

which was also a pub for a time, dates from 1812. The single-storey building ahead is the Cross Bath. There has been a bath on this site since Roman times, but the present building, by Thomas Baldwin, dates from the 1780s.

Walk to the left of the Cross Bath and look along Bath Street to the King's Bath. Having now walked much of the old city, you can appreciate how different Bath Street is to the narrow, unplanned streets that characterise the rest of it. Although there were determined efforts, starting in the late eighteenth century, to improve the look of the city's historic core, this remains the only fully-realised piece of enlightened urban planning within the old walls. In 1909, however, there was a proposal to demolish the north side of Bath Street and rebuild

WALK 1: WITHIN THE WALLS

it in Edwardian Baroque style. The ensuing outcry led to the birth of the Bath preservation movement.

Nevertheless, Bath Street has not escaped unscathed. To your left, a faux-classical bit of post-modernism, which has come in for a lot of flak from architectural critics, houses a window display for BHS. Over to the right is the entrance to the new spa, designed by Nicholas Grimshaw, which ousted an eighteenth-century shopfront.[1] An original fanlight can be seen, however, a little way along on the right at No 6. The narrow building to the right of the spa was Bath's first museum, opened in 1797 and known as the House of Antiquities. The two crumbling figures in the niches above the entrance are believed to have come from the old Guildhall in the High Street.

Fanlight in Bath Street
The Hetling Pump Room

Continue round to the right to see the entrance to the Hot Bath. Built by John Wood the Younger in the 1770s, it replaced an earlier building which stood where Hot Bath Street now runs. It now forms part of the new spa, whose glass walls tower above it. Opposite is the Hetling Pump

1 The shopfront has been preserved and can now be seen in the Building of Bath Collection.

Room, a private establishment which closed in 1875 and now houses the Spa Visitor Centre. On the other side of the alleyway is the chapel of St John's Hospital, built in 1723 and refashioned in the nineteenth century. It also serves the parish of St Michaels Within, the site of whose original church you saw a few minutes ago.

Walk round the back of the Cross Bath to the entrance to St John's Hospital, founded in 1174 to offer refuge for the needy and still providing almshouse accommodation over 800 years later. **Go through the archway into the courtyard and turn left into the chapel.**[1]

Carry on through the courtyard to Westgate Buildings, where you turn left, passing Chandos House, built by John Wood for the Duke of Chandos in 1729-30. After passing an alleyway, you come to Abbey Church House, dating from the middle ages but rebuilt in the late sixteenth century and restored after bomb damage in 1942. In 2007 it was

acquired by a hotel group to provide conference facilities. Over to your right – outside the city walls – are the uncompromisingly modern buildings of the City of Bath College, with the wooded slopes of Beechen Cliff beyond.

Abbey Church House as it looked before the bombing raids of 1942

Carry on past Abbey Church House, following the line of the walls, as the street – called Lower Borough Walls – curves to the left of the Hobgoblin pub. On your right, look out for the old dairy sign over Moss's shop. To your left is the old Royal United Hospital (RUH). Whereas the General (or Mineral Water) Hospital was established to treat people from outside the city, the RUH was for local people. Designed by John Pinch, it was built in the 1820s as the Bath United Hospital, combining the functions of two earlier hospitals. When a new wing, named after the recently-deceased Prince Albert, opened in 1864, it became the Royal United Hospital. The RUH moved to its present site west of the city in 1932, and this building was taken over by Bath Technical College. The college sold it in 2005, and part of it has since been demolished as part of a scheme to convert it to a hotel.

The green space a little way along on the right (unofficially known as Pigeon Park) was the cemetery for another of Bath's lost churches,

---

1 The chapel is normally open between 9am and 5pm Monday to Friday. If it is closed, go along the alleyway beside the Hetling Pump Room rather than through the courtyard of St John's, and turn left.

St James's. This church lasted much longer than the others whose sites you have seen. Rebuilt in the eighteenth century, it was badly damaged by bombing in 1942, but its ruins survived until 1957 when they were demolished. If you look ahead, you can see where it once stood; a Marks & Spencer store now occupies the site. The old South Gate stood to the right of the church.

A map of 1852 showing St James's church and cemetery, and the old United Hospital

The coat of arms above the entrance to Bellott's Hospital

In the centre of the old cemetery is a recently-erected memorial to victims of road accidents. To the left of the cemetery, the Chapel Arts Centre occupies the old church hall. The building to the right of the cemetery was originally a Quaker Meeting House. It was built on the site of a Roman Catholic church which opened in 1780 but was burnt down a few months later by a drunken

mob in the worst night of rioting the city has ever seen. The priest was chased through the streets, narrowly escaping with his life, and troops had to be brought in to restore order. A footman called John Butler was hanged for his part in the riots. The Hobgoblin pub was later built on the site of his execution.[1] **Turn left along Bilbury Lane beside the Lamb & Lion pub.**[2] The name Bilbury is a corruption of Binnebury, an Anglo-Saxon word meaning 'within the borough walls'. **After 50 metres you come to Beau Street**, originally known as Bell Tree Lane. Few people linger long at this rather gloomy crossroads, hemmed in by tall buildings, yet it is one of the most intriguing spots in the city.

To your left, on the south side of Beau Street, is the monumental façade of the old RUH. Looking ahead you can see an archway into Bath Street, with St Catherine's Hospital on the right. When St Catherine's was founded in 1435, it stood on the corner where the old RUH stands today.

---

1 The story of the riots can be found in *Awash With Ale*, published by Akeman Press.

2 Due to the conversion of the old RUH into a hotel, Bilbury Lane is closed for 18 months from 6 February 2012. Until it reopens, you need to retrace your steps along Lower Borough Walls, turn right along Hot Bath Street and right again along Beau Street for 40 metres.

It was rebuilt on its present site in 1829. To your right, on the south side of Beau Street, is yet another hospital – Bellott's, founded in 1609 and rebuilt in 1859. Finally, to your left, are the sheer glass walls of the new spa, reflecting the Bath stone buildings around them. There cannot be many crossroads with old hospitals on three corners and a spa offering health treatments on the fourth – but this distinction does not exhaust the fascination of this little-known corner of Bath.

Reflections in the new Spa

The King's Bath, the Cross Bath and the Hot Bath were built where Bath's three hot springs came to the surface. There have been baths on these sites since Roman times, but before that the springs ran unchecked, creating a steamy and mysterious marsh, its edges stained bright orange by the iron-rich waters. For the people who lived here before the Romans it must have been a hallowed and mysterious place. The area has been so comprehensively built over that virtually no evidence of anything pre-Roman survives. Archaeologists have, however, found traces of a pre-Roman causeway running into the heart of the marsh where the three springs ran together. It stood roughly where you are standing now. Here, an unimaginably long time ago, when the springs ran freely, open to the sky, offerings would have been made to the goddess of the springs in this unearthly place.

Turn right along Beau Street. At the end, on the left-hand corner of Stall Street, there was once an inn called the Bell. On 20 July 1727, workmen were 'digging to make a common sewer in the middle of the street ... near the Bell Inn' when, some 15 feet down, they chanced upon the bronze head of a statue. Some, like John Wood, said it was the head of Apollo; others that it represented Pallas Athenae. Today, as the head of Minerva (Pallas's Roman incarnation), it takes pride of place in the Roman Baths Museum.

Turn right along Stall Street and left into Abbeygate Street.[1] If you look to your left as you pass the bottom of Swallow Street you can see, built into the wall, a copy of a fragment of masonry from the Bishop's Palace that once stood here. Although most of the buildings in Abbeygate

---

1 Despite this being one of Bath's busiest streets, there is a dearth of dropped pavements here. To avoid high kerbs, you may need to continue to the end of Stall Street, cross over and head back to Abbeygate Street.

Street are modern, the one at the end, with semi-circular headed windows on the first floor, dates from the 1630s and was an inn for over 200 years. Originally called the Raven, it became the Freemason's Tavern and was refronted in grand style in 1832. The modern archway to the left stands on the site of the gateway to the Abbey precinct which was demolished in 1733.

Another street once ran south from here, but disappeared when the Marks & Spencer store was built. St James Street South contained one of the grandest early-eighteenth-century houses in the city. It survived a near miss in April 1942 when a bomb fell less than 30 metres away, only to be demolished less than 20 years later.

Take the alleyway to the right of the former Raven and carry on up a slope to Gallaway's Buildings. These were built around 1749 for an apothecary called William Gallaway. By the early nineteenth century, the elegant residents they were intended for had long abandoned them in favour of more fashionable lodgings. They became slum tenements, and around 1870, as part of a campaign to improve their image, the corporation renamed them North Parade Buildings. On the wall of the first house on the right is graffiti from 1774. The building whose gable end faces down the street dates from the 1620s and is one of the oldest in Bath. The opening in its gable end was a roost for owls, which were encouraged as a way of controlling vermin.

Part way along Gallaway's Buildings, turn down the alley on the left. The courtyard on the right-hand side indicates the original ground level.

Looking north along Gallaway's Buildings to Lilliput Alley

Far left: The alley from Gallaway's Buildings to Abbey Green

Left: The plane tree in Abbey Green casts its shadow on a seventeenth-century building refronted in the eighteenth century

Right: Early morning in Lilliput Alley

Just past it, you will see some seventeenth-century mullion windows, with the ground-floor one blocked up.

The alley leads into Abbey Green, dominated by an enormous plane tree. The building to the left of the archway in the far corner is the north side of the old Raven, whose grander façade you saw earlier. You can see how a two-storey extension was later squeezed in between it and the eighteenth-century Bath-stone building at No 4. This in turn had been tacked onto the side of No 3, which dates from 1689 and whose rubble stone would originally have been covered with render.

In the 1980s, a Roman mosaic was discovered in the cellar of the Crystal Palace pub opposite, but this has since been covered over. To the right of the Crystal Palace is a double bow-fronted shopfront dating from the late eighteenth century. The 'crinoline railings' were designed so that prospective customers could lean forward to inspect the items on display in the window. The fanlight above the door is modern and constructed from coat-hangers.

To your right the Bath Sweet Shop and the Bath Bun Tea Shop occupy a seventeenth-century building which was refronted in the eighteenth century. The wooden beam running the length of the façade is a bressummer, a common feature in eighteenth-century buildings.[1] While the façades of grander buildings generally had two courses of stone, most buildings only had one. This was a less robust method of construction, and, if settlement occurred after the building was completed, there was a risk of collapse. Bressummers absorbed settlement and reduced the risk. Even so, cracks still appeared in walls – one such crack, patched up with twenty-first century expertise, can be seen in the wall on the corner of the alley you have just walked along.

Turn right beside the sweet shop along North Parade Passage. Originally known as Lilliput Alley, this was renamed for the same reason

---

1 Wooden beams were known as 'summers'; 'bressummer' is a contraction of 'breast-summer'.

as Gallaway's Buildings, but is still generally referred to by its original name. No 2, on the left, was the post office where Ralph Allen came to work around 1710. Beyond it are two of Bath's longest-established and most popular restaurants – Demuth's, one of the country's top vegetarian restaurants, and Tilley's Bistro.

Carry on along Lilliput Alley to Sally Lunn's tea rooms. Although a plaque on its wall states that it dates from around 1482, a glance at the map on page 10 shows that, over a century later, there were no buildings here at all. It can, in fact, like the other buildings in the row, be dated fairly precisely to around 1622. Although Sally Lunn's is one of Bath's top tourist attractions, few visitors realise that what is now the front of the building was originally the back. Today, the original façade lies hidden in a yard down a grimy alleyway, but for over a century after it was built it looked out over a bowling green, as you can see from the map on page

11. To the right of Sally Lunn's is the building you saw from the other end of Gallaway's Buildings. It was originally a pub called the Star & Garter and now forms part of the Huntsman next door.

Carry on to the end of Lilliput Alley and look over the railings on the right, where the old city wall can be seen cutting across at an oblique angle. The wall continued across the open space where the fountain now stands towards the East Gate. To your left is the Huntsman pub, built as a coffee house in the 1740s, which is visited in the second walk. The alleyway to the right of it leads down to the original frontages of Sally Lunn's and the other buildings in Lilliput Alley.

To return to the starting point, **turn left and left again along York Street.** Just past the Greek Revival-style Friends Meeting House on the left – built as a Masonic lodge in 1819 – look through a gate to see, in an abandoned courtyard, the richly-ornamented house John Wood built for Ralph Allen in 1727 at the back of the old post office. **A few metres further on, you come to the Visitor Information Centre and the end of the walk.**

2

PALLADIAN PLEASURES
The Georgian Expansion

Distance *3 miles*
Time *3-4 hours*
Accessibility *Step-free and on pavements throughout*
Public toilets *Charlotte Street (just west of the north side of Queen Square)*
Starting point *Kingston Parade (outside Visitor Information Centre)*

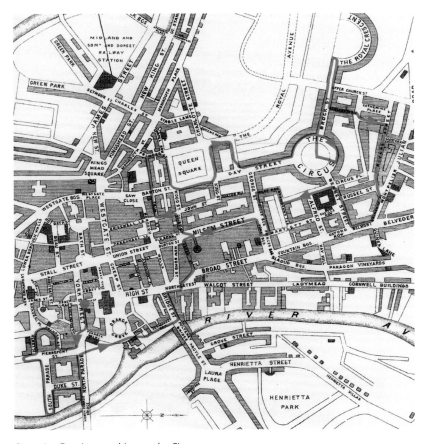

Opposite: Evening sunshine on the Circus

To make a just comparison between the publick accommodations of Bath at this time, and one and twenty years back, the best chambers for gentlemen were then just what the garrets for servants now are.
John Wood, 1749

Bath ... to be sure, is an earthly paradise, The Square, the Circus, and the Parades, put you in mind of the sumptuous palaces represented in prints and pictures; and the new buildings ... look like so many enchanted castles, raised on hanging terraces.
Tobias Smollett, *Humphrey Clinker*, 1771

In the early eighteenth century, Bath embarked on a period of unprecedented expansion. By the end of the century, the city's population was between ten and twelve times greater than it had been at the beginning.[1] This growth was fuelled almost entirely by the leisure industry. Historians still argue over the exact combination of circumstances that led to this, but the discussions always seem to come back to one man – Beau Nash. To what extent Nash was the mastermind behind Bath's meteoric rise and to what extent he was the right man in the right place at the right time is open to debate, but he dominated social life in Bath from 1704 – when he was appointed Master of Ceremonies – until his death in 1761.

Two other men played pivotal roles in the transformation of Bath. In 1710, a young Cornishman called Ralph Allen moved to Bath to work as a clerk in the post office. He rose rapidly through the ranks, taking over as the city's postmaster two years later. He then drew up plans for a reform of the national postal service that was so successful he made himself a fortune in the process. He used the money to acquire the stone quarries south of Bath, streamlined production and built a tramway to carry the stone down to the city. He made Bath stone available in sufficient quantities and at a low enough price to facilitate the large-scale building projects that transformed the city. As Bath's most prominent and influential citizen, he also played a major role in its development until his death in 1764.

The third member of this illustrious trio was John Wood, a young architect from Yorkshire who arrived in Bath in the mid-1720s with a dream of transforming the city into a showpiece such as had not been seen since the days of the Romans.[2] Although his plans were often frustrated, from the early 1730s he set the benchmark for architectural design in the

---

1 Bath had a population of around 3,000 in 1700; by the time of the 1801 Census, the city and its suburbs had a population of around 35,000.

2 Until the mid-twentieth century it was accepted that John Wood was a Yorkshireman. Discovery of a possible reference to his being educated in Bath and a record of a John Wood being born in 1704 to the wife of a Bath builder called George Wood led to him being claimed as a Bathonian. Although this cannot be discounted, opinion seems now to be shifting back to acceptance of him as a Yorkshireman.

city. After his death in 1754, his work was carried on by his son, John Wood the Younger.

People flocked to Bath in the eighteenth century for two reasons – health and pleasure. The Georgians were as obsessed with healthy lifestyles – and with enjoying themselves – as we are. The difference is that their leisure activities were regimented. Dancing masters instructed visitors not only how to dance but how to walk, how to greet strangers and how to behave in polite society, while Beau Nash drew up a comprehensive list of rules of conduct. There were fixed hours for specific activities, as this description of the pleasures of Bath, written by Oliver Goldsmith in 1762, makes clear:

> The amusements of the day are generally begun by bathing ... The hours for bathing are commonly between six and nine in the morning ... The amusement of bathing is immediately succeeded by a general assembly of people at the pump-house, some for pleasure, and some to drink the hot waters. Three glasses, at three different times, is the usual portion for every drinker; and the intervals between every glass are enlivened by the harmony of a small band of music, as well as by the conversation of the gay, the witty, or the forward. From the pump-house the ladies, from time to time, withdraw to a female coffee-house, and from thence return to their lodgings to breakfast. The gentlemen withdraw to their coffee-houses, to read the papers, or converse on the news of the day, with a freedom and ease not to be found in the metropolis. People of fashion make public breakfasts at the assembly-houses, to which they invite their acquaintances, and they sometimes order private concerts; or when so disposed, attend lectures upon the arts and sciences, which are frequently taught there in a pretty superficial manner, so as not to tease the understanding, while they afford the imagination some amusement ...
>
> Thus we have the tedious morning fairly over. When noon approaches, and church (if any please to go there) is done, some of the company appear upon the parade, and other public walks, where they continue to chat

Public Bathing at Bath: or Stewing Alive

Robert Cruikshank's depiction of bathers in the King's Bath in 1826 and amuse each other, till they have formed parties for the play, cards, or dancing for the evening ...

When the hour of dinner draws nigh, and the company is returned from their different recreations, the provisions are generally served with the utmost elegance and plenty ... After dinner is over, and evening prayers ended, the company meet a second time at the pump-house. From this they retire to the walks, and from thence go to drink tea at the assembly-houses, and the rest of the evenings are concluded either with balls, plays or visits ... Every Tuesday and Friday evening is concluded with a public ball, the contributions to which are so numerous, that the price of each ticket is trifling. Thus Bath yields a continued rotation of diversions, and people of all ways of thinking, even from the libertine to the Methodist, have it in their power to complete the day with employments suited to their inclinations.

This walk visits the places frequented by eighteenth-century visitors to Bath. You will also see how John Wood and his son transformed Bath from a small provincial town to one of the most visually arresting cities in the world. You saw the King's Bath and the Pump Room – where eighteenth-century visitors began their day – in the first walk, so this walk starts with their next port of call, the coffee house.

From the Visitor Information Centre, head east along York Street. Turn right at the end, walk along to the Huntsman and look east along North Parade. Had you stood here 300 years ago, during the early years of Beau Nash's reign, you would have been on the rampire atop the city walls looking east over open country. Bath was still a small and not especially fashionable spa town. Cooped up behind its ancient walls, it was crammed with old – and generally not very salubrious – buildings. To your left would have been a bowling green; behind you would have been the houses in Lilliput Alley. The idea that buildings as grand as those

on your right would one day arise here would have seemed preposterous.

But arise they did, courtesy of John Wood, in the 1740s. They were built on embankments to raise them high above the floods that frequently inundated the low-lying ground. And, while they may have looked like palaces,

North Parade

they were not. They were not even homes. North Parade, like most of Bath's grand eighteenth-century terraces, was built as lodging houses. Here wealthy visitors would rent a suite of rooms for a few months during the season, where they would install their families and servants.

Today, the road beyond the traffic lights is one of the busiest in Bath. Originally, however, it was, as its name suggests, devoted to parading or what the Italians call *passegiatta* – strolling around to see and be seen, a combination of gentle exercise and social intercourse. The height of the Bath season in the eighteenth century was in the winter, when walking in the countryside was often difficult. This urban parade allowed visitors to take a constitutional without getting their feet or clothes muddy. It was also easy to retreat indoors if it came on to rain.

The Huntsman was built around 1740 as the Parade Coffee House, a sort of gentlemen's club. Local and national newspapers were kept and well-heeled male visitors could renew old acquaintances and catch up on the latest gossip. There were several coffee houses in Georgian Bath – including one for ladies – but this is the only one to have survived.

There were also two sets of Assembly Rooms nearby – the first, opened around 1705, stood roughly where the fountain on the traffic island is today; the site of the other, which opened in 1735, is now occupied by York Street. With all these facilities, it is not surprising that North Parade took over from the Orange Grove as the most fashionable outdoor space in the city.

There was also a theatre just around the corner. To find it, **walk along to the traffic lights, turn right by Good Buy Books and then right again through an archway into Pierrepont Place.** This leads into Old Orchard Street, still paved with pennant-stone setts.[1] No 1, on the left, with a particularly fine doorway topped by pineapples, was home to the Linleys, a famous musical family. Among them was the celebrated beauty Elizabeth Linley, whose elopement with Richard Brinsley Sheridan in 1772 caused such a sensation that a play about it appeared on the London stage.

Follow the street round to the left and walk along to a building on the left with a large plaque. Although it may look much like the

other buildings in this quiet, half-forgotten backwater, this was Bath's first Theatre Royal. Built by Thomas Jelly, it opened in 1750; in 1768 it became the first theatre outside London to be granted a royal patent and for a time was the most fashionable provincial theatre in the country.

Bath's first Theatre Royal, now a Masonic Hall

1 Setts are often described, incorrectly, as cobblestones, to which they bear no resemblance. Cobbles are those round stones used for paving streets in other towns and cities, which are a torment to walk on.

On the opposite side of the street, the building that now houses a Spiritualist church was the theatre tavern, known as the Pineapple. Old Orchard Street was once, hard though it may be to believe today, one of the busiest and most fashionable streets in the city. It ended at the theatre, where steps led down to a paved area with room for around 50 carriages. Beyond that were orchards, open fields, the river and the wooded slopes of Beechen Cliff.

Although it was altered and extended in 1774, the theatre was too small and in 1805 was replaced by a new theatre on the other side of town. The old theatre became a Catholic chapel, but since 1865 has been a Masonic Hall. There are guided tours of the interior – one of the most atmospheric and fascinating buildings in the city – several times a week.

At the end of Old Orchard Street, cross the road and turn left along Henry Street. The church with the spire straight ahead is St John's, which the Catholics moved to when they left the old theatre. St John's church is on many visitors' itineraries, not because of its architecture but because a pair of peregrine falcons nest on the spire. They first bred here successfully in 2006, after the Hawk & Owl Trust installed a nest platform, and have hatched young here every year since. On your right is another church, built in classical style in 1844 by the Swedenborgians, a sect which counted Sir Isaac Pitman, the inventor of the most famous form of shorthand, among its members. A window is dedicated to him in the church, which now houses a branch of Deloitte.

A fledgling peregrine falcon gears itself up for its first flight from St John's church

Turn right at the end of Henry Street, cross the road at the pedestrian lights, turn left and then right along South Parade. South Parade was built at the same time as North Parade and originally enjoyed uninterrupted views over open country. Unlike North Parade, it is still a cul de sac. If you **walk to the end** you can look across to what, in the eighteenth century, were water meadows. Steps from here led down to a ferry which took visitors across the river, from where they could set off on country

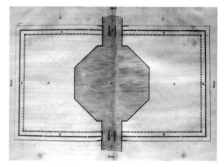

Above: John Wood's design for an octagonal basin on the River Avon in Bath

Below: Water features designed by John Wood at Bramham Park in Yorkshire

Bottom: A plan of the Parades and surrounding area by John Wood

walks. Looking along South Parade, with its wide pavement still intact, it is possible to recapture something of its original elegance and grandeur, and imagine what it would have been like when crowded with fashionable visitors.

North and South Parades were part of a much grander plan. John Wood wanted to build more terraces to the south, as well as on the other side of the river. He also had plans to dam the river and create a large octagonal basin where boats could moor up. The idea may have dated back to one of his earlier projects. In 1722, he designed some water features, including canals and octagonal basins, at Bramham Park in Yorkshire, which can still be seen today.

South Parade is linked to North Parade by other rows of lodging houses, with no gaps in between, so that, even after walking all round, you cannot glimpse what lies behind them. When you consider that each house has a garden, this lack of access seems even more peculiar. The way into this secret world is, of course, at basement level – the original ground level – through vaults under the road.

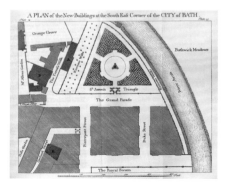

Top left: South Parade, where glazing bars have been replaced by large panes of glass and many first-floor windows have been lengthened.

Top right: A stark contrast between soot-blackened and newly-cleaned stone on the west side of Duke Street. Note that the glazing bars have been restored in the house on the right.

Above: The east side of Duke Street also illustrates the way in which the lengthening of first-floor windows mars the sense of symmetry

One thing that has marred the appearance of many of Bath's Georgian buildings – including several on South Parade – is the replacement of their original glazing bars by large panes of glass. In the eighteenth century, glass-making technology was not up to making large panes. Georgian architects turned this limitation to their advantage by making glazing bars echo the proportions of the windows they formed part of, as well as the proportions of the building as a whole. Symmetry was everything, and you do not have to be an architectural expert to sense that Georgian windows with original (or restored) glazing bars are more aesthetically satisfying than windows with large panes of glass. John Betjeman came up with a phrase that sums up the look of windows that have lost their glazing bars perfectly – 'blind and bombed'.

Head back part way along South Parade and turn right into Duke Street. Some of the buildings on the left give an idea what all Bath's Georgian buildings looked like until the 1960s, when the city's chimneys belched forth smoke, and the stone was impregnated with soot. You will notice that the ground floors of Nos 6 and 7 have been painted white. This was once common practice, as a way of relieving the near-universal gloom of the streets. After the burning of coal was banned in Bath, a programme of stone-cleaning got under way, with most of the city's buildings restored to their former glory. There are now fears, however, that pollution from traffic fumes poses as great a threat to Bath stone as soot once did.

The left-hand side of Duke Street also demonstrates another way in which the symmetry of Georgian buildings has been compromised. If you look at the first-floor windows of No 6, you will notice that they are longer than those on either side. This is because they were lengthened in the nineteenth century to admit more light, thereby destroying their relation to the proportions of the building as a whole. As you walk round the city, you will see many more examples of this.

Turn right at the end of Duke Street and walk a little way out onto the bridge, built in 1836 to turn what was formerly a cul-de-sac into a through route. If you look over the parapet you will see a grotto at the end of North Parade, now incorporated into the patio of a restaurant. It dates from the early eighteenth century, long before the bridge was built, and originally stood in a secluded spot by a riverside path. Legend has it that Sheridan and Elizabeth Linley met here while plotting their

King Edward VII Memorial

Slippery Lane

elopement. Looking the other way, towards Pulteney Bridge, you have one of the classic views of the city.

Turn and walk back along North Parade – noting the particularly fine doorways on Nos 12 and 12A. **At the traffic lights, cross the road to the right and carry on beside the balustrade.** On your right is Parade Gardens, laid out in the nineteenth century on the site of walks designed in the early eighteenth century by the owner of the Assembly Rooms. The green angel by the steps is a memorial to King Edward VII. On the other side of the river, originally served by ferry, was Spring Gardens – Bath's first pleasure gardens – where concerts, dancing, public breakfasts and afternoon teas were held.

Carry on as the road curves right and then left alongside the river. Ahead is Pulteney Bridge, built between 1769 and 1774. **At the end of Grand Parade, cross the road straight ahead** (with care because only half the crossing is controlled by lights) **and turn left up Bridge Street. At the top of Bridge Street, turn right along Northgate Street.** The alleyway you pass on the right, beside a barber's shop, is Slippery

Lane, the only surviving section of a medieval lane that ran outside the city walls.

At the traffic lights by the Podium, cross to the traffic island, cross again to the right and carry on towards St Michael's church before turning left into Green Street. On the corner, over the entrance to Belushi's, is a bas-relief of Dr Oliver, a celebrated eighteenth-century

Clockwise from above: Dr Oliver

The bowling green that gave its name to Green Street, on a map of around 1700

Looking east along Green Street to St Michael's church

The Old Green Tree

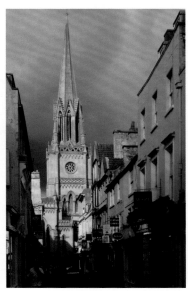

doctor who made a fortune by treating invalids who came to Bath to take the waters. He invented a biscuit, still made today, called the Bath Oliver, which he advised his gouty patients to eat. It was sold here.

Green Street was one of the first streets built outside the walls in the early eighteenth century, and gives an idea of the standard of architecture before John Wood arrived on the scene. It was called Green Street because it was built on the site of a bowling green. At one end of the green was a large tree which shaded players and spectators on hot days. After it was cut down, its place was taken by a tavern called the Old Green Tree. Built around 1716, it is still open today, and is one of Bath's most traditional pubs, with three small wood-panelled rooms, a selection of ales from local breweries and home-cooked food at lunchtimes.

With the exception of the single-storey buildings on the right, most of the buildings in Green Street date from around the same time as the Old Green Tree, and a very mixed bunch they are. They were put up by different builders, each working according to his customer's budget, taste and requirements. There was no attempt to create a unified whole, and gables stand cheek by jowl with parapets. Green Street House, two doors along from the Old Green Tree, is particularly fine, yet defiantly asymmetrical, with the windows on the first and second floors unevenly spaced. At the other end of the street is a shell porch over the entrance to No 3. Try to imagine the building as it would have been without the shopfronts on either side of it, and you end up with something not unlike the vernacular buildings in the villages around Bath. What characterises the buildings in Green Street above all else – and it was something that had characterised vernacular architecture for centuries – was diversity. That was what John Wood set out to change.

At the end of Green Street, turn right into Milsom Street. Two doors along on the right, the entrance to the Octagon Chapel will, if you are lucky, be open. Currently the chapel is used for temporary art shows and exhibitions and is closed at other times. As it is one of Bath's most spectacular buildings, however, you should take the opportunity to visit it if you can. It opened in 1767 and was the most fashionable of Bath's proprietary chapels, built for wealthy visitors unwilling to mix with the hoi polloi in the Abbey. They had to stump up a hefty fee, but were rewarded with celebrity preachers, elegant surroundings and top musicians. The Octagon's first music director was William Herschel. He resigned in 1781 after discovering Uranus and deciding to devote himself to astronomy full-time.

Cross Milsom Street and head west along Quiet Street. The row of shops on the right-hand side – which would not look out of place in Paris – was built by Major Davis in the 1870s, replacing a row of early eighteenth-century buildings. On the left, the building with statues of Commerce and Genius in its niches and Mercury atop the pediment was designed in 1825 by HE Goodridge as an up-market bazaar. Today it is the Eastern Eye Indian Restaurant, with one of the most sumptuous interiors in Bath.

At the end of Quiet Street, look over to the right to the north side of Wood Street, where the row of early eighteenth-century buildings was not, as with Quiet Street, demolished, but suffered the indignity of having single-storey extensions, with ponderous pillars, imposed onto them in the 1870s. The name of the perpetrator is not known, but Major Davis seems a likely candidate.

Mercury on the former bazaar in Quiet Street

Turn left down Queen Street, passing another of Bath's top real-ale pubs, the Raven, famous for its pies. Like Old Orchard Street, Queen Street is still paved with pennant-stone setts. Most of Bath's streets were once paved with setts, which have either been ripped up or covered over. Where they survive, as here, they complement Bath's Georgian buildings far better than tarmac.[1]

Queen Street in the mist

1 It has also been pointed out that, where they have been restored, they are better at traffic-calming than more visually and environmentally intrusive initiatives – an eighteenth-century solution to a twenty-first-century problem.

Go under the archway (known as St John's Gate) into Trim Street. This was built in 1707 by George Trim, an influential member of the corporation, and was originally known as Backward Buildings. Although it was the first new street to be built outside the walls since medieval times, it was some time before all the building plots were taken. No 5, the house with an exuberant Baroque façade to your left, for example, was not built until around 1720. It was the home of General Wolfe's parents, and Wolfe was staying there in 1759 when he was ordered to lead an assault on Quebec. Although he led British forces to victory over the French, he died of his wounds. The military trophies in the tympanum of No 5 were designed to honour his memory.

Opposite, at No 12a, is one of the finest shopfronts in the city. The shop on the corner, to the right of No 14, was occupied, between 1802 and 1805, by William Smith, 'the father of English geology'. His work as surveyor to the Somersetshire Coal Canal gave him the opportunity to study strata, and in 1799 he produced a large-scale geological map of the Bath area. He later produced a geological map of the whole country, which has become known as 'The Map that Changed the World'. The shop was a showroom, where his maps, along with his collections of fossils and minerals, were displayed. By coincidence, another famous visitor to Bath, Jane Austen, stayed in Trim Street for a few months in 1806. She would certainly have passed Smith's showroom on a daily basis, and probably took the opportunity to examine its cabinets of curiosities as well.

Turn right and, as you **walk to the end of Trim Street,** note the dates on the building on the left: 1724 is when it was built; 1897 is when the doorway was blocked up and the building was converted to a stay (or corset) factory. The surviving doorway, a little further along, still has a splendid shell porch. At the end is the old Unitarian church, designed by John Palmer in 1795, and now an Irish pub. At the crossroads, you are confronted by modern buildings on three sides. This is not the result of wartime bombing but of redevelopment in the 1960s.

Carry straight on into Beauford Square, one of Bath's hidden gems. It was the work of a Bristol architect called John Strahan. As in Green Street, the buildings are of different heights and styles, but Beauford Square is about 15 years later than Green Street, and, while there may not be the kind of uniformity Wood would have imposed, there is at least a unanimity of intent. Curiously, Wood described its architecture as 'piratical', implying that Strahan stole elements of the design from him. The developer was John Hobbs, a Bristol merchant who was also involved in developing the area around Queen Square in Bristol. A magnificent townhouse built for him by Strahan on Prince Street in Bristol is now the Shakespeare Tavern. Hobbs was also the driving force behind the building of the Avon Navigation between Bristol and Bath, and named

Beauford Square after the scheme's major sponsor, the Duke of Beaufort. It is unclear, however, why it is not called Beaufort Square.

Originally, Beauford Square only had buildings on three sides – to the south it looked across to Beau Nash's house in the Sawclose, which you saw in Walk 1. The building dominating the southern side of the square is the Theatre Royal, which opened in 1805. This was originally its main entrance, but after a fire in 1862 it was rebuilt with the main entrance in the Sawclose.

Before moving on, take a closer look at the buildings on the east side of the square, to the left of the theatre. Although the southern end of the row is eighteenth century, the northern end is less than 50 years old. In the 1960s, there were plans to redevelop much of central Bath, and Beauford Square was in line to be flattened. The bulldozers actually moved in and knocked down part of the east side before a public outcry forced the council to reconsider. For a while, the site was used as a car park, until it was decided to build a replica of the original building.

At the end of Beauford Square, turn right up Princes Street. Beauford House, on the right, was a pub called the Beauford Arms. Although now converted to offices it retains its Victorian façade. Look up to the left to see the impressive sign of the Shepherds Hall friendly society. More impressive lettering can be seen if you turn and look back at the rooftop ironwork advertising 'J Ellett: Smith & Plumber'.

At the top of Princes Street is Queen Square, John Wood's first major project in the city, built between 1728 and 1736. The patch of grass and shrubs over to your left marks the site of a proprietary chapel Wood built for the square's residents. It was demolished in the 1860s to widen the road, which is still known as Chapel Row today. The monument that stands on the site of the chapel was recovered in the 1960s from the garden of 14 Queen Square in a

Above: Mask on the Theatre Royal in Beauford Square

Right top: Shepherd's Hall in Princes Street

Right centre: Victorian lettering in Beauford Square

Right bottom: Monument on the corner of Queen Square

A map of 1740 showing Queen Square as originally built

The obelisk commemorating the visit of Prince Frederick

poor state of repair and has since been restored. Its provenance is unknown: it may have been constructed from fragments of the chapel, although it may have come from the Queen's Bath. Chapel Row includes one of Bath's oldest and most popular restaurants, the Beaujolais Bistro, opened in 1970 by expat Jean-Pierre Auge.

If you look up the west side of the square, you will notice that the central section is different to the buildings on either side of it. The other three sides of the square were built as terraces, but the west side originally consisted of three blocks, with the central one set back behind a garden. The central block was demolished in 1830 and replaced by the Greek Revival building which is now home to the Bath Royal Literary & Scientific Institute.

The obelisk in the centre of the square was erected, like the obelisk in the Orange Grove, by Beau Nash in honour of a royal visitor. In this case it was Frederick, Prince of Wales. Like Nash, the prince was a Freemason, and John Wood designed the obelisk to represent that most potent of Masonic symbols – a ray of light emanating from the sun. It originally came to a point at the top until it was struck by lightning.

Turn right and walk along the south side of the square, looking out for the carvings of a satyr's head and a cherub over the doors of Nos 11 & 12. The east end of the row was destroyed by bombing in 1942 and rebuilt in 1953.

As you **turn and walk up the east side of the square**, look out for the grotesque carvings on the doorposts of Nos 2 and 3. As you approach the traffic lights, the north side of the square appears, uncluttered by

trees but probably cluttered by traffic. **At the traffic lights, carry straight on across the road to look at the building on the corner of Gay Street** with a full-height semi-circular bay. It was built by John Wood and has another grotesque carving over the entrance. If you look through the ground-floor window to the right of the entrance you will see a small powder room, with a shell niche, blue-and-white Delft tiles and a marble basin. Here eighteenth-century gentlemen would have withdrawn to powder their wigs.[1]

Next door is the Jane Austen Centre, with a gentleman who is no stranger to powdered wigs likely to be on duty outside. Bespoke, bewhiskered, bewaistcoated and bedecked in full Regency array, Martin Salter, the Jane Austen Centre's meeter and greeter, was declared in September 2011 to be 'England's most photographed man'. Interviewed on television after the announcement, he was asked for his top tip when having your photograph taken. His advice – 'try to keep your eyes open'.

Cross at the traffic lights and walk halfway along the north side of the square. It is difficult, with a constant stream of traffic flowing past and large trees blocking the view, to appreciate the full grandeur of Wood's achievement – but if you cast your mind back to Beauford Square or Green Street, you will get some idea how groundbreaking Queen Square must have seemed in the 1730s.[2]

---

1 Although it has long been accepted that this is what the room was used for, it has recently been suggested that the room adjoining it was a dining room, and this is where glasses were washed.

2 A model of Queen Square as originally built can be seen in the Building of Bath Collection.

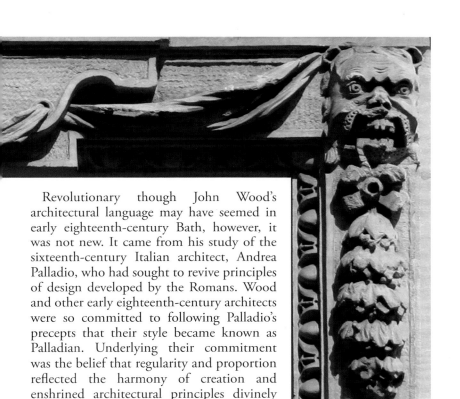

Revolutionary though John Wood's architectural language may have seemed in early eighteenth-century Bath, however, it was not new. It came from his study of the sixteenth-century Italian architect, Andrea Palladio, who had sought to revive principles of design developed by the Romans. Wood and other early eighteenth-century architects were so committed to following Palladio's precepts that their style became known as Palladian. Underlying their commitment was the belief that regularity and proportion reflected the harmony of creation and enshrined architectural principles divinely transmitted to the earliest builders.

Where John Wood was revolutionary was in taking an architectural style developed by Palladio to build palaces and applying it to the construction of lodging houses. The north side of Queen Square was designed to look like a palace, and was far grander than the south and east sides.[1] It also included certain features which thereafter became obligatory for grand buildings in the city – not only throughout the eighteenth century, but for much of the nineteenth and twentieth centuries as well. Its monumental central section, with a pediment supported on six columns and a rusticated ground floor, is echoed in buildings across the city.[2] It is not only the

1 As an architect almost obsessively wedded to ideas of symmetry, Wood wanted the west side of the square to be like the south and east sides, but was forced to bow to commercial pressure from two wealthy shareholders who did not want to live in a terrace in this prestigious development.

2 Rustication was a way of cutting individual blocks of stone so that, when laid together, the joints between them were emphasised. Deeply-incised groves between each block of stone were believed to lend weight to buildings, but could only be used sparingly, otherwise the effect would be ponderous and overwhelming.

Above: The north side of Queen Square

Opposite: Some of the metopes on the Circus and an early photograph of Stonehenge

traffic that hinders appreciation of John Wood's achievement; the various indignities it has suffered – loss of glazing bars, lengthening of windows and a Virginia creeper smothering the western end – do not help either. Nevertheless, it remains an astonishing building.

Walk to the end of the north side, turn right and walk uphill. The row of buildings at an angle off to your left is Queen's Parade, built by John Wood the Younger around 1766 – possibly to demonstrate that even the best architects can have an off day, or possibly in a fit of pique after his plans to build assembly rooms here were thwarted. Although no one would describe Queen's Parade as an architectural showpiece, it would look a lot better if the extensions at the front – containing lavatories – had not been added in the nineteenth century.

Turn right at the corner into Queen's Parade Place (originally known as Back Lane). Over to your left are the war memorial, the gates to Royal Victoria Park and steps up to the gravel walk. The two single-storey lodges on your right were originally shelters for sedan chairmen. The row on the left at the end of the street was originally one building longer. When the end house was demolished in 1870 to widen the street, a new end wall was designed by Major Davis, incorporating a feature no eighteenth-century architect would have dreamed of – a balustrade in the entablature.

Turn left up Gay Street, keeping a look out for the elaborately carved façade of No 8. The carvings were added by a sculptor called Prince Hoare who created the statue of Beau Nash in the Pump Room. A little further up, on the other side of the road, No 25 was, in 1805, the home of Jane Austen.

WALK 2: PALLADIAN PLEASURES

Gay Street leads into the Circus – or to give it its full title, the King's Circus. Its foundation stone was laid on 7 February 1754. Less than four months later, with work hardly started, its architect, John Wood, was dead. Although his son took over the project, it was another twelve years before it was complete. The design of the Circus was heavily influenced by Stonehenge, which Wood had surveyed and written about at great length. In a book called *An Essay on Bath*, he attempted to prove that Bladud had introduced the druids to Britain, appointed himself arch-druid

and established Bath as a druidic capital in 480BC. Wood saw the Circus as an eighteenth-century equivalent of Stonehenge, a druid temple for the modern age. The acorns on the parapet recalled the oaks that were sacred to the druids – perhaps Wood hoped the Circus would be the acorn from which the oak of modern druidism would spring. They also alluded to the legend of Bladud – after all, pigs are notoriously fond of acorns. Wood went much further, however, leaving clues to the mystical significance of the Circus in the strange collection of carvings or metopes on the frieze running round it. The received wisdom is that they are Masonic symbols, but there are hints of something more esoteric.

Turn left and walk along to the corner of Brock Street. Here you can see carvings not only of the sun, the moon and a star, but also a bearded, goatlike head in profile – a possible allusion to the Knights Templar. The rose is one of many to be found in the Circus – possibly indicating the influence of Rosicrucianism.

Cross the road and continue walking round the Circus. The cockle shells to the right of No 11 are emblems of St James of Santiago de Compostela, who is linked with the alchemical tradition; the owl next to them is also an alchemical symbol. On No 13 is an oroberus – a snake with its tail in its mouth, symbolising eternity – alongside another rose. On No 14 the Ten Commandments appear with a sword across them, an emblem of the Knights Templar. The carving showing the sun's rays reflecting off a mirror alludes to the work of one of Wood's great heroes, Sir Isaac Newton. Newton not only conducted experiments into the nature of light, he was, like Wood, an astronomer, and if you walk along to No 15 you will see a carving of a telescope. Even more significant, as far as John Wood was concerned, Newton was an alchemist who had studied the Hermetic Tradition that many of the metopes in the Circus allude to.

The number three is everywhere in the Circus. Three orders of columns – Doric, Ionic and Corinthian – run round it and three streets lead out of it. If lines were to be drawn across the Circus from the entrances to these streets, they would create an equilateral triangle. A triangle in a circle is an important Masonic and alchemical symbol, which can also be seen in several of the carvings. In a work entitled *The Origin of Building*, John Wood elaborated on its significance:

> In the works of the Divine Architect of all things, we find nothing but perfect figures, consisting of the utmost regularity, the sweetest harmony, and the most delightful proportion: And as his works universally tend to a circular form, and are as universally constituted of three different principal parts, so those three parts generally carry with them, in the whole, and severally, the properties of use, strength and beauty.

The Circus was not intended as a stand-alone development, but as part of a grander symbolic scheme. If you **walk across to the centre of the Circus** and stand on the block of concrete over an underground reservoir, you can look south to where Gay Street runs down to Queen Square. If you look to your right, you can see Brock Street running along to the Royal Crescent. Gay Street and Brock Street are both the same length, a clear indication that they formed part of a grand plan. However, if you look to your left you will see Bennet Street, leading nowhere in particular and turning to the right a few metres along. The question of why Bennet Street is the odd one out must wait until later – for now, **walk back to Brock Street and head along it.**

Brock Street was built by John Wood the Younger in 1767-8 and has some splendid Venetian windows. The left-hand side has, like Queen Square Place, been disfigured by extensions and porches, while the right-hand side has had shopfronts tacked on. Nevertheless, it remains an

Above: Brock Street during the First World War

Below: The entrance to Brock Street Chapel

Bottom: An advertisement for a cycle-riding school in the chapel

CYCLE RIDING SCHOOL FOR LEARNERS.
BROCK STREET HALL, BATH.

Over 400 Ladies and Gentlemen taught since last October.

PURCHASERS OF MACHINES
TAUGHT FREE OF CHARGE.

Jas. Steers,
CYCLE DEALER
AND LESSEE

Office: 11, John St., Bath

All Lessons given strictly Private.

Ladies and Gentlemen of mature age taught to ride perfectly. Special attention given to this Class of Learners.

elegant thoroughfare, with one of Bath's most popular restaurants – the Circus – on the right.

Towards the end of the street, there is a particularly fine window with coupled Ionic columns and blind sidelights over the archway between Nos 20 and 21. The archway, which is modern, stands where the entrance to a proprietary chapel once stood. After the chapel closed, it had a varied career as a cycle rink, swimming bath, badminton court and warehouse, before being destroyed by bombing in 1942. It was in the Gothick style, and, if you look across the street, you will see that there is a Gothick porch on No 16. Whether there was any connection between the two, however, is unknown.

At the end of Brock Street, look to the right along Upper Church Street – also by John Wood the Younger – where there are some fine wrought-iron balconies. In the distance, you can see Lansdown Place East high on the hillside with the tower of St Stephen's behind it.

Cross the road and carry on into the Royal Crescent, one of the great set pieces of Georgian Bath and one of the most instantly recognisable buildings in the world. As you approach the Crescent, there is no hint of what is to come, until, as you reach the corner, its full sweep and majesty is revealed. This is architecture raised to the level of the grand dramatic gesture. Built by John Wood the Younger between 1767 and 1775, nothing like it had been seen before. It was not just the design that was new, it was the way Wood the Younger forged a new relationship between that design and the natural world. The concept of *rus in urbe* – the countryside in town – was a fashionable one in Georgian England, and had already found its expression in pleasure gardens and riverside developments like North and South Parades. The Royal Crescent took the idea one step further, creating a building that fitted into the landscape and commanded the sort of view you might expect from a grand house in the country. It broke out of the straitjacket of streets and squares, throwing its doors open to the fields and woods. It was, in effect, an urban building reinvented as part of the landscape.

The building of the Royal Crescent also marked a turning-point in the fortunes of the Upper Town. The Parades, which had taken over from the Orange Grove as the most popular place to see and be seen, fell quiet as the crowds flocked here. This was not just the most fashionable address in Bath; it soon became the most fashionable place for parading as well. On one sunny January morning in 1780, for example, a visitor wrote that he had seen between 3,000 and 4,000 people promenading in front of the Crescent, and that it was 'quite full from point to point'. Six years later, Betsy Sheridan wrote that 'the Crescent fields … is the present Mall of Bath and I think the pleasantest I ever was in as one is literally walking in the fields with a most beautiful prospect all around at the same time that you meet all the company that is now here. There is something whimsical yet pleasing in seeing a number of well-dressed people walking in the same fields where cows and horses are grazing.'

The first house in the Crescent has been restored and furnished in eighteenth-century style by the Bath Preservation Trust and is open to the public. Here you can get an idea of the lifestyles of the Crescent's first residents. The first-floor windows of this house have also been restored to their original length. Looking along the Crescent, you will see that every other house has had its first-floor windows lowered, disrupting the proportions of the original design.

What the Royal Crescent symbolises – as its name suggests – is the moon. The marriage of the sun and the moon is central to alchemy – and here the moon is linked, by Brock Street, to the Circus, which symbolises the sun. John Wood claimed that the druids had built temples to the sun and moon on Lansdown, and building the Circus and Crescent was his way of reviving an ancient tradition.[1] If you are wondering how Queen Square fitted into this scheme, in alchemical cosmology a square symbolises the earth. So it seems that these three set pieces, joined by roads of equal length, were intended to symbolise the earth, sun and moon. Wood may also have had plans to go one step further – but to discover what these plans might have been, you need to head east.

Head back along Brock Street, taking the second left along the traffic-free enclave of Margaret's Buildings. On the corner is Alexandra May's – one of the finest shopfronts and most glittering window displays in the city. A little way along, at No 15B, is the Gothick-style side entrance to the old Brock Street Chapel. Opposite, to the right of the excellent Rustico Bistro Italiano, look for the old Bass advertising sign – the oldest trademark in the world – painted over but still very much visible.

There was heavy bombing in this area in April 1942 and part of Margaret's Buildings was rebuilt after the war. One notable survival is the antique shop towards the end on the right – once a branch of Cater, Stoffel & Fortt's provision merchants. The mosaic in the entrance lists their other stores, and many original fittings survive inside. On the corner of Margaret's Buildings, in a modern building, is Bath Old Books, an essential stop for bibliophiles, with a good selection of books on Bath.

Cross the street at the end and head straight on up Catherine Place (also known as Catharine Place), built by John Wood the Younger between 1777 and 1784. The building on the corner is a modern replacement; the original fell victim to the same bomb that destroyed the building where Bath Old Books stands today. At the top of Catherine Place is Rivers Street, also by Wood the Younger. Some of the houses at the west end of the street are modern replacements for more buildings destroyed by bombing.

---

1 The Romans also paid homage to Sol, the sun god, and Luna, the moon god, with carvings of them facing each other across the temple courtyard of Aquae Sulis. It is not known whether John Wood was aware of this.

Turn right along Rivers Street. The Chequers — now a gastropub — was built for sedan chairmen, who would have been in serious need of refreshment after carrying their fares uphill. The New Bath Loyal Society of Chairmen was founded here in 1794. If you look down Rivers Street Mews, you will see that the backs of the houses in Catherine Place are a real hotch-potch. Beyond a rather splendid bow window, there is a tiny extension supported on brackets. This is, as you might guess, a lavatory. Such cantilevered extensions were known as 'hanging loos' and were very popular for a time — which is understandable, given that the only other options were a chamber pot under the bed or a trip to the privy down the garden. After some spectacular collapses, however, they fell out of favour, and the type of extension you can see further along, built up from ground level rather than cantilevered out, became the norm.

The full-height canted bay facing down Russel Street

An Edwardian postcard view of Christ Church

23 BATH. — Christ Church. — LL.

Continue along Rivers Street and cross the top of Russel Street. From here, there is a good view down to the Assembly Rooms. Notice how the house on the left-hand side of Rivers Street has an imposing full-height canted bay, built as an eye-catcher or *point de vue* for anyone looking up the street.

A few metres further on you come to Julian Road, with Christ Church across the road. Built in 1798, this was the first free church consecrated in England since the Reformation. It was for the servants and artisans who lived and worked in the Upper Town and could not afford the pew rents charged by proprietary chapels.[1] The

1 The gallery, however, was for the charitably-minded upper classes, who, by paying pew rents, funded the church.

long building to the left of it was an eighteenth-century riding school. When it was converted to flats in the 1970s, part of it was demolished and replaced by a modern extension. Between the riding school and the church, set back at the top of a flight of steps, is a Royal Tennis Court dating from 1777. Today, it houses perhaps the most fascinating museum in the city, built around a Victorian mineral-water factory and engineering works. In the Museum of Bath at Work, you can find out how Bath stone was quarried and cut, see a car made in the city in 1914 and learn what life was like for the vast majority of Bath's inhabitants. As a healthy antidote to the rose-tinted Jane Austenisation of the city's heritage, and in default of a museum devoted to the city's history, this extraordinary museum should feature on every visitor's itinerary.

As you **turn right along Brunswick Place**, look back to see, above the small white building tacked onto the end of Rivers Street, an old sign for the Red House Bakery – a long-forgotten piece of the city's commercial heritage.

Carry on to the busy crossroads on Lansdown Road. Although not a place many people tarry, this too may have formed part of the Woods' grand plan. Unlike the Circus and the Royal Crescent, however, this part was never realised.

If you look at the map from the early 1770s on page 62 and imagine Bennet Street heading north-east from the Circus in a straight line, you can see that it would have ended at this crossroads. It would

Above: Two views in the Museum of Bath at Work

Below: Sign for the Old Red House in Rivers Street

also have been the same length as Gay Street and Brock Street.[1] Unlike the other parts of the Woods' grand plan, this crossroads has been here for centuries – Lansdown Road was the old road from Bath to the north; the road that crosses it was built by the Romans. In the mid-eighteenth century, however, it was virtually in open country – another greenfield site ripe for development. And, as you can see from the glimpses of distant hills, now mostly blocked by tall buildings, it would have had spectacular

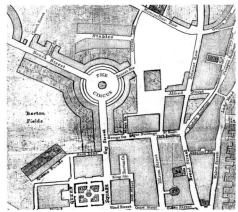

A map from the early 1770s showing the land between the stump of Bennet Street and the crossroads on Lansdown Road still undeveloped. Looked at in this way, it seems likely that the Woods intended Bennet Street to be another grand street running straight to another showpiece devlopment.

views. But what would the Woods have made of it? The writer Tobias Smollett, who knew them, provides a possible answer. In his novel *Humphrey Clinker*, published in 1771, that archetypal grumpy old man, Matthew Bramble, writes to a friend from Bath:

> The same artist who planned the Circus has likewise projected a Crescent; when that is finished, we shall probably have a Star.

This has always been treated as a joke. But was it? What if there were plans to build a Star? And was this where they planned to build it? If Bennet Street had been extended to the crossroads, it would have created five ways – representing a star – on a site even more dramatic than that of the Royal Crescent. Perhaps Montpelier – the row of four buildings on the north side of Julian Road, and remarkably similar to the buildings in Brock Street – marked the first stage of the development. And was it any coincidence that the inn built at the bottom of the road opposite in the 1760s was called the Star?

You can get an idea of what such a Star might have been like by looking once again at Bramham Park, where John Wood worked before coming to Bath. The gardens were laid out before he arrived, but his ideas of urban design seem to have been inspired by the avenues, circuses and crescents of formal hedges he found there. There was also a Star at Bramham,

---

1 The distance from the top of Gay Street to the corner of Queen Square, and from the east end of Brock Street to the end of the Royal Crescent is 187.5 metres; 187.5 metres in a straight line from the corner of Bennet Street takes you to the corner you are standing on.

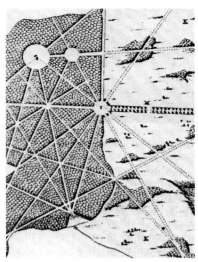

Above: A plan of part of the gardens at Bramham Park, where John Wood worked before he came to Bath

Below: One of the 'stars' at Bramham

Bottom: Belmont

with five avenues meeting at a central point. This was a standard element of eighteenth-century garden design; there is a similar feature – still known as the Star – in the Great Park at Cirencester. What makes Wood's translation of garden design to an urban setting more likely – and more intriguing – is that the gardens at Bramham were laid out by Robert Benson, who later became Lord Bingley. He was Grand Master of the Old Grand Lodge at York, which styled itself the Premier Assembly of English Freemasons, and he designed the gardens according to Masonic principles. But if John Wood the Younger did plan to bring his father's dream to fruition by building a Star in Bath, he was frustrated. A consortium of other developers acquired the land he needed to realise the project and built on it.

Given the lack of documentary evidence to support these theories, they must for the moment remain speculative. When it comes to the frustration of John Wood the Younger's plans for the Assembly Rooms, where we are now headed, we are on somewhat firmer ground. Here encroachment of a particularly brutal kind certainly did take place. You can see the first stage of this encroachment if you look over at Belmont, the row of houses running downhill on the opposite side of the road. You will notice that there is something very odd about it: the first eight houses are not stepped down the hill, but raised up to form a level terrace. The pavement in front of them is also level, so that, by the time it reaches the eighth house, it is high above the road. From this point, however, the houses in the row step down the hill at a steeper angle than the hill itself, so that, at the bottom, the pavement is only slightly higher than the road. It is an odd arrangement, and suggests that the first eight houses were built first and the rest came later.

If you **walk down Lansdown Road, take the first right into Bennet Street** and walk along to No 19 – once home to Admiral Phillip, the first governor of Australia – you will have a good view of the Assembly Rooms – although in this context 'good' is a somewhat relative term. The *Pevsner Architectural Guide to Bath* echoes the general view of the building when it describes it as 'a large and noble block, tucked away behind the Circus in an unimaginative urban arrangement'. But what if it was not John Wood the Younger's imagination that was at fault – what if he actually planned his Assembly Rooms to be viewed from the east, over what were, when he drew up his plans, pleasure grounds called the Hand & Flower. Take away the squat, gabled extension he stuck onto the east end when his grand design had been hemmed in by buildings, imagine seeing the Assembly Rooms across verdant lawns, and you have a truly imposing building.

It was Thomas Atwood who scuppered his plans. Unlike the Woods, Atwood was well connected and knew how to work the system. A plumber by trade, he not only became mayor of Bath but was also appointed city architect. By the 1760s he was one of the most successful developers in the city.

Belmont seems to have been built between 1770 and 1773, blocking the view eastward from the Hand & Flower grounds. It was almost certainly built by Thomas Jelly, a close associate of Atwood, who had collaborated

with him on several projects. If you look back towards Belmont you can appreciate the devastating impact this development would have had.

It was what Atwood did next, however, that put paid to John Wood the Younger's plans altogether. The council owned the freehold of

Belmont from Bennet Street

the Hand & Flower grounds. In March 1773, Atwood persuaded them to dispossess the leaseholder, a Mr Rogers, and transfer the lease to him. Within weeks, the grounds were transformed into a building site. The block facing you on the south side of Bennet Street was the result. With the prospect of the Assembly Rooms from the east ruined, there was little reason to preserve the architectural coherence of its east end, and in 1777 John Wood the Younger added a squat extension to it, which housed a card room. As well as enhancing the facilities of the Rooms, this must have caused great annoyance to the residents of Saville Row – and given Wood the Younger at least a modicum of satisfaction.

Today, this area, although full of perfectly respectable Georgian buildings, lacks the visual excitement of Queen Square, the Circus, or the Royal Crescent. And while praise for the interior of the Assembly Rooms is matched by lack of enthusiasm for the exterior, its intended façade lies hidden behind an extension, down a narrow alley. How different it could have been if the Woods' plans had not been thwarted by eighteenth-century insider dealing.

Cross over and continue along Bennet Street, past the single-storey extension on the north side of the Assembly Rooms that once housed a row of shops. As you walk past the bottom of Russel Street, look up to see how successfully the canted bay at the top closes the view.

Turn left to the entrance to the Assembly Rooms, which are open to the public unless events are being held. If the outside of the Rooms fails to set the pulse racing, the interior is another story. The Rooms have had an eventful history. After a long period of decline, they were bought in 1931 by Ernest Cook, who three years earlier had sold the travel agency business founded by his grandfather and moved to Bath to become a patron of the arts. He donated the Rooms to the Society for the Preservation of Ancient Buildings, who passed them on to the National Trust. After being restored at great expense, they were reopened by the Duchess of Kent on 19 October 1938. Less than four years later, they were burnt out by incendiary bombs during an air raid on the city. After the war there was much debate about what should happen to them, with many favouring demolition and replacement by housing. Fortunately, the preservationists won, the Rooms were restored and reopened once more in 1963. In 1987 part of the ballroom ceiling collapsed due to a fault in the plasterwork, and there was another restoration.

The Assembly Rooms after the air raids of April 1942

If you visited Bath's two other great eighteenth-century rooms – the Pump Room and the Banqueting Room – in the first walk, the ballroom may come as something of a shock. Not only is it more austere; its windows are very high and very small. There were two reasons for this: first, with nobody able to see out – and nobody able to see in – you were effectively cut off in a sort of fantasy world where different values prevailed; second, balls were held at night, so the issue of how much daylight was admitted to the room was irrelevant. Try to imagine the ballroom, not as it appears when cold, empty and echoing in the unforgiving light of day, but as it would have been at the height of the season, with the light from hundreds of candles shimmering through the prisms of the chandeliers. Here is how a visitor described it in 1778, seven years after it opened:

> On a ball night, in a full season, when all the benches are filled with ladies in full dress, the Rooms magnificently lighted by wax, the splendour of the lustres, girandoles, and the superlative charms of so many lovely women, whose natural beauties being awakened by the variety of amusements which, on all sides, surround them – renders it one of the most pleasing sights that the imagination of man can conceive; and what, we are convinced, no other part of Europe can boast of.

The Octagon at the heart of the Rooms is dominated by a superb portrait of Captain Wade, the first Master of Ceremonies at the New Rooms (as they were originally called to distinguish them from the Old Rooms on Terrace Walk). It was by Gainsborough, who deliberately made Wade's body elongated to counteract the foreshortening effect of seeing the painting from below.[1]

The tea room, where refreshments were taken midway through the evening, seems even more austere to modern eyes than the ballroom. Its bare stone has the purplish hue that Bath stone acquires after being subjected to intense heat, giving the room an antique, Pompeian look.

Leaving the Assembly Rooms, you are confronted by the backs of the building in the Circus – a motley collection of extensions and excrescences. To the south is Alfred Street. The bust of Alfred over the doorway of the second house dates from the time of its first occupant, Catherine Macaulay, a celebrated historian whose hero was King Alfred – hence the name of the street. Today Alfred Street is home to Wood's, one of Bath's best-loved restaurants, opened by David and Claude Price in 1979.

---

1 At the time of writing the portrait of Captain Wade was on loan to the Victoria Art Gallery.

Go down St Andrew's Terrace (beside Alfred Street), and turn right and then left into Miles's Buildings, built by John Wood the Younger in the late 1760s. The Porter pub on the corner is well-known for vegetarian food and live music; less well-known is the sphinx perched on the parapet of the building.

Turn left along George Street. A few doors along, you come to Edgar Buildings, designed by Thomas Jelly and built around 1761. The pediment at the centre of its palatial façade faces down Milsom Street, designed by Jelly as part of the same grand plan. Shopfronts, traffic, street furniture and 250 years of tinkering with Jelly's design have ensured that one of Bath's grandest set-pieces has effectively disappeared from view. The grandiose Victorian porch below the central pediment dates from when the Bath Constitutional Club occupied the building. The steps in front, where an impressive lamp post stands today, were the original site of the Edward VII memorial now in Parade Gardens.

The two large buildings flanking the top of Milsom Street date from 1865 and 1875 respectively and were, until recently, banks. Totally out of keeping with their surroundings, they provide a glimpse of what Bath might have looked like if the Victorians had really got their teeth into it. To your left, on the corner of Broad Street, is the Royal York Hotel, built by John Wood the Younger and opened in 1769 as the York House Hotel.

Carry on to the pedestrian lights, cross, turn right and then left down Milsom Street. This was laid out in 1762 on 'a piece of ground lately known by the name of Milsom's Garden'. It is almost impossible to imagine it as it was when originally built – a quiet street of refined lodging houses away from the hurly-burly of the city centre. Although the leases

Opposite page, from left: The bust of King Alfred in Alfred Street; a sedan chairmen's ramp in Miles's Buildings, now disfigured by the addition of modern security fencing; the sphinx on the Porter pub

Above: Edgar Buildings

Left: The former National Provincial bank on the north-east corner of Milsom Street

of the properties stipulated that they should not be used for trade, this was soon ignored. As early as 22 November 1770, a bookseller called Andrew Tennant placed a notice in the *Bath Chronicle* informing his customers that he had moved from the Abbey Church Yard to 'the large shop at the corner house at the top of Milsom Street'. On 9 September the following year, a Mrs Ford thanked the 'many indulging friends' who had patronised her milliner's shop in Milsom Street, which she was handing over to her niece, Mary Plura. By the end of the eighteenth century, Milsom Street was Bath's most fashionable shopping street and has remained so ever since. Few reminders of its residential origins survive, although one can be found on the left at No 33, where there is an early fanlight.

33 Milsom Street

Across the road, the main entrance to Jolly's was designed in 1879 by Major Davis. A little further along on the left, at Nos 37-42, is Somersetshire Buildings, built by Thomas Baldwin in the 1780s. The land here was not developed until then because it had been set aside for a poor house. This is not only the grandest set of buildings in the street; it is one of the grandest in the city. Yet, because it is in a busy shopping street and its ground floor has received so many inappropriate makeovers, most people do not give it a second glance. The trick, as with so many of Bath's buildings, is to raise your eyes to the upper floors, where the integrity of Baldwin's design, with a central full-height bay and grand pavilions at either end, survives.

For all its magnificence, though, there are problems with Somersetshire Buildings. For a start, there is its location. Baldwin had no control over that, of course, but he did not have to design something that failed so spectacularly to fit into the existing streetscape. Somersetshire Buildings demands to be seen from a distance, but instead looks across a narrow

Somersetshire Buildings in the early twentieth century and today

Above: 43 Milsom Street

Left: The cherub at the end of Milsom Street

street. Then there are those monumental, over-dominant engaged columns – and making a full-height bay the central feature effectively cuts the façade in two. Somersetshire Buildings seems to look back beyond the Palladianism of John Wood to the Baroque, and in doing so looks forward to the nineteenth century – to Brighton's grand asymmetrical terraces, for example, or to the Victorian banks at the top of Milsom Street. As a palatial front, Somersetshire Buildings seems too compressed (it is less than two-thirds the length of the north side of Queen Square), with too much detail crammed into a narrow space. Baldwin was not accustomed to accommodating his grand designs to cramped or awkward sites, nor, it seems, was he one to compromise. Bath Street, the Guildhall, Great Pulteney Street – all are masterpieces of urban design. The ideas on display in Somersetshire Buildings would – had they been applied in a building with a site and setting chosen by Baldwin – doubtless have produced something equally memorable. As it is, Somersetshire Buildings is a magnificent example of trying to fit a quart into a pint pot. But – and just to prove that no expense was spared – it also has one of the finest plasterwork ceilings in Bath, on the ground-floor of the central building, now the Nat West bank.

Next to Somersetshire Buildings, at No 43, painted lettering still advertises the circulating library that once operated from here. The cherub you can see in a niche below the royal coat of arms at the end of the street once formed part of a seventeenth-century cross that stood in the Cross Bath. If you look back from here to Edgar Buildings, you will see how skilfully Jelly planned the view up the street. You can also appreciate the crass insensitivity of the architects who designed the two banks at the top.

And so you come to Green Street once again – pre-John Wood Bath in all its asymmetrical glory – where you turn left to retrace your steps to the starting point.

3
A CONSTELLATION OF CRESCENTS
The Northern Slopes

Distance *3 miles*

Time *2-3 hours*

Accessibility *On pavements or paved surfaces throughout, with one flight of steps and a step-free alternative*

Public toilets *Monmouth Street (off Kingsmead Square)*

Starting point *Kingston Parade (outside Visitor Information Centre)*

> *I cast my eye around, and next observe*
> *The Royal Crescent with its graceful curve,*
> *And then above where other crescents grow*
> *That seem to emulate the curve below.*
> Thomas Haynes Bayley (1797-1839)

This walk looks at how the ground-breaking design of the Royal Crescent inspired other architects, with tier upon tier of crescents built on the city's northern slopes in the half century following its completion. In the realm of domestic architecture, few forms are more dramatic than the crescent, and this walk includes some of the most stunning urban panoramas you are likely to find anywhere.

You will also see how architectural styles developed in the late Georgian period. John Wood's classicism was derived from Roman models as reinterpreted by Palladio; he did not seek inspiration from the architecture of ancient Greece because he – like his contemporaries – was unaware of it. The rediscovery of Greek architecture in the latter half of the eighteenth century had a profound impact on design, and this walk takes in several examples of what became known as Greek Revival style. You will also see examples of the folksy neoclassicism that enjoyed a brief vogue in the 1980s and 1990s, largely due to the influence of Prince Charles, and built by one of his favourite architects, William Bertram.

While the craze for crescent building in the late eighteenth and early nineteenth centuries owed much to John Wood the Younger, it was also inspired by someone who was not an architect at all – William Hogarth. Although best known for satirical works such as *Marriage à la Mode* and *The Rake's Progress*, he was not only a very accomplished painter but also an influential aesthetic theorist.

Opposite: Cavendish and Lansdown Crescents

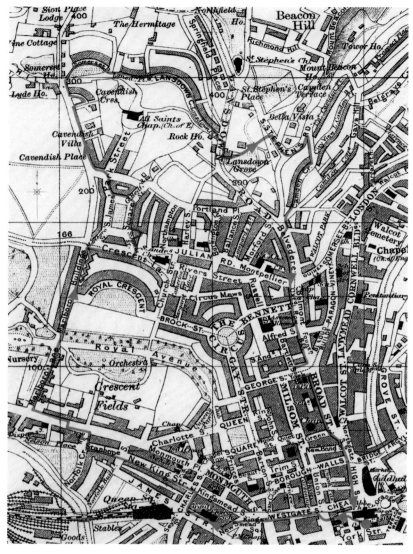

John Wood and many of his contemporaries had reacted against the excesses of the Baroque by looking back to Palladio, and using him as the inspiration for an architecture of rationalism. This was, after all, the Age of Reason, and their architectural designs were informed by the desire to create a rational society. They believed that buildings whose form was derived from rational principles and based on precepts laid down in antiquity were an essential prerequisite of such a society. However odd John Wood's ideas of druidism and alchemical fusion may seem today, for him they were ways of returning to first principles, as he made clear in a long and somewhat rambling treatise called *The Origin of Building*.

John Wood's aim as an architect was, above all, to rediscover and reapply these fundamental architectural principles. Tradition was everything; the waywardness of Baroque architecture, where the inspiration of the individual was paramount, represented for him the triumph of unreason and irrationality over divine truth. But, although Wood's Palladianism chimed with the spirit of rationalism that characterised the early eighteenth century, the forces of irrationality and inspiration never really went away, and by the time of his death in 1754 they were already beginning to reassert themselves.

William Hogarth's *Analysis of Beauty*, published in 1753, a year before John Wood's death, was a seminal text in this move away from the austerity of Palladianism. In it, Hogarth repudiated straight lines and symmetry in favour of what he called the 'line of beauty' – a serpentine line which echoed natural forms rather than intellectual concepts. Such lines had characterised the work of Baroque architects such as Borromini which Wood and other Palladians regarded as debased.

Later writers developed Hogarth's ideas, moving ever further away from the aridity of rationalism towards an aesthetics of sensation and inspiration, in which instinctive ideas of beauty – and of the picturesque – were all important. The most influential of these was Edmund Burke, who in 1757 published a *Philosophical Enquiry into the Origin of Our Ideas of the Sublime and the Beautiful*. In it he declared that the perception of beauty was instinctive rather than rational. Somewhat chauvinistically, he also suggested that the reason Hogarth's 'line of beauty' was so seductive was because it echoed the curves of the female body.

Burke's ideas on the sublime were even more groundbreaking. He argued that the feeling of awe aroused by the grandeur or mystery of natural or man-made phenomena had its origin in instincts of self-preservation. Elevating our instinctive apprehension of the sublime to the same level as our appreciation of beauty initiated an aesthetic revolution whose effects are still felt today.

In the latter part of the Georgian era, as Palladian ideals faded, the sublime became ubiquitous, with a craze for Gothic novels reflected in architectural fantasies such as the Royal Pavilion in Brighton and Beckford's Tower in Bath. Although this walk includes nothing so extravagant, you will see, as you climb the city's northern slopes, how the ideals espoused by John Wood were gradually displaced by a pursuit of the picturesque and the sublime.

Starting from the Visitor Information Centre, **head over to the left of the Abbey and turn left through Abbey Church Yard. Turn right into Stall Street and left along Westgate Street. At the end of Westgate Street, carry straight on into Kingsmead Square**, laid out in the late 1720s.

As you will see, the south side of the square is the only one with any semblance of uniformity. The western end of the terrace was bombed in 1942 and later rebuilt, and in 1969 the whole of the south side narrowly escaped demolition.

To the left of it is Avon Street, which runs down to the river. Today it is lined with modern buildings. Yet, blameless though its reputation is today, this street was once the most notorious in Bath. Built in the 1730s as lodging houses, it was soon abandoned by anyone with pretensions to gentility. In 1742 John Wood wrote that 'from a regular and tolerable beginning' Avon Street had 'fallen into an irregularity and meanness not worth describing'. It was the epicentre of Bath's red-light district; the prostitutes who plied their trade here were known as 'the nymphs of Avon Street'. It was also appallingly overcrowded. At the time of the 1821 Census, 1,500 people – over 5% of Bath's population – were crammed into its 90 or so buildings. Nothing now survives to remind us of a part of the city that was once – although for far different reasons – as well known as the Circus or Royal Crescent.

Kingsmead Square never fell as far out of favour as Avon Street, but by the early nineteenth century it was well off the radar as far as genteel visitors were concerned. In the 1840s the Chartists held mass meetings here and during the General Strike there were daily trade-union rallies.

The north side of Kingsmead Square contains some imposing buildings, but the overall effect is ruined by their different floor levels, so that even

Clockwise from above:
The south side of Kingsmead Square

Avon Street in the late nine-teenth century

The north side of Kingsmead Square

WALK 3: A CONSTELLATION OF CRESCENTS

Above: Atlantes on Rosewell House
Below: Two of the carvings on the keystones and the Rosewell rebus

the windows do not line up. To the west is Kingsmead Street, now a dead end with steps leading down to a car park, but, before it was destroyed by bombing in April 1942, a busy through route lined with shops.

The most intriguing building in Kingsmead Square is Rosewell House, built in 1735, on the southern corner of Kingsmead Street. Although

Above: Kingsmead Square in the early twentieth century, when Kingsmead Street was a busy through route

Below: The former labour exchange, pockmarked by shrapnel

Right: Holy Trinity, destroyed by bombing in 1942

contemporary with Queen Square, its Baroque exuberance – and especially the two bearded atlantes flanking the central first-floor window – hark back to an earlier architectural tradition. Over the second-floor window is a datestone with carvings of a rose and a well. This is a rebus indicating that the house was built for Thomas Rosewell. It was almost certainly this building that John Wood had in mind when he wrote that 'the houses in King's Mead Square have nothing, save ornaments without taste, to please the eye.'

The buildings to the left of Rosewell House were demolished in the 1860s to make way for a new street – called appropriately New Street – giving improved access to the Midland Railway station. As you can no longer head west along Kingsmead Street, **walk down New Street to James Street West.**

This area of the city suffered badly from bombing in April 1942. The single-storey building on the opposite side of James Street West – a former labour exchange – still bears the pockmarks made by shrapnel 70 years ago. To your right, the modern block on the north side of the street stands on the site of Holy Trinity church, which was destroyed. The only reminder of it is the name of the Trinity pub on your left.

Turn right along James Street West. At the crossroads, look over to the old Midland Railway station. A row of nine Georgian buildings was demolished to make way for it. Opened in 1870, it closed in 1966 but has since been restored. Despite the lack of trains, it remains one of the finest Victorian stations in the country.

Turn right up Charles Street, cross at the pedestrian lights halfway up and carry straight on along New King Street. This was a continuation of Kingsmead Street and another busy through route, with tram tracks down the middle.

On your right, the side wall of the Christadelphian Hall still carries an advertisement for a cycle shop that closed over a century ago. The Percy Community Centre, a little further along, stands on the site of a Methodist church whose foundation stone was laid by John Wesley in 1776. Rebuilt in 1847, it was destroyed by bombing in April 1942. Just beyond the community centre, you can see a step that once led to the doorway of a house which suffered the same fate.

New King Street was built in the 1760s and has had several famous residents. Jane Austen, however, was not among them. She looked at houses here with her mother in May 1801, but was not impressed. 'They were smaller than I expected to find them,' she wrote to her sister. 'One in particular out of the two was quite monstrously little; the best of the sitting-rooms not so large as the little parlour at Steventon, and the second room in every floor about capacious enough to admit a very small single bed.'

Opposite the Community Centre a plaque marks the site of a house where the dramatist Richard Brinsley Sheridan lived when he first came to Bath in 1770. An even more famous visitor – Lord Nelson – stayed for a time at No 17. Nelson's wife Fanny moved here in 1794 – along with Nelson's father – while he was away at sea. On the evening of Sunday 3 September 1797, after four years' separation, Nelson arrived at New King Street unannounced. He had lost his right arm at the Battle of Santa Cruz seven weeks earlier. The stump of his arm was infected and he was in great pain. He could only sleep with the aid of opium and feared that the infection would prove fatal. Happily, he recovered and went on to even greater glory. But, although his wife – along with his father – stayed on in Bath after he returned to sea the following April, he never came back to the city. Soon afterwards, he met and fell in love with Lady Hamilton, and the rest is history.

Two doors along, at No 19, is the house where the astronomer William Herschel once lived. It was while scanning the night sky through a telescope from here in 1781 that he discovered Uranus, which he originally called Georgium Sidus (George's Star) in honour of King George III. He was rewarded with the post of 'King's Astronomer' and a handsome pension, on the strength of which he gave up his day job as organist at the Octagon chapel and moved closer to London. His house, which still looks much as it did in the late-eighteenth century, contains a fascinating museum devoted to Herschel and his sister Caroline, who assisted him in his work.

St Ann's Place

Carry on along New King Street to St Ann's Place, on the right. This little-known gem nearly disappeared in 1972 because of plans to build a road tunnel under the city. Swathes of old houses in this area would have disappeared to make way for approach roads.[1] The building at the end of St Ann's Place with the skewed roof – once covered in thatch – was the Royal Oak pub, which closed in 1961.

At the crossroads carry on into Great Stanhope Street. The façade of No 24, on the left, was designed by Edward Davis in Greek Revival style in the 1830s.[2] You will notice that there is something peculiar about the right-hand window on the first floor of No 24 – behind it, as behind other first-floor windows in the street, there is a landing. This is a feature of many of Bath's Georgian buildings, a consequence of their being built back to front. In the early eighteenth century, houses were built to a standard design, with the stairs at the back and the rooms arranged symmetrically at the front. This facilitated the symmetrical arrangement of the windows on the façade. It meant, however, that, in most cases, the view from these

1 You will see the area earmarked for the eastern approach roads in Walk 4.

2 Edward Davis was the uncle of Major Charles Davis, some of whose buildings you saw in Walks 1 and 2.

windows was of the houses on the other side of the street, when there were often far better views from the back. Streets also tended to be noisy and smelly, while the backs of the houses often enjoyed semi-rural tranquillity. As the century wore on, architects started to rotate the interiors of those houses with good views at the back through 180 degrees, but continued to design symmetrical facades which no longer lined up with what was behind them. You will see the results of this uneasy compromise many more times as you walk round the city.

At the end of Stanhope Street, you are suddenly confronted with the breathtaking sweep of Norfolk Crescent on the left. It was started in 1792, but in 1793 a major financial crisis, caused by the failure of the Bath Bank, brought work to a stop. It did not start again until the early 1800s, and it was 1822 before the last house was completed. This corner of Bath is dedicated to the memory of Lord Nelson. Norfolk Crescent recalls his home county, Nelson Place lies ahead, while to the right is Nile Street, commemorating his elevation to Baron Nelson of the Nile. It did not start out like that, however. Norfolk Crescent was named after the Duke of Norfolk, Nelson Place originally formed part of Great Stanhope Street, and Nile Street was Howard Street – Howard being the Duke of Norfolk's family name. What the duke thought of the renaming in the wake of Nelson's victory at Trafalgar – or whether he himself suggested it – is not known.

The original design for Norfolk Crescent was by John Palmer, but when work was resumed John Pinch made significant changes. He added wrought-iron balconies to the first floor and moved the windows of the attic storey from behind the pediment. The balconies were an inspired touch, but the addition of what amounted to an extra storey to the façade – while it must have been appreciated by the servants who lived in the

Norfolk Crescent around 1910

attics – created a design problem that Pinch failed to resolve. You will notice that, although the façade is very plain, apart from the rusticated ground floor, there are several heavy bands above the second floor, running the entire length of the building. This is the entablature and, in the original design, the central pediment would have sat on top of it. The insertion of an extra row of windows, separating the pediment from the Ionic pilasters that support the entablature in the centre and at either end, breaks all the canons of architectural propriety. The Woods would have been horrified – but Pinch had such a sure sense of what would look right that he was prepared to go ahead and break them anyway. The north end of the Crescent was gutted by incendiary bombs in April 1942. When the first seven buildings were rebuilt some 20 years later, most of the original entrances were blocked up.

Norfolk Crescent is the only one of Bath's crescents built on level ground at the bottom of the valley. However, it was beside the river, and the prospect of green fields on the far bank must have been delightful. How could the developer have known that, by the end of the nineteenth century,

The watchman's shelter in Norfolk Crescent on an early twentieth-century postcard

it would look across to railway marshalling yards, engine sheds and factories? Today, the railway and the industry have gone, and it looks across to a supermarket car park – or would do, if trees did not hide it. Despite all the vicissitudes it has suffered, Norfolk Crescent remains one of Bath's finest architectural showpieces. It also boasts one of the city's little-known Greek Revival gems, in the shape of the watchman's shelter on the corner, based on the Choragic Monument of Lysicrates in Athens.

Turn right along Nile Street and left along the Upper Bristol Road. Cross at the pedestrian lights, continue along

the Upper Bristol Road and turn right up Marlborough Lane. After 200 metres you will pass a pair of sphinxes guarding the entrance to the Royal Avenue. Opposite is a pair of Greek Revival arches designed in 1830 by Edward Davis. The obelisk beyond them was built in 1837 to celebrate the accession of Queen Victoria.

Carry on uphill past Marlborough Buildings, with magnificent views of the Royal Crescent to your right. Nos 13-15 Marlborough Buildings, facing the entrance to the Crescent, were built around 1787 as a stand-alone development before the rest of the row and are more ornate. As you continue uphill, late Victorian and early twentieth-century full-height porch-cum-loo extensions proliferate, reaching their apogee in the

Looking through the Sphinx Gates to the Victoria Obelisk, flanked by Edward Davis's Greek Revival gates. This view dates from the 1860s when none of these structures was much more than 30 years old

Nos 13-15 Marlborough Buildings, originally built as a stand-alone development

over-the-top French-chateau-style extension to No 25. As you walk past the back of the houses in the Royal Crescent notice once again how the symmetry of the façade gives way to an architectural free-for-all. At the top of Marlborough Buildings is the Marlborough Tavern, built, like the Chequers in Rivers Street, for sedan chairmen and now a gastropub.

Turn right along Julian Road, once known as Cottle's Lane after a local landowner. It follows the course of a Roman road once thought to have been called the Via Julia – hence its change of name. The Romans, however, did not name their roads, but gave them numbers – this one was Highway 14. The Via Julia theory was an elaborate hoax perpetrated by a literary forger called Charles Julius Bertram, who claimed to have discovered an ancient manuscript giving details of the route. So convincing was the forgery that the antiquarian William Stukeley was taken in, along with Richard Colt Hoare, who popularised the use of the name. Somewhat embarrassingly, therefore, Julian Road perpetuates not the name of a lost Roman road, but the middle name of an eighteenth-century fraudster.

After 125 metres, look out for No 15 Crescent Lane on the right. This is the back entrance to the Royal Crescent Hotel and was designed in

St Andrew's, bombed in 1942 and demolished in 1960

1986 by William Bertram as a sombre exercise in self-conscious neoclassicism. If you look ahead you will see a wide expanse of grass. This has a curious history. When John the Wood the Younger built the Royal Crescent, the land was set aside for a proprietary chapel and 'burying ground'. Both John Wood the Younger and his father – who had been buried in a temporary grave at Swainswick – were going to be interred here, but the chapel was never built. In the early nineteenth century, a villa was built at the far end, but in the late 1860s it was pulled down to build a church. St Andrew's was designed by George Gilbert Scott in full-blown Gothic Revival style with a 67-metre spire – 18 metres

WALK 3: A CONSTELLATION OF CRESCENTS

higher than the Abbey. It fell victim to the Luftwaffe in April 1942 – Nikolaus Pevsner, writing thirteen years after the end of the war, described it as 'happily bombed', which, given that he was German, seems a tad insensitive – and the site was eventually cleared in 1960.

Cross at the zebra crossing, turn left and then right up St James's Street. St James's Wine Vaults, on the left, has been a pub since it was built in 1791. **Turn right under an archway into St James's Place.** The launderette here was once a butcher's and the hooks for hanging meat survive overhead. The courtyard beyond it is one of the city's most atmospheric hidden corners. The oldest building in the area lies ahead. It may have started life as a farm, although it is more likely that, when the workmen arrived to build St James's Square and the streets around it, they built this house first to provide themselves with lodgings. The braces holding the building together suggest it was built hastily, with walls only one course thick.

As you **carry on through the archway at the end of the courtyard**, you will see Curiosity Cottage – once a shop – on the right. Above its nameplate is a link snuffer. Links were torches of burning pitch carried through the streets by link boys to guide pedestrians home through the dark and often dangerous streets. When they arrived at their destination,

these snuffers were used to extinguish the links.

When you emerge into St James's Square, look to the left to see two plaques. One records that Walter Savage Landor lived here, the other that Charles Dickens 'dwelt' here. The distinction is important. Dickens' association with this building was confined to being invited to dinner by Landor on several occasions.[1] That was enough for the worthies of the Bath Dickens Society, however, anxious to honour the great man's somewhat tenuous links with the city.[2]

As for Curiosity Cottage, Dickens is believed to have come up with the character of Little Nell in *The Old Curiosity Shop* while discussing the novel over dinner with Landor. This later gave rise to the story that Dickens based the character of Little Nell on a girl he saw working in the shop at the back of Landor's house. The former shop has now been renamed Curiosity Cottage, setting the seal on the legend.

Turn right up the east side of St James's Square. Built by John Palmer between 1790 and 1793, the *Pevsner Architectural Guide* describes this as the 'most complete Georgian square in Bath'. Like Queen Square, the

---

1 Landor was a famous writer whose star, unlike that of Dickens, has faded.

2 For more on Dickens' links with Bath, see *Literary Walks in Bath*, published by Akeman Press.

north side has a palatial façade with a central pediment. Unlike Queen Square, however, St James's Square retains, despite the cars parked around it, much of the tranquillity its original residents would have known. Great Bedford Street, leading out of the north-east corner of the square, was intended to be one of the showpieces of late-eighteenth-century

The east side of St James's Square

The north side of St James's Square in the 1950s

WALK 3: A CONSTELLATION OF CRESCENTS

Bath, a wide thoroughfare running up to the junction of Lansdown Road and Lansdown Place East and lined with magnificent houses. Only the first few of those houses were ever built and those on the east side were destroyed by bombing in 1942.

Turn left along the north side of the square and right up Park Street. Park Street was begun by John Palmer around 1790, but work stopped three years later. It was not until 1808 that work resumed on the remaining houses, this time to designs by John Pinch. Here once again the landings of the houses on the left can be seen through the first-floor windows, indicating that their interiors are back to front.

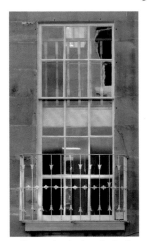

Turn left into Park Place and right into Cavendish Place, both built by John Pinch between 1806 and 1816. Cavendish Place is one of the city's architectural highlights, with superb fanlights and ironwork, and a Vitruvian scroll and cornice flowing uphill in a series of graceful sweeps. Its location, overlooking the green slopes of High Common, sets it off magnificently.

Continue uphill past Winifred's Dale, built by John Pinch around 1810, an early and very fine example of the semi-detached villas that would soon spread over the hills around Bath as terraces and crescents fell out of favour.

Above: A window in Park Street

Below: Cavendish Place

Bottom: Cavendish Lodge

Just beyond it comes the shock of the nearly new, in the form of Cavendish Lodge, a post-modernist apartment block set back behind two lodges. It was designed by William Bertram and built, amid great controversy, in 1996. Opinion is still divided as to its merits, for, while it employs Georgian motifs, its Southfork-like ostentation and folksy dry-stone walling are a world – or at least an ocean – away from the Georgian ideal. Fifteen years on, it seems surprisingly dated. The world has moved on and the semiotic irony of dropping a chunk of neo-Georgian kitsch into a Georgian setting no longer raises the wry smile it was presumably intended to – although many failed to see the joke in the first place.

A few metres further on, turn right and walk round Cavendish Crescent, designed by John Pinch and built between 1815 and

1830. Small-scale, tucked away and supremely understated, it is a model of taste and decorum, relying for impact on its picturesque setting. It has no pillars or pilasters, no central feature, little in the way of ornament, and, as at Norfolk Crescent, the servants' windows are not hidden behind the pediment. It was the last crescent to be built in Bath, the final flowering of a style that had epitomised gracious living for over half a century. From now on, at least for the well-to-do, detached or semi-detached villas were the way forward. Cavendish Crescent did have at least one notable resident, however – Sir William Holburne, who, until his death in 1874, lived at No 10, where he squirrelled away the paintings and *objets d'art* now on display in the Holburne Museum.

At the end of the crescent carry on uphill. On your left is Doric House, built by Joseph Gandy for the painter Thomas Barker in 1805. It is one of the earliest and most monumental Greek Revival buildings in the

city, and looks forward, in its mausoleum-like austerity, to the portentous heaviness of Victorian architecture. On the other side of the windowless wall is a vast mural by Barker – a work of jaw-dropping sublimity depicting the massacre of 25,000 Greeks by Ottoman troops on the island of Chios during the Greek War of Independence.

Ahead of you at the crossroads, rising above the telephone box, is Somerset House, built around 1790. On the wall of the building on the right a faded sign reveals that it was once a post office. At one time it was also Moger's Dairy, and it survived as a newsagent's and corner shop until the mid-1990s.

Above: Doric House

Right: Recalling a long-lost post office

Below: When the old post office was still a shop. Sadly, the splendid sign for Moger's Dairy over the door has since been obliterated

Head up the flight of steps to the right of Somerset House – looking back to see the range of false windows on the old post office.[1] At the top is Somerset Place, designed by Bath's most maverick architect, John Eveleigh. Originally from London, Eveleigh worked as a builder for

Somerset Place

Thomas Baldwin before setting up as an architect in 1787. Work on the central section of Somerset Place began around 1790, but was abandoned when Eveleigh went bankrupt in 1793. Although it was eventually resumed some 15 years later, Somerset Place was never completed, leaving an uneven number of buildings on either side of the central feature. It is a crescent in all but name and has some wonderful touches, such as the ironwork, the ice men on the central keystones and a superb broken pediment. Notice though that while the buildings on either side step gently down, the plat band and cornice do not. They slope down instead, giving the casual observer the impression that the row is level. When you become aware that it is not, the illusion is ruined, and Eveleigh's innovative solution to the problem of the sloping site seems somehow unsatisfactory. Somerset Place was badly damaged by bombing in April 1942. The three houses at the western end are total rebuilds; much of the rest of the crescent was rebuilt behind the façade as student accommodation in the 1950s. In 2006 it was bought by developers who plan to convert it to townhouses and apartments.

Walk along the pavement to the east end of Somerset Place and look over into a garden on the other side of the lane. This garden, which predates the buildings around it, originally belonged to a house – long demolished – called St Catherine's Hermitage. It was built around 1774 by Philip Thicknesse, a larger-than-life character who is said to have amassed a fortune through blackmailing the rich and famous. The turret-like bay, five storeys high, which rises from the garden, was added to the end house in Lansdown Place West sometime between 1852 and 1886, and once housed a collection of curiosities gathered together by Guy Stickney Blaine.

As you climb the astonishingly steep slope of Lansdown Place West, Lansdown Crescent comes into view ahead. This is architecture as high drama. Lansdown Place West forms a unified and coherent whole with Lansdown Crescent and Lansdown Place East at the far end. Here is

---

1 To avoid the steps, bear right up the road and take the first left.

Hogarth's line of beauty snaking ineluctably over the contours high above the city. Despite its sinuous curves, its proportions are assured and the iron overthrows framing each doorway provide the perfect foil to its restrained minimalism. To see it at dusk when the lamps are lit – especially if there is a touch of mist in the air – is to experience one of Bath's finest visual treats.

So accomplished is the design of Lansdown Crescent that it may come as a surprise to learn that its architect is unknown. It has been attributed to John Palmer, but its dissimilarity to Palmer's other buildings – and the lack of any documentary evidence – must cast doubt on this. It may have been designed by a local banker called John Lowder, who designed buildings elsewhere and was involved with this development.[1] It was common for substantial buildings to be designed by men who were not architects. Marlborough Buildings, for example, were designed by John Fielder, a tiler and plasterer, James Broom, a carpenter, and Thomas King, a statuary. But, as for Lansdown Crescent, until documentary evidence turns up, the question of who designed it must remain open.

The archway linking Lansdown Place West to Lansdown Crescent was not part of the original design, but added by William Beckford, who owned the houses on either side. The house with the full-height bay at the other end of Lansdown Crescent – No 1 – was built by 1786 as a detached villa called Lansdown Place.[2]

Above: No 1 Lansdown Crescent, originally built as a detached villa

Opposite: Lansdown Crescent at dusk

Three years later, it was decided to continue building westward and create a crescent. The whole development, including Lansdown Place East and West, was complete by 1795.

1 Another candidate is Thomas Baldwin. In 1893, a local author called REM Peach, who wrote several books on Bath's history, ascribed Lansdown Crescent to Baldwin, but its marked dissimilarity to any of Baldwin's other buildings makes this unlikely.

2 The villa still appeared in lordly isolation on a map published by Savage and Meyler in 1805, although the rest of the crescent had been in existence for a decade.

During the Bath Blitz in April 1942, bombs fell in the meadow below the crescent, causing extensive damage. The craters can still be seen, although today the scene is one of pastoral tranquillity, with the turf nibbled by sheep, as it would have been two centuries ago. The original residents had much more extensive views, however, as there were no tall trees below the meadow.

Carry on down Lansdown Place East, and, when you reach Lansdown Road, cross with care and head downhill. Hope House, on the right, was originally called Rock House. It dates from 1790, but has been greatly extended and is now a school.

Turn left in front of the Lansdown Grove Hotel. Although this looks late nineteenth century, the central section was built around 1740, when it was known as Sandpit House. It was extended in 1860 and again in 1913. Haygarth Court, on your right as you continue uphill, was built as a nursing home in 1888 and has now been converted to apartments.

On the left you will see through the trees an eighteenth-century Gothick loggia in the gardens of the Lansdown Grove Hotel, with a modern building stuck onto the back of it. As you continue uphill, the front of this extension – with a Dutch gable, Lutyenesque doorway and diagonal chimneys – comes into view. It was designed by William Bertram in 1987.

Facing you at the end of the road is Heathfield, an Italianate villa built around 1845 by James Wilson. If you look through its Doric gateway, you will see an assortment of columns and capitals, believed to have come from John Wood's chapel in Queen Square when it was demolished in the 1860s.

Turn right downhill and, as you follow the road round when it curves to the left, take a look at the footpath carrying straight on down. Until the early eighteenth century, this was the main road into Bath from the north – the original Lansdown Road. It was rerouted, along a gentler gradient, after Queen Anne's coach, climbing out of the city, started rolling back downhill. A nasty accident was averted when several onlookers rushed over to check its downward progress. As you carry on along the road, one of the finest panoramas of the city opens up on the right.

The crest of the Earl of Camden

Follow the road as it doubles back downhill to the right. As you approach the junction at the bottom, with a nineteenth-century terrace across the road – and a palm tree adding a Riviera touch – there is no hint of what awaits you around the corner. When you get there, however, Camden Crescent is suddenly revealed in all its glory. Camden Crescent was built by John Eveleigh for Charles Pratt, Earl of Camden, whose crest – an elephant's head – can be seen over its doorways.

Camden Crescent

The first stone of the crescent was laid on 9 April 1787. Inscribed 'nil desperandum – auspice Camden', it weighed two tons and was drawn by six horses decorated with blue ribbons. It was accompanied by twelve quarrymen wearing blue cockades, who cried 'prosperity to the city and corporation of Bath' as they passed the Guildhall.

If you **turn right and walk along to the centre of the crescent**, you will see Pratt's coat of arms in the tympanum. You will also see that the entablature is supported by five Corinthian columns on a rusticated base. It was an inviolable rule for architects working in the classical tradition that there should always be an even number of pillars. Whether Eveleigh was unaware of the rule or whether he was deliberately setting out to be a maverick is unclear. What we do know is that whoever chose the site for the crescent made a profound error of judgement.

If you look ahead, you will see that there are ten houses to the east of the central pair, the last one adorned with four columns on a rusticated base. If you look the other way, there are only four houses, with no columns or rustication on the end house. This is not the result of Eveleigh's waywardness – or of the money running out – but of subsidence. There were to have been six more houses, giving an equal number on either side. The end house, on an outcrop high above valley, was started first, but, when work began on the ones in between, the ground gave way. The part-completed house at the end survived for a few years as a romantic ruin, until it too collapsed one night in a mighty thunderstorm, along with the promontory it stood on. As sublime endings go, that takes some beating.

A view of Camden Crescent from around 1805, showing the ruins of the house at the east end which survived until the promontory it stood on collapsed in a thunderstorm

Carry on along Camden Crescent. Beyond the last house in the crescent are five more houses forming a flanking wing. There were to have been five similar houses running downhill at the other end. At the side of the last house is a magnificent full-height bay with a first-floor balcony commanding a superb view of a busy crossroads. **Continue downhill, crossing to the left beside a single-storey lodge, and turning left across Upper Hedgemead Road a few metres further on. Turn left down Lansdown Road, cross over (using the pedestrian island) and carry on downhill.**

This part of Lansdown Road is known as Belvedere, and was one of the earliest developments in the Upper Town: the *Bath Journal* advertised a house to let here on 25 June 1753. In the nineteenth century, many of the buildings on the west side and some on the east were converted to shops. A particularly fine and well-preserved shopfront can be seen across the road on the old pharmacy at No 29. Three doors down, the alleyway beside the Indian restaurant once led to Wellington Terrace, which disappeared after a series of landslips in the 1880s. No 34 – Antique Textiles – has a sphinx atop the parapet. The path leading into Hedgemead Park, a little further down, was originally lined with houses. The park was created in 1889 after the houses had been cleared away and the land condemned as unfit for building.

Cross Julian Road and continue downhill.[1] As you cross Alfred Street, look across to the bottom of Belmont to see a two-storey porch with a

---

1 There are no dropped pavements at this difficult crossing, so if this poses a problem, you will need to turn right along Julian Road before crossing by Christ Church.

serpentine front, evoking once again the line of beauty. Just below it is the rusticated entrance to Fountain House, with an elaborate Venetian window above it. Fountain House was built some time before 1740 as a detached residence. It stood on the corner of a byway called Back Lane, which ran to the right of it. Back Lane was closed in the 1750s and houses were later built on the site. In the 1770s Fountain House was extended to the north and in the nineteenth century part of it became a shop. Despite these alterations, it remains an imposing building. It is on the site of a spring – or fountain – where a chapel dedicated to St Werburgh stood in the middle ages. After the chapel was deconsecrated it became an alehouse, before being pulled down to make way for Fountain House. In 1860, a drinking fountain and horse trough fed by the spring were built on the corner further down. They were removed in 1938 to widen the road.

Fountain House, built on the site of a spring where a chapel dedicated to St Werburgh stood in the middle ages

Turn right at the crossroads and cross at the pedestrian lights. Turn left, walk back to the crossroads, turn right down Broad Street and carry on along Northgate Street and High Street to return to the starting point.

4

BEYOND THE NORTH GATE
Walcot Street, the Paragon & Broad Street

Distance *2 miles*

Time *1.5-2 hours*

Accessibility *On pavements or paved surfaces throughout; several flights of steps, with step-free alternatives available*

Public Toilets *Podium Shopping Centre, Northgate Street*

Starting point *Kingston Parade (outside Visitor Information Centre)*

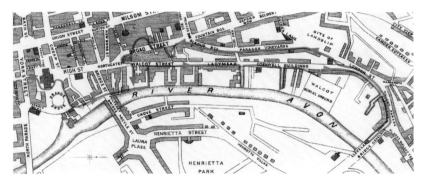

> *Most residents of the city are mere occupiers. For them the social organisation of its space is a given fact. They simply use what is left over after the wealthy and powerful have taken their shares. Their place in it is allocated to them and it forms for them the spatial condition of their consciousness. Such consciousness becomes manifest in social movements rather than in building.*
> RS Neale, *Bath: A Social History*, 1680-1850

> *Streets are the space left over between buildings.*
> Rebecca Solnit, 2001

Until the beginning of the eighteenth century, there were only three streets outside the city walls – Broad Street and Walcot Street to the north and Southgate Street to the south. There is nothing left of the old Southgate Street, but Broad Street and Walcot Street bear many reminders of bygone days and are among the most fascinating parts of the old city. Together with the Paragon, built in the eighteenth century, they form the subject of this walk.

Opposite: Looking west along Walcot Street with the Paragon high above

From the Visitor Information Centre, walk towards the Abbey and turn right along Kingston Buildings. The building ahead, now the Seventh Day Adventist church, was originally the studio of Lucius Gahagan, an Irish sculptor who settled in Bath in the 1820s. His works include the bust of Garrick over the entrance to the Garrick's Head pub and the statues of Commerce and Genius on the former bazaar in Quiet Street. To the left of the studio, you can see the backs of the early eighteenth-century gabled buildings on the south side of the Orange Grove. Although the fronts were transformed beyond recognition by Major Davis in the late nineteenth century, the backs have changed far less. Despite their proximity to some of the best-known buildings in Bath, these backs – unlike anything else in the city, with an almost Scottish look to them – are known hardly at all.

Bear left past the east front of the abbey, bear left again and then turn right over two sets of pedestrian lights. Bear right past Brown's and Garfunkels, and turn left along Grand Parade. At the end, cross the road straight ahead (with care because only half the crossing is controlled by traffic lights) and carry straight on under a metal archway.[1] After climbing the steps, keep to the right, following a sign for the Riverside Walkway. From here there is a good view of the unglamorous north side of Pulteney Bridge. Walk down the long flight of steps ahead and carry on along the cantilevered walkway. The old buildings across the river, now converted to flats and offices, were once part of the Northgate Brewery, which started out around 1770 on this side of the river but soon outgrew the site. A tramway bridge was built across the river and the brewery continued to expand on the other side. It became the biggest brewery in the west of England before closing

Above: Construction work around the old Northgate Brewery buildings on Grove Street in September 1980

Right: Looking across to Grove Street from the Riverside Walkway today

1 For a step-free route, turn left up Bridge Street, right along Northgate Street and carry on along Walcot Street to the Hilton Hotel.

in 1868. The brewery buildings on this side went long ago – all that remains is the shell of those on the far bank.

After climbing another flight of steps, turn right along a pavement until you come to a locked gate with steps on the other side of it. The riverside walkway once continued down here, although, as it came to a dead end a little way along, the decision was taken to close it. You are probably thinking that, if there was a competition for the ten worst riverside walks, this would be a strong contender. And it may not be much consolation to learn that there is a campaign – albeit one opposed by some local residents – to extend it 700 metres to Cleveland Bridge. If that ever happens, it will be a superb facility for visitors and residents alike, transforming their experience of this part of the city and bringing regeneration in its wake.

For now, though, **turn left, walk up to Walcot Street, turn right and walk along to a viewing platform over the car park.** At one time there were public toilets here. After being closed – like most of Bath's toilets – by the council, they were demolished in June 2003 as part of a site-specific art installation during Walcot Nation Day – more on that later.

Walcot Street is one of the most historic streets in the city. People have lived and worked along it since Roman times. It was the Saxons, however, who came up with the the name Walcot – which, given what Walcot means, was a bit of a cheek. After the Romans abandoned Bath – or Aquae Sulis as they called it – the people left behind settled down, making the best of things and trying to stay out of the way of ravaging hordes. Eventually one ravaging horde – the Saxons – scored an overwhelming victory at the Battle of Dyrham, eight miles to the north, in AD577. They then occupied Aquae Sulis and established a settlement within the Roman ramparts. They called the bit inside the ramparts Akemancester; the bit outside, where the native population continued to eke out a precarious existence, they called Walcot – from the Saxon word 'wealh' meaning 'foreigner'. Wales and Cornwall – both names coined by the Saxons – have a similar derivation. The fact that it was the Saxons who were the foreigners seems to have passed them by.

The attitude of the Saxons has summed up the official view of Walcot Street – as somewhere rather beyond the pale – ever since. In 1742, for example, John Wood wrote that Walcot Street had 'one of the finest situations for building in that nature is capable of producing' but added that, 'instead of finding it covered with habitations for the chief citizens, it is filled, for the most part, with hovels for the refuse of the people.'

In the twentieth century, town planners made at least three attempts to get rid of it altogether. In 1938 came the Walcot Street Improvement Scheme, with a plan to demolish all the buildings on the east side of the street between Northgate Street and Old Orchard. The outbreak of war put the plans on hold, but in 1945 a report prepared for the Bath & District Joint

Planning Committee by Sir Patrick Abercrombie revived them in an amended form. A new dual-carriageway was to be built alongside the river, with Walcot Street replaced by something remarkably similar to the new Southgate. The scheme never got off the ground, but in 1964 came the Buchanan Report, which came within a whisker of being implemented. Had it been, Walcot Street would be no more than a distant memory, and where you are standing would have been an approach road running down to a motorway-style tunnel under the city.

Things came to a head in 1972. Despite public opinion being overwhelmingly against it, the council was determined the tunnel should be built. Walcot Street was saved by that year's local government elections. An action

Above: The southern end of Walcot Street cleared for redevlopment

Left: Posters urging voters to elect Sam Farr

group fielded candidates against councillors who supported the tunnel. The result was decisive, with a famous victory over Elgar Jenkins, one of the scheme's supporters, by Sam Farr, a photographer with the *Bath Chronicle*.

Even though the tunnel was killed off, much damage had been done. Walcot Street was full of empty properties, where people had moved out believing the bulldozers were about to move in. Many buildings had already been demolished. From that nadir, Walcot Street slowly fought back, re-establishing itself as a community and

Walcot Nation Day ... gone but not forgotten

reinventing itself as Walcot Nation, a countercultural cornucopia of artistic endeavour and passionate opposition to everything the tunnel had stood for. Once a year the street was closed to celebrate Walcot Nation Day. They were heady times, but, while their spirit lives on, especially in places like the Bell Inn, the last Nation Day was in 2005 and many now fear that gentrification is eroding what made Walcot Street special. It is ironic that Walcot Street has been rebranded Bath's 'artisan quarter' by the image makers at a time when many of the artisans are being forced out by rising rents and redevelopment.

This stretch of road, which now looks over a car park, was once home to dozens of shops and businesses – including an inn where Dr Johnson is reputed to have stayed – with a maze of courts and alleyways behind.

If you look across the river you will see an elegant Georgian building – once the city gaol – with Sham Castle high on the hill above. To the left of the car park, the building shored up with scaffolding is the old Corn Market, built some time before 1817. The service road beside it is on the site of the old cattle market. The YMCA across the road was built in 1972 on the site of an inn called the George, which closed around 1868. Harvest, a Walcot Street institution for over 30 years, stands where carts once trundled through to its yard.

Left: The Corn Market, from a painting by Nick Cudworth

Above: Walcot Street in the mist

Below: The tramshed in 1938

Bottom: Looking eastwards along Walcot Street

Carry on along Walcot Street, past the impressive façade of the Corn Market, added in 1855, to the entrance to Beehive Yard. The red-brick Tramshed was built in 1903 for the electric trams introduced the following year. After the trams were scrapped in 1939, the building found various uses – most notably as an antiques market – before being converted to a bar, offices and apartments in 2002.

Through the gates of the yard is the old Walcot Foundry. Beehive Yard was named after the Beehive Inn which occupied the building on the corner, part of which now houses a language school.

In the mid-eighteenth century Walcot Street underwent a subtle re-branding. The first – and grittiest – part of the street, which you have just walked along, continued to be known as Walcot Street. The next part, however – beginning at the Beehive – was renamed Ladymead. This was an old name for the area, the lady in question being Edith, wife of Edward the Confessor, who had owned the land. The final stretch was renamed Cornwell Buildings after a well fed by the Corn (or Carn) brook that once stood there. This tripartite arrangement lasted until 1905, when the council

Buildings in Ladymead, the pavement covering what was once their front gardens

decreed that the entire street should revert to its original name. The old names survive, however, carved ineradicably into the stonework.

Next to the old Beehive, the Shannon furniture store occupies a building dating from around 1700. The left-hand side was once an inn called the Catherine Wheel. Tiny though it was, it not only brewed its own beer but provided 'well-aired beds' for travellers. After it closed around 1909, a horsemeat butcher took over the premises. Later it became a grocer's and then the Pandora Café. The buildings here originally had gardens in front of them, which were removed in 1829 to create 'an excellent causeway … for the accommodation of foot passengers'. The wide pavement, whose kerb follows the line of the garden walls, was later pressed into service as an extension to the cattle market, with sheep pens set up here on busy days.

No 84 – the left-hand side of John's Bikes – has a datestone of 1736. Although Frost's Antiques occupied this building for much of the twentieth century, the right-hand side of John's Bikes has been a cycle shop for well over a century. The three cycle racks in front, spelling out WALCOT, along with the one-eyed-alien bollards, are part of the Walcot Street Artworks project, conceived in 1999. This is a good place to survey the buildings looming above you on the other side of the road, and to try to imagine the impact they must have had when they were built. Up to the left, the palatial façade with a pediment at its centre belongs to Bladud's Buildings, probably designed by Thomas Jelly and built between 1755 and 1762. Although you are looking at the back, it is as grand as the front – such buildings are described as having a 'double elevation'.

Two views of the Paragon from Walcot Street

The flight of steps opposite runs between Bladud's Buildings and the Paragon. The Paragon was designed by Thomas Atwood and built between 1768 and 1775. Taking his lead from the Royal Crescent, he designed it as a curved terrace, following the lie of the land. It is not its curve that strikes you most forcefully from below, however, but its scale. The massive retaining walls, holding back who knows how many thousand tons of earth, are astonishing enough; to build what amounted to eighteenth-century skyscrapers on top displayed an audacity bordering on recklessness.

To the right of the steps is a drinking fountain and horse trough designed by Major Davis in 1860, which gave many local residents access to clean drinking water for the first time. After years of disuse and neglect, it was restored (although not connected to a water supply) in 2006.

Continue along Walcot Street to St Michael's church hall, a superb art-nouveau building designed in 1904 by Wallace Gill, and now a restaurant. The Thai restaurant on the other side of Old Orchard was originally the Bladud's Head Inn,

opened in 1792, with stables and a brewery in the yard at the back.

Turn right down Old Orchard. On your right is a small courtyard lined with workshops and studios. At the far end is the studio of Bronwyn Williams-Ellis, where you can not only admire a fascinating array of ceramic tiles and sculptures, but also see old hooks surviving from when the building was a slaughterhouse. Like much of Walcot Street, there have been buildings on this site for almost two thousand years, and, because it was always a working area, building materials were recycled rather than discarded. It is anyone's guess how many of the blocks of stone you can see in the walls date back to medieval or even Roman times. A little further down is a row of eighteenth-century cottages, with a bressummer running its entire length. On the right is the bottom entrance to Beehive Yard, where the old brass and iron foundry has been converted to offices.

Head back up to Walcot Street and turn right. As you pass the Old Red House Bakery – now Mastershoe – look out for little faces leering at you from the wall opposite. Beside the bakery is the entrance to a yard, still paved with setts, giving a glimpse of the old workaday world of Walcot Street, now fast disappearing. The main entrance to the yard is a little further along. It belonged to Hayward & Wooster, builders and contractors, who moved here in 1881. The Arts and Crafts-style office and showroom to the left of the entrance dates from 1905 and blocks

the view of an eighteenth-century house where Robert Southey, poet laureate from 1813 to 1843, spent much of his childhood. In 1977 the yard was taken over by Walcot Reclamation, an architectural salvage firm. The company went into voluntary administration in 2009, and the showroom has now been taken over by Eton Design.

Opposite page, from top:
The carving of St Michael on St Michael's church hall
Three of the Walcot Street gargoyles
Entrance to one of the yards on Ladymead

Below: The boundary between Walcot and St Michael's parishes

Beyond the showroom is a former penitentiary where 'females of fallen reputation' could find 'shelter, advice and encouragement to return to the paths of virtue'. In 1816 a lock hospital was opened, where women suffering from sexually-transmitted diseases were confined. It lasted for nine years before being converted to a chapel. If you look up, you can still see the words 'Penitentiary Chapel' above the first-floor windows; through the windows you may also be able to see the domes in the chapel ceiling. Down at ground level, look for the letters WP StMP. They mark the boundary between St Michael's parish and Walcot, which follows the course of the Corn or Carn Brook. It continues eastward under the street before swinging to the north 60 metres further on. A gateway at the end of the building opens onto the courtyard of Ladymead House, once a grand mansion with gardens running down to the river, but incorporated into the penitentiary in 1805. The building has now been converted to apartments.

If you look through the next set of gates, you will see a building with a tall chimney. This was a pin factory, whose opening in 1815 was recorded in the *New Monthly Magazine*:

> A pin-manufactory has recently been established in Bath, where the poor of Walcot parish, chiefly children, are exclusively employed in habits of early industry. They are thus kept from roving about the streets and forming improper acquaintance, and bring their honest earnings home to the assistance of their parents, which must eventually occasion a very great reduction of the poor rates of that extensive parish.

If you look up to the wall on the far side of the gateway, you will see that you have reached Cornwell Buildings. The superb – and very unusual – concave shopfront here dates from around 1820, when a pub called the Walcot Wine Vaults opened. It would almost certainly have had a standard bow front if the entrance to the yard of the Bell Inn had not stood opposite. Carts and wagons needed a wide turning circle to enter the yard and this dictated the design of the frontage.

The Walcot Wine Vaults, which closed in 1914, has an important place in the history of darts. A group photograph taken outside the pub around 1907 shows a dartboard with three crosses chalked on it, presumably indicating where three darts had hit the board to clinch a match. Not only is this the second oldest photograph of a dartboard ever seen, the design is unlike that of any other dartboard known.[1]

The second oldest photograph of a dartboard ever seen, taken outside the Walcot Wine Vaults around 1907

Turn right down Chatham Row, built in 1762 and originally called Pitt Street. It was named after William Pitt, MP for Bath, and renamed four years later when he became Earl of Chatham. The toothing stones jutting from the wall of the last house on the right indicate that the row was originally intended to continue downhill. The stones were left so that the wall of the building next door could be keyed or bonded in. In the event, the land was used for the gardens of the houses on the left. Access to them is through vaults under the road.

The dedication of the street to such an eminent person as Pitt confirms what its layout seems to suggest – that this was a fashionable, upmarket development. The house at the bottom of the row, with a charming Venetian window and riverside view, is particularly attractive. It has a chequered history, however. By 1856, it housed a shop and soup kitchen run by the Society for Improving the Condition of the Working Classes in Bath. After the street was condemned in 1967, this house was used by the fire brigade to test the fire-resistant properties of Georgian buildings. It is remarkable that this burnt-out shell should, over two centuries after it was built, have survived to become the jewel in the crown of a revitalised Chatham Row. The gate opposite once led down to the river, but is now kept permanently locked.

---

1 I was alerted to the existence of this photograph by Dr Patrick Chaplin, an authority on the history of darts, who would dearly love to find out more about the Walcot Street dartboard, so, if anyone can shed any light on it, please get in touch via info@akemanpress.com and I will pass the information on,

As you **head back up to Walcot Street**, look up to the buildings above the Bell. The building with a two-storey canted bay marks the end of the Paragon. To the right of it is Axford's Buildings, built by members of the Axford family, who were prominent local Unitarians. The land it stands on was once part of a large garden attached to the Bell Inn, which extended all the way up to the Paragon and along to Walcot churchyard. The corporation, which owned the land, assigned the lease to the Axfords in 1768 and Axford's Buildings were completed five years later.

A map from 1852 showing Chatham Row, the Bell, the Walcot Wine Vaults and the Penitentiary. Gibb's Court and Cornwall Terrace, to the north of Chatham Row, are, however, long gone.

The origins of the Bell are lost in obscurity, but it has certainly been an inn since the early eighteenth century. Today it is one of the city's top music pubs, with live music on Monday and Wednesday evenings and Sunday lunchtimes. It also serves an extensive range of real ales and bar snacks, and in the summer the yard at the back is one of the most popular pub gardens in the city. Above

the ground-floor windows on the left is a mark that looks like a letter W. This has led to some confusion as to which parish the Bell is in. It seems to suggest it is in Walcot, but if you look at the right-hand side of the building you will see StMP on the wall. The mark on the left is a red herring; despite being at the heart of Walcot life for over 250 years, the Bell is actually the last building – on this side of the street – in the parish of St Michael's. The building next door – demolished after bomb damage in 1942 – would have had a matching WP sign. The current building on the site is the home of Bath Aqua Glass, where visitors can watch glass-blowing demonstrations and buy handmade glass jewellery.

Carry on along Walcot Street. Beyond Aqua Glass is a delightful row of small eighteenth-century houses with Venetian windows, some of them still with their original glass. On your right, gates guard the entrance to an old school, opened in 1904 and now converted to flats. **At the far end of the next row of buildings** – a Georgian pastiche dating from around 2001 – **turn right down Walcot Gate.** The mortuary chapel on your right, built in 1842, is now used for art exhibitions. The large field beyond

Top: Cottages in Walcot Gate before restoration in 2001

Above: Jack & Danny's, one of Walcot Street's best-loved institutions

Below: The gloriously unrestored facade of Scott Antiques

it, leading down almost to the river, was once part of the cemetery. Ahead is a row of old cottages, long derelict but recently restored and incorporated into TR Hayes furniture store.

Go up the steps opposite the field.[1] This narrow byway – known as George's Buildings – marks the end of Walcot Street and the beginning of London Street. Opposite is Walcot parish church, dedicated to St Swithin. There has been a church on this site for over a thousand years, but the present church, designed by John Palmer, dates from 1777-80.

As you **turn right up London Street**, take a look into the window of the Nick Cudworth Gallery at 5 London Street, where evocative views of Bath sit alongside enigmatic interiors and still lifes. Carry on past the gloriously unrestored (but for how long) Scott Antiques to the old Hat & Feather Inn. Once one of the epicentres of Walcot Nation, it closed in 2004 and is now the Hudson Bar & Grill. The row it

1 To avoid the steps, retrace your steps to Walcot Street and turn right.

Sadly missed – the old Hat & Feather

stands in dates from 1902, when the buildings that formerly stood here, projecting much further into the road, were demolished. There had, however, been an inn called the Hat & Feather here since at least the mid-eighteenth century, and probably much earlier. Behind it was a warren of courts and cottages known as Hat & Feather Yard, which led down to the river. The row of cottages you saw from Walcot Gate is all that remains of them. Archaeological investigations have revealed that the area around Hat & Feather Yard has been occupied – possibly continuously – since Roman times. It has even been suggested that this may have been the original heart of the Roman settlement. There seems to have been a river crossing near where Cleveland Bridge now stands, and there are indications that a fort was established nearby in the early years of the Roman occupation. This would have provided a natural focus for settlement, and, although the Romans wasted little time in developing bathing facilities and establishing a temple around the hot springs, it seems that, initially at least, there was little commercial or domestic development there. All of which suggests that Walcot may have been the original Bath.

At the other end of the row, the building that now forms the entrance to TR Hayes furniture store was originally another inn, called the Three Crowns, which closed in 1917. The terracotta mouldings around the entrance and the frieze of vine leaves you can see through the window suggest it was a fairly sumptuous establishment. If you look down the lane beside it, you can see the backs of the old cottages whose fronts you saw earlier.

On the other side of the lane is a particularly well-preserved nineteenth-century butcher's shopfront, with its grilles, canopy, hooks, shutter keeps and shutter slots all intact, and the old shutters converted to windows. Its position on a corner meant that windows could be opened on two sides, helping to create the through draught so essential to keep temperatures down before the advent of refrigeration and air-conditioning.

Continue past the Methodist church of 1815 and turn right into Cleveland Cottages, with faded advertisements painted on the wall on your left and segregated entrances to the old church school on your right. Carry on past a row of cottages until you reach what looks like an old chapel, but was actually a factory built in the 1870s by an organ-builder called William Sweetland. He also built the house tacked onto the row on the left, where he spent the latter part of his life. The factory was designed like a chapel because most of the organs made here were intended for churches or chapels, and Sweetland wanted a

The Methodist church on London Street

building with appropriate acoustics to try them out.

Retrace your steps and turn right along Cleveland Terrace, which, as you round the corner, turns into Cleveland Place West. The shopfront at 4 Cleveland Terrace, dating from around 1830, is particularly fine, as is the ironwork on the balconies. Cleveland Terrace and Cleveland Place

were named after the Marquess of Cleveland, who owned the Pulteney Estate on the other side of the river and funded this development in the 1820s.[1] They were designed in Greek Revival style by Henry Edmund Goodridge, at around the same time that he was drawing up plans for Beckford's Tower (which is visited in the ninth walk). The columns in the garden of Sweetland's house at the end of the row come from John Wood's chapel in Queen Square.

Across the road, Cleveland Place East includes the Eastern Dispensary, where medical care was provided for people who could not afford doctor's fees. The toothing stones at the side indicate that there were originally plans for a building next door. Goodridge designed Cleveland Place East and West as an imposing entrance to Cleveland Bridge, which the Marquess of Cleveland commissioned in 1827 as a short cut from the London Road to the

A column in Sweetland's garden, with the organ factory behind

1 William Vane, Earl of Darlington, was made Marquess of Cleveland in 1827 and Duke of Cleveland six years later.

Cleveland Bridge

Pulteney Estate; it was originally a toll bridge, but tolls were abolished after the corporation took it over in 1927.

As you turn to **retrace your steps along Cleveland Place West**, the view ahead is dominated by Walcot Parade. It dates, like the Royal Crescent, from the 1770s, but looked out, not over rolling lawns but from the highest pavement in the city. The intention in each case was the same – to provide commanding views over what was, to all intents and purposes, open country. Until Cleveland Bridge was built, the view would have been of the tree-lined river and the village of Bathwick beyond. Unlike the Royal Crescent, however, Walcot Parade presents a curiously jumbled face to the world – some houses with two bays, some with three, some double-fronted – very much a place to see from rather than to be seen.

Turn left, retracing your steps along Cleveland Terrace and London Street. Just past the Nick Cudworth Gallery, cross the street (with care, as it is busy), walk up two short flights of steps and turn left alongside the churchyard.[1] In the churchyard can be seen the gravestones of the novelist Fanny Burney and the Rev George Austen, Jane Austen's father.[2] The spire of St Swithin's church, which was added in 1790, was dismantled and renovated in the 1990s. Beyond the church a gateway leads into the old graveyard. The sexton's house by the entrance predates the present church, although it has been extensively remodelled. The inverted and

1 To avoid the steps walk along to the corner and turn left.

2 Both of these have been moved from their original, somewhat obscure positions because of the posthumous fame of Fanny Burney and Jane Austen.

extinguished torches on the walls of the mausoleum alongside it symbolise death.

The view that would have greeted early eighteenth-century visitors as they walked uphill past St Swithin's bore no relation to what you see today. On the right, where the railings of Hedgemead Park now stand, were a row of buildings, some of them dating back centuries. Ahead, what is now the main road along the Paragon was a muddy, rutted track – known as Back Lane – through vineyards. The main road – such as it was – branched up to the right, following the course of the old Roman road.

All that changed in the mid-eighteenth century when the developers moved in. Just past the mausoleum, you come to the long row of buildings whose backs you saw from Walcot Street. First is Axford's Buildings. The builder put in charge of the project by the Axfords was Daniel Aust, who also built the Star Inn opposite. Major building projects required an enormous amount of manpower and building was thirsty work. There were plenty of other pubs nearby, so, to make sure his men used the Star, Daniel Aust arranged to pay them there. It was a cunning way of ensuring that much of the money was returned to him in beer sales. The Star is coffin-shaped, as an aerial photograph in the pub clearly shows. This may have been because it had to fit onto a cramped site; equally, it may have been because Daniel Aust was also a coffin maker – with a rather peculiar sense of humour.

When the Star was built, the only entrance was at the back, on the old main road. It is still there today, and, if the Star is open, it is well worth heading round to the original entrance to discover a building that, in its essentials, has hardly changed for the last 150 years.[1] Not only does the Star still have many of its Victorian fittings; it is also divided up into a series of small rooms, as most pubs were in the nineteenth century. It is not a museum piece, however, but a pub that still works supremely well today. And, if you feel so inclined, you can ask the landlord why the bench near the bar is called Death Row.

Back on Axford's Buildings, take a look at the curious columns flanking the entrance to No 36 before walking along to Nos 28-32, which were

---

1 There are no dropped pavements on the north side of the street.

112   WALK 4: BEYOND THE NORTH GATE

Above: Axford's Buildings with the Paragon beyond
Opposite: The spire of St Swithin's and an upturned torch on the mausoleum
Below: Bomb damage in Axford's Buildings, April 1942

rebuilt after being flattened by a bomb in 1942. No 27 marks the boundary of Walcot and St Michael's parishes. Axford's Buildings consists of 16 houses and runs without a break into the Paragon, a curved terrace of 21 houses, slightly grander and with rusticated bases on the houses at either end. From No 21 – the first house in the Paragon – there is a good view of the buildings opposite. To the right, rising above the Star, are the former Walcot Schools, shoehorned into a difficult site by the architect James Wilson in

1840. To the left of the steps is the Admiral's House, so called because Admiral Cochet lived there in the early nineteenth century. If you compare it with the end house in the Paragon, you will notice enough similarities to suggest it was built at the same time and by the same architect – Thomas Atwood. The terrace to the left of the Admiral's House – originally known as Harlequin Row – is a glorious architectural free-for-all – Venetian windows, Baroque mouldings, Gibbs surrounds, full-height bays and bows – with a jaunty swagger that suggests Brighton rather than Bath. Although there is Bath stone in the facades, there is also brick covered in render. It was built sometime after 1756, when the vineyards here were divided into building plots, but look back to an earlier style of architecture – it is as though John Wood, with his ideas of conformity and decorum, had never existed.

Harlequin Row

The Paragon

Delightful as it is today, it would have been even more so when first built, with open fields at the back and a view down to Walcot Street and the river in front.

Turning back to the Paragon, notice that, while it echoes the design of the Royal Crescent, it lacks a central feature. Nikolaus Pevsner described the Paragon as 'the second of Bath's crescents', but most architectural historians have insisted it is no such thing, arguing that Atwood simply took the idea of building a curved row of houses but, instead of placing it in lordly isolation, made it one side of a curved street. Had Atwood called it a crescent there would be no argument and historians would be debating to what extent Atwood redefined the term. As it is, he called it a Paragon – a model for others to follow or, as the *Oxford English Dictionary* has it, 'a pattern of excellence'. Modesty was not Atwood's strong suit, nor, it seems, was enumeration – as you **continue along the Paragon**, notice that J is substituted for 1 in the house numbers all the way along. Atwood did inspire other architects, however

– most notably in Clifton, where John Drew's crescent-like Paragon, built in 1809-14, occupies an even more dramatic site.

At the end of Harlequin Row is the Countess of Huntingdon's Chapel. Selina, Countess of Huntingdon, was a follower of John Wesley who formed a breakaway Methodist sect called the Countess of Huntingdon's Connexion. This chapel, built in 1765, 'after the Gothic taste in a plain but very elegant manner', is the earliest Gothick building in the city. The architect is unknown, although marked similarities to an orangery at Frampton on Severn by Thomas Halfpenny of Bristol suggest it may have been him. The building facing the street is not the chapel but the minister's house – the chapel is behind it. This was one of the most fashionable places of worship in the city and many considered the singing better than that in the Abbey. It now houses the Building of Bath Collection, but its interior is largely unchanged, and it is still possible to imagine it packed with a patched, peruqued and powdered congregation belting out revivalist hymns. To the left of the chapel is another terrace, less flamboyant than that on the right, but no less harlequinesque.

The defiantly unrestored building at the west end of the Paragon was where the Leigh-Perrotts, Jane Austen's aunt and uncle, lived. Jane stayed here on her early visits to Bath. Next to it is a bit of infill between the Paragon and Bladud's Buildings, with steps leading down to Walcot Street.

Until the mid-eighteenth century, Back Lane, whose course the modern road along the Paragon has followed so far, swung up to the right to emerge on Lansdown Road. In 1754, however, Bladud's Buildings were built and the road was rerouted. A new pedestrianised way up to Lansdown Road – called Hay Hill and aligned on Alfred Street – was later opened up.[1] Bladud's Buildings, designed by Thomas Jelly, must have made an impressive contribution to Bath's streetscape when first built. Like the

Steps leading down to Walcot Street

north side of Queen Square, they were designed to look like a palace, with a central pediment. As with Edgar Buildings, however, Jelly's grand design has been marred by the insertion of shopfronts, while its symmetry has been compromised by the addition of a full-height segmental bow on No 6 and semi-circular-headed windows on the ground-floor of No 2. A location beside one of the city's busiest crossroads hardly aids appreciation of its finer points either.

---

1 In the early nineteenth century, Hay Hill was also known as Belmont Place.

At the end of Bladud's Buildings, you come to Broad Street, which dates back to medieval times, when this crossroads marked the edge of the urban area. The layout here was very different, however. The main road to the north ran up Broad Street and Lansdown Road, but George Street, which lies ahead, was a narrow byway called Foss Lane. Although the section of road you have just walked along did not exist until the mid-eighteenth century, a lane ran eastwards from here down to Walcot Street. It disappeared when Bladud's Buildings were built.[1]

Turn left down Broad Street.[2] The double row of Venetian windows on your right belonged to assembly rooms added to the Royal York Hotel around 1807 and rebuilt after a major fire in 1827.

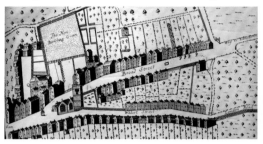

A map showing Broad Street and Walcot Street around 1700. The lane from the top of Broad Street down to Walcot Street can be seen branching off Lansdown Road on the extreme right.

Broad Street decorated for Queen Victoria's diamond jubilee in 1897

---

1 When the land where Bladud's Buildings stand was advertised for sale in the *Bath Journal* on 25 November 1754, it was described as 'a piece of ground reaching from the top of Broad Street to the top of Ladymead'.

2 If you are following a step-free route, cross over at the top of Broad Street, turn left downhill and walk down to the old King Edward's School.

After 40 metres, turn left along an alley by the foundation stone of the old YMCA. This leads to a courtyard by the entrance to the new YMCA. If you turn right and go down a few steps, you will find the last of the Walcot Street Artworks, a floating globe unveiled in 2010. In the eighteenth and nineteenth centuries, this oasis of calm was one of the grimmest and most densely-populated parts of the city. If you look down the steps to Walcot Street, you will see, partway down, an old gabled building on the right with a blocked mullion window. If you look along the alley towards Broad Street, you will see traces of fireplaces in a chimney breast – the ghostly legacy of some of Bath's most miserable back-to-backs. These were hovels thrown up in the eighteenth century to house people who flocked to Bath to find work, and are as much a part of the city's Georgian heritage as the Circus or the Paragon. This particular development

Gracious Court, running between Broad Street and Walcot Street, in 1852. The row of five little boxes to the right of No 18 were the five privies that catered for the dozens of people who lived here.

Steps from Gracious Court to Walcot Street

was built by Gracious Stride, who called it Gracious Court. That, unfortunately, was the only gracious thing about it. As you head along the alleyway back to Broad Street, notice that, while the wall on the left bears the name Gracious Court, that on the right bears the name Broad Street Place – another example of the council renaming a particularly notorious street in an attempt to improve its image.

Cross Broad Street and carry on down to the old King Edward's School, built in 1752 by Thomas Jelly. Its alumni include Thomas de Quincey, author of the *Confessions of an English Opium Eater*. By 1954, the school had outgrown the building. There were plans to demolish it and build a new school on the site, but in the event the school moved out – in stages – to a new site in Bathwick, finally vacating the Broad Street building in 1990. It has remained empty ever since, although permission was granted in 2010 to convert it to a hotel and bar.

Buildings once ran all the way along the east side of Broad Street, but in 1970 those opposite the school were demolished to create a one-way system in preparation for the planned tunnel under the city. The new street linking Broad and Walcot Streets was called Saracen Street, after the nearby Saracen's Head Inn.

If you look across to the Bodrum Takeaway at No 34, you will see how the building was refurbished – on the cheap – in the late eighteenth century. Originally it had a gable end facing the street, like some of the buildings further down. When gable ends went out of fashion, the wall was built up on either side to create a parapet. Over two centuries later, the outline of the gable is only too apparent.

Above: King Edward's School

Below left: The outline of a gable end still visible over two centuries after efforts were taken to conceal it

Below right: A seventeenth-century building hidden away behind Broad Street

Opposite: One of the few examples of timber framing still visible in Bath

Just past the old school, turn right into Milsom Place. Clearly there are old buildings here, but just how old is not clear until you look more closely. If you **climb the steps on the left**[1] and look over the wall at the back of the buildings in Broad Street, you will see what appears to be a seventeenth-century rubble-stone extension, with mullion windows, stuck onto the back of an eighteenth-century building – but of course it can't be. Broad Street was once much wider than it is today and this seventeenth-century 'extension' faced onto it; the building that towers above it was tacked onto the front in the eighteenth century, drastically reducing the width of the street. The same thing happened all the way along.

Go back down the steps, turn right to double back on yourself, go through an archway and look to the left. Beyond more blocked mullion windows, the join between seventeenth- and eighteenth-century buildings can clearly be seen.

In the middle ages, Broad Street was home to many broadloom weavers, who settled here because it was outside the jurisdiction of the city guilds. Among them was Chaucer's fictional Wife of Bath, who was so skilled at 'cloth-making' that she surpassed those 'of Ypres and of Ghent'. Chaucer was at pains to stress that she was from 'bisyde Bathe' – in other words, outside its walls.

The yard you are standing in once belonged to an inn called the Kings Arms. The Cote restaurant was its stables – look how the corner of the building was canted so that carriages could negotiate the sinuous route into the yard. The old inn, on the right of the archway into Broad Street, also has a chamfered corner.

Before heading back to Broad Street through the archway, **carry on, past tables and chairs, to where a rubble-stone building, with a modern window inserted into the ground floor, juts out.** If you look to the left, you will see, at the top of a fire escape, part of a half-timbered building, a rare survival from a time when most of Bath was built not of stone but of wood, lath and plaster.

Now **head back to Broad Street.** Ahead, at No 41, is part of Rossiters, housed in a gloriously asymmetrical building from around 1720 – four bays wide with a pediment over the second bay. It once had two more storeys but these were removed in 1973. Two doors to the left, No 38 (also part of Rossiters) is one of the most impressive double-gabled

---

1 If you are following a step-free walk, head to the left of the steps and go on to the next paragraph.

The Saracen's Head in the early twentieth century

buildings in the city. It had a datestone of 1709, but this has been removed.

The Saracen's Head Inn, also double-gabled but with more of a country-town feel to it, has the date 1713 chiselled into its left-hand gable. Its main claim to fame is that Charles Dickens stayed here – albeit somewhat reluctantly – in 1835, while reporting on a major political rally for the *Morning Chronicle*.

The Cath Kidson shop, facing the inn, occupies the building whose half-timbered side you saw earlier. The façade, which is modern, gives no hint of what lies behind, but if you walk up a magnificent eighteenth-century staircase to the first-floor, sixteenth-century roof beams are exposed to view.[1]

Next to the Saracen's Head is St Michael's church, which was under construction at the time of Dickens' visit. Designed in Early English style by George Manners, it is the fourth church on the site. Its predecessor lasted less than a century. In 1731, it was decided to demolish the old church, which was not only too small but also dilapidated. John Wood offered to build a replacement, on condition that pews were reserved for the residents of Queen Square. His offer was declined and the job went to one of the churchwardens, a stonecutter called John Harvey. When it was consecrated in 1743, the design met with near-universal condemnation. John Wood declared that Harvey had designed it 'in a taste so peculiar to himself that the very journeymen workmen, to mortify him, declared that a horse, accustomed to the sight of good buildings, was so frighted at the odd appearance of the church, that he would not go by it till he was hood-

---

1 The staircase was moved here from the Octagon chapel in 1980, although the Octagon seems not to have been its original home, and it was probably moved there from another building.

winked'. Pierce Egan, writing in 1819, described it as 'an annoyance to the admirers of architecture in Bath'. Happily, the church that replaced it has no such record of scaring horses and is acknowledged to be one of the finest nineteenth-century buildings in the city.

The eighteenth-century church of St Michael's – so ugly that horses had to be hoodwinked to go past it

You are now very near the end of the walk, with the site of the North Gate just ahead – but before you get there, one more secret corner (which involves climbing a flight of steps) awaits. **Cross Broad Street, go round St Michael's church and walk a little way along Walcot Street.** On the way, look out for the quirky carvings across the road on the Podium. **When you reach the back of the Saracen's Head, cross over and walk up a broad flight of steps.** The structure hidden by vegetation on your left is a ventilation shaft from an underground car park. The broad courtyard ahead lies on the site of St Michael's burial ground. A path led through the graveyard to a Baptist chapel on the left-hand side, where the Hilton hotel now stands. When the Hilton – then known as the Beaufort – opened in 1972, the company that owned it boasted that the architect had 'caught the dignity, the style appropriate to Bath's rich tapestry of history, while at the same time infusing the clean lines of modern architectural practice. It is a combination that … illustrates the company's policy of observing and respecting the need for harmony with the local background.' How times change. The *Pevsner Architectural Guide to Bath*, published in 2003, called it 'the most reviled building in Bath', a judgement few would argue with. We can at least be grateful that the tunnel whose entrance it was to have overlooked was never built.

Head straight on through a large archway leading to the Riverside Terrace and turn right. The contrast with the busy street you have just left could not be more marked. On your right is the library, ahead is an entrance to the Podium, but the chances are that you will have this bleak and lofty terrace to yourself, with time to savour a view of the unfashionable side of Pulteney Bridge and the hills beyond before heading back to the starting point.

5

INTO THE EAST
Larkhall & the London Road

Distance *5 miles*

Time *3 – 3.5 hours*

Accessibility *On pavements or paved surfaces throughout; several flights of steps, with step-free alternatives available*

Public toilets *Larkhall Square*

Starting point *Kingston Parade (outside Visitor Information Centre) – or at the east end of Walcot Street*

> *To the most indifferent traveller, who scarcely 'reads as he runs'; or, perhaps, labouring under the mental debility of ennui – the entrance to Bath cannot fail in removing this frigid apathy, and awaken his feelings to the numerous interesting objects which, in rapid succession, present themselves to his notice.*
>
> Pierce Egan, 'The Entrance to Bath from the London Road'
> *Walks Through Bath, 1819*

This walk picks up where the last one left off, at the far end of Walcot Street. It takes in some of Bath's least-known Georgian terraces, along with a surrealist folly, a lost spa and long-forgotten pleasure gardens.

From the Visitor Information Centre head north past the Abbey along the High Street and Northgate Street, and continue along Walcot Street. At the end of Walcot Street, go up the steps on the left just past Walcot church[1] and cross the zebra crossing.[2] Go up the flight of steps straight ahead. These once led to rows of narrow streets lined with terraced houses. After a series of landslips in the late nineteenth century, the hillside was cleared and made into a park. The only buildings to survive were Gloster Villas, which you pass on the right. **After going under a bridge, turn left through a gate into the park. Turn left downhill and left again past an**

---

1 For a step-free route, carry on along the right-hand side of Walcot Street and continue along London Street. At Cleveland Place, cross and continue along London Road. After 200 metres, cross at the pedestrian lights, turn left and then right up Snow Hill. After 250 metres, pick up the walk by turning right into Kensington Gardens.

2 The zebra crossing was out of use at the time of writing due to building work, and replaced by temporary pedestrian lights up to the left. The crossing was due to be reinstated after the completion of the work.

Opposite: The sinuous curve of Grosvenor Place

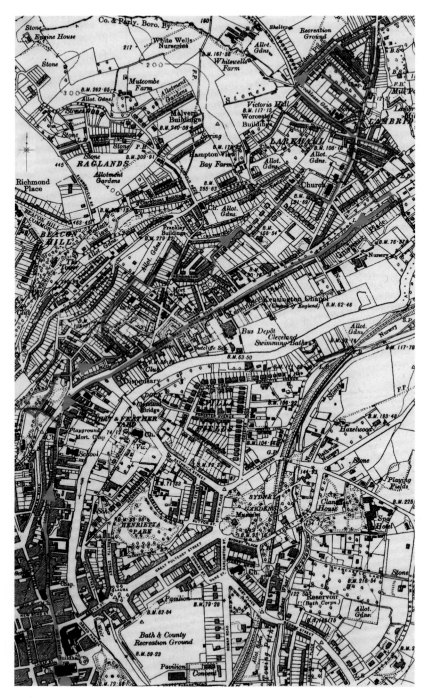

Above: The footpath leading up through Hedgemead Park

Left: Dover Place

Right: Highbury Place

ornate drinking fountain to cross the bridge. Follow the path as it curves gently downhill, but carry on up to the left as it drops steeply away and go through a gateway onto Lower Hedgemead Road. Turn right downhill and, at the crossroads, carry straight on into Pera Road. The large building straight ahead is the Clarence Street Malthouse, a legacy of one of Bath's most important nineteenth-century industries.

Walk down past the malthouse and turn left at the end up Thomas Street. The former chapel on the left was, like the rest of the street, built in the late 1820s. Lyndhurst Terrace, at the top, also dates from the early nineteenth century, and is worth a diversion if only to appreciate the view across the valley. Below Lyndhurst Terrace, however, you need to bear right up a footpath past Lyndhurst Cottage and into Seymour Road. The long row of terraced houses you can see curving above you is Belgrave Crescent – a late-nineteenth-century take on the Georgian idea. As you near the end of Seymour Road, railings on the right give a view down Dover Place, another hidden Georgian gem, built in 1816.

At the end of Seymour Road, turn right down Bennett's Lane and take the first left past Highbury Cottages, built on the site of a row of almshouses. Above them is Highbury Place, elegant and spacious, with copious false windows and dating from around 1815. After a row of semi-detached houses, you come to Highbury Terrace, multi-coloured and running delightfully downhill behind a row of front gardens.

Walk down Highbury Terrace, taking extreme care on the steep flight of steps past the bottom house, which was once a pub called the Highbury Arms. If you look up to the left you can see the end of Frankley Buildings, another multi-coloured terrace running down the hillside, with a pediment on the central house.

Turn right downhill and take the first left into Kensington Gardens (where those who selected the step-free option rejoin the walk). As you approach the end of the road, one of Bath's most dramatically-sited – and least-known – Georgian buildings comes into view ahead. Hayes Mount, with its superb range of Venetian windows and graciously bowed façade, was probably built by Thomas Jelly in the 1770s. An evocative trompe l'oeil painting can be seen on the right-hand false window on the top floor.

Turn left and right past Hayes Mount and along Upper East Hayes.
The villas on the right, including Hayes Mount, cannot be viewed from the front. What you see instead are their backs, asymmetrical, unadorned, but full of character. This row of villas is one of the earliest in the city, marking a decisive break with the ubiquity of terrace design and initiating a paradigm of suburban development that is still with us today. On the left is the extravagant folly of Casa Dali, with a classical statue in all its naked glory, and old doors leading into walls.

As you **turn right downhill at the end**, there is a superb view across the valley. **Turn left into Belgrave Road, and at the crossroads carry on into Dowding Road**, where there are views ahead to Little Solsbury Hill. There were once plans to build a large square here: Worcester Square

appeared on maps of the city until well into the nineteenth century, but it was never built. **Take the next right down Holland Road**, past St Saviour's church, an adaptation by John Pinch of his design for St Mary's, Bathwick and consecrated in 1832. The chancel was added 50 years later. The two-storey building on the opposite side of the crossroads was a pub called the Queen, which closed in 1928.

Opposite: Hayes Mount

Top: Trompe l'oeil window in Hayes Mount

Above: Metal cranes in Upper East Hayes

Below: The Larkhall Inn

Turn left along St Saviour's Road past Victoria Place, built around 1840. The Rondo Theatre, on the left, is housed in the former church hall. A little further on is Larkhall Square, the heart of the village, dominated by the Larkhall Inn. The origins of the inn are shrouded in mystery; it may have started life as a pair of cottages before being converted to a country residence called Lark Hall, and later becoming an inn. When developers started building on the land around it in the late eighteenth century, they called the area Larkhall.

Turn left at the inn and go along the road to the right of the public toilets. Brookleaze Buildings, on the left, probably date from the late 1830s. As you can see, many of the

Bath stone buildings along here are painted, presenting not only a cheerful face to the world but also a barrier to the traffic fumes that may pose as great a threat as soot once did. The last house in Brookleaze Buildings has acquired an extra storey and a porch. Beyond it is Avondale Buildings, dating from later in the nineteenth century.

At the end of the street, cross and carry on for a few metres before crossing again and turning right along Eldon Place. This is an example of what much of Larkhall would have looked like if the planners had had their way. The early nineteenth-century buildings that once stood here were demolished in 1969 to make for those you see today. Several other streets were earmarked for redevelopment, but a combination of protests and delays spared them just long enough for an official change of heart.

A little further along on the right is an earlier piece of redevelopment. The large red-brick building on the corner of Dafford Street was built as a pub called the Royal Oak in 1898. It was later taken over by Brains Brewery and renamed the Brains Surgery, but closed in 2009 and is now student accommodation.

Turn right down Dafford Street, another delightful row of early-nineteenth-century cottages. On the left is Mandds Villa, a small single-storey building with a basement. Originally called Dafford Villa, it was built some time before 1859. Further along Dafford Street is a former Methodist chapel, built in 1832. The Rose & Crown at the end opened in the 1840s.

BLADUD SPA.

Turn left along St Saviour's Road to find the site of Larkhall's lost spa. Known as Bladud Spa, it consisted of several buildings. The first you come to, on the right, is Lambrook House, originally called Spa Gardens. Screened by trees, it lies across a bridge behind a private forecourt. A little further on, past the entrance to Spa Lane, the wide bridge across the Lam Brook was the entrance to the spa. The children's play area to the right marks the site of the single-storey Greek-revival building that sat over the well; the footing of one of its walls can be seen near the bridge. A two-storey building known as Spa House stood behind it. The spring

Above: Bladud Spa on an 1886 Ordnance Survey map
Opposite below: Bladud Spa around 1840
Opposite above: Mandds Villa

that fed the spa was discovered in 1832 when a Mr Blackwin sank a well for a brewery here. The water from it tasted so foul that he sent it away for analysis. The results showed that he had discovered one of the most potent chalybeate springs in the country, so instead of building a brewery he opened a spa.

It closed in 1930 after the spring dried up. The building was used as a chapel for a time before being demolished. It bore a striking resemblance to Mandds Villa, which not only suggests it was by the same builder but also raises the question of what Mandds Villa was built as, and whether it had any connection with the spa.

You can, if you wish, carry on along St Saviour's Road for 100 metres to the Bladud's Head, an inn occupying a row of three old cottages on the edge of the country. Otherwise, **head back along St Saviour's Road** past the Rose & Crown and two charming cottages with full-length balconies. A little further along, **turn right along Dafford's Buildings** to discover some of the oldest houses in Larkhall. A little way along on the right you come to a row of two-storey, early-nineteenth-century houses, beyond which is a range of larger, late-eighteenth-century houses, some of which have been subdivided.

At the end of Dafford's Buildings, turn left along an unmade road and left again along Larkhall Place. On the right are the backs of a row of houses built at various times from the late eighteenth century onwards. Elsewhere – on Upper East Hayes, for example – when you see the back of a row of buildings, the front often remains a closed book. Here, though, you get to see the front – and, if this is a secret corner, the pathway along the other side feels like a secret world. To get there, **turn right at the end**

Looking west from Larkhall Place

WALK 5: INTO THE EAST

and right again up a short flight of steps (unless you are following a step-free route). Not only does this lead past a fascinating range of buildings; it also leads to what must surely be the classic view of Larkhall, with the yard of the Larkhall Inn in the foreground and the tower of St Saviour's church rising above the rooftops.

Head back to St Saviour's Road, turn right and walk along to Larkhall Square. The large sign bracket over the butcher's on the right-hand corner

once carried a sign for the White Lion Inn, which closed in 1959. Opposite, words on the walls of the chemist's recall more of Larkhall's history.

Turn left along Upper Lambridge Street. On the left, the Titfield Thunderbolt Bookshop, which specialises in local books and transport titles, is well worth a visit. On the right is the back of Lambridge Place. To see the front, **turn first right and carry on round**. Here again, the Bath stone façades have been painted a splendid assortment of colours.

At the end, turn left and left again into Beaufort Place – less grand than Lambridge Place, but no less colourful and no less charming, with a splendid full-height bay on the end house. This leads past Lambridge Mews to the London Road. On the right is Beaufort East, a terrace built around 1790. Although it is set back from the road behind tree-shaded lawns, its front doors open directly onto the pavement. On the left is Lambridge, a terrace of Regency villas varying in style and size, set back behind gardens. Only a few years separate the two, but the shift in mood between the late eighteenth century and the early nineteenth could not be

Looking east along the London Road around 1910 with Beaufort East on the left

more marked – regularity and sociability giving way to individuality and the quest for greater privacy.

Turn left along the London Road to the pedestrian lights, cross and turn right, heading back towards the city. Shortly after crossing the end of Grosvenor Bridge Road, Grosvenor Place, the first of a series of grand terraces, appears ahead, with a late-nineteenth-century extension tacked onto the end. A little way along, **turn up a short flight of steps into Grosvenor Place.**[1]

The London Road, which you will be following back into town, is one of the most fascinating, yet least known, parts of the Georgian city, and contains some of its finest buildings. It is also, as you will not need telling, horrendously busy, with about the worst air quality in the city. It was once very different. In 1742, John Wood wrote that it was one of the most popular places around Bath 'for taking the air and exercise'. Its development over the ensuing century preserved and indeed enhanced its semi-rural atmosphere, transforming it into a wide boulevard with elegant terraces and villas set back behind long lawns or screened by trees. In parts, it seems more like Cheltenham than Bath – an impression aided by its level site – but most of what you see here is earlier, raising the intriguing possibility that Cheltenham's developers – such as Bath's Harcourt Masters – were influenced by what they saw here.

As you can see from the photograph on the previous page, London Road was still a tranquil haven in the early twentith century. Trying to appreciate the architectural heritage of the London Road today, however, is like trying to listen to the slow movement of a Schubert string quartet while someone behind you puffs on a cigar and chunters into a mobile phone. This is not just a heritage issue. Automotive culture has effectively marginalised the London Road as a place for social interaction, individual exploration and living. A constant flow of heavy traffic fills the air with poisonous fumes and shreds the nerves of even the most stalwart. To try to recapture something of the semi-rural calm that once prevailed here is impossible. All you can do is look at the buildings that have survived and hope that one day – although probably not in any of our lifetimes – a modicum of peace will return.

Grosvenor Place was designed by John Eveleigh in 1791. With its sinuous line, flowing forward towards the centre of the terrace, it takes the idea of the crescent and runs with it. Convention dictated that the central building in a terrace or crescent – if it was to be distinguished from those on either side – should have a pediment, but, although Eveleigh was content to follow precedent with Somerset Place and Camden Crescent, here he opted for a radically different approach. It is one that Hogarth – and indeed Antoni Gaudi – would have approved of.

---

1 To avoid the steps, carry on along the London Road and turn left into Grosvenor Place further along.

Beaufort East

The centrepiece of Grosvenor Place is one of Georgian Bath's most delightfully quirky buildings. It was designed as the entrance to pleasure gardens. Work started on the gardens in the spring of 1791 and, although still far from complete, they opened the following summer. In 1793, Eveleigh went bankrupt. After struggling on under a succession of owners, the gardens finally closed in the early 1800s.

Eveleigh's maverick approach to architectural propriety is much in evidence here. Not only does the central building have an even number of bays, the central column sits over the front door. It is not just Eveleigh's waywardness that the building bears witness to, however, but also his failure, for the building was never completed. Three of the cartouches on which animals were to have been carved remain blank, and the lower set of bands around the columns are ungarlanded. But at least the wonderful icemen, one of Eveleigh's trademarks, make their appearance above the ground-floor windows.

Carvings of a lion and an iceman above the entrance to Grosvenor pleasure gardens

As you continue along Grosvenor Place, look out for the Greek Revival splendour of No 13 and the elaborate carvings above some of the front doors. At the far end – beyond No 1 – is Grosvenor House. Most of its windows facing the main road are blank (including one with a trompe l'oeil blind) because there are windows on the west

A map of 1793 showing Grosvenor Pleasure Gardens – or Grosvenor Garden Vauxhall as it was known – flanked by Cumberland and Grosvenor Streets, which, like Worcester Square, were never built

side. Grosvenor House was intended as the first house in a street – to be called Grosvenor Street – running down to the river. Although it appears on early nineteenth-century maps, it was never built.

Carry on along the London Road. The next terrace, Alexander Buildings – supremely elegant and built around 1815 – is set back behind gardens. Beyond it comes Percy Place, largely built in the late eighteenth century but with later infilling. Opposite is Worcester Terrace, also built around 1815, although with what appears to be an earlier semi-detached building at the west end. Look out for the cat waiting patiently outside No 6. The leather shop on the corner of Upper East Hayes is an extraordinary Edwardian concoction, which looks as though it was inspired by an alpine hunting-lodge. A couple of doors along is a curious Italianate building dating from 1862 with, at its centre, a Venetian window above an archway and a chimney in the form of a bell turret.

Opposite the bell turret, **turn left through an ironwork arch to walk along Kensington Place**, designed in the 1790s by John Palmer. There is some fine ironwork here – and look out for the columns and balls supporting the porch of No 17. Kensington Place consists of two terraces, each with a pediment above the central building. If you look across the London Road when you reach the gap between the two terraces you

Top: Grosvenor House and Alexandra Buildings

Above: Gardenalia

Below: The Worcester Terrace cat

will see a single-storey shop with 'Kensington Nurseries' chiselled into its pediment. Now a launderette, it was once the entrance to large nurseries laid out on the slopes behind it. To the left of it is Gardenalia, a garden store with a fascinating array of antique, reclaimed and contemporary garden ornaments. **Continue along Kensington Place** past a former proprietary chapel, recently converted to apartments. As you **rejoin the London Road**, look across to Hanover Street, laid out in the early 1790s and originally intended to lead to a grand square called Hanover Square, which, like so much else, was never built.

Carry on along the London Road and across the entrance to a supermarket car park. The remaining stretch of the London Road – although only 400 metres long – is far too fascinating and complicated to be dealt with at the end of a walk which has already covered so much ground. It will instead be covered in Walk 14. For now, **carry on along the London Road, continue over the traffic lights at Cleveland Place and head on to Walcot Street to return to the city centre.**

6

A PLACE IN THE COUNTRY
Lyncombe & Widcombe

Distance *3.5 miles*

Time *2-3 hours*

Accessibility *Mostly on pavements or paved surfaces, although with one country footpath; several flights of steps, with step-free alternatives available*

No public toilets

Starting point *Kingston Parade (outside Visitor Information Centre)*

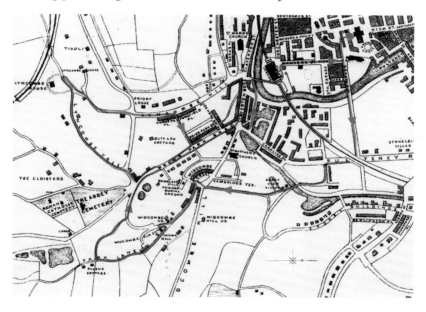

Widcombe, so named from the great breadth of the dent wherein it stands, is a village beginning upon a high nap of ground on the south side of the dent, not unjustly styled Mount Pleasant. Some of the citizens of Bath have here their little villas. The village of Lyncombe was anciently situated at the bottom of the dent of that name; and Lyn signifying water, the name itself imports the water or watery bottom.

John Wood, 1742

Opposite: Eighteenth-century dovecote in Widcombe

Hither from noisy crowds I fly;
Here dwells soft ease, and peace of mind;
Yet think not Fancy's curious eye
To these deep solitudes confined.
Would I fair Eden's bloom restore!
Lo! Widcomb's cultivated vale,
Where Flora paints her slopes for Moore,[1]
And all Arabia's sweets exhale.
Luxurious thus I freely rove.
Nor at the sons of wealth repine;
Mere tenant of each hill and grove,
Which sovereign Fancy renders mine.

Richard Graves,
Lines Written near Bath, 1755

This walk heads across the river to Lyncombe and Widcombe. These two parishes, united in the sixteenth century, have long if somewhat obscure histories. By the early eighteenth century, Lyncombe had fallen on hard times – according to John Wood, by 1742 'few of the houses of this village' remained – but Widcombe was an important weaving centre.

Lyncombe and Widcombe saw less expansion in the eighteenth century, however, than almost anywhere else in the immediate vicinity of Bath. This was largely because wealthy landowners moved in early, built grand houses and bought up the land around them. Ralph Allen may be the best known, but there were several others. Lyncombe also developed a reputation as a country retreat, where visitors could escape the dust and bustle of the city. Over two centuries later, the Georgian ideal of *rus in urbe* is more tangible here than almost anywhere else in Bath.

From the Visitor Information Centre, head south along Church Street, turn left into Lilliput Alley (North Parade Passage), carry on along North Parade and cross at the traffic lights. Continue along North Parade and cross the river. At the end of North Parade Road, cross Pulteney Road, turn right and take the second left up Pulteney Gardens. The road curves up to the right past Lime Grove Cottage, one of the oldest buildings in the area and originally surrounded by nurseries. Continue uphill past a modern building and over the canal. Beyond the lock on the left is a recently-restored and very decorative chimney, all that is left of a pumphouse which drew water up from the bottom of the flight to replenish the water lost when boats went through the locks.

When the road forks, bear right and take the first right into Abbey View Gardens. This leads to one of the most delightful views of the city, with a striking view to the west of Beechen Cliff rising above the spire of St Matthew's church.

---

1 Edward Moore (1712-57), poet, dramatist and friend of Henry Fielding.

Retrace your steps along Abbey View Gardens and turn right uphill. When the road forks, bear right along the Tyning. This name occurs frequently in the Bath area, and probably comes from the Old English word, 'tynan', meaning a plot of land enclosed by a hedge.

At the end of the Tyning, cross to Church Street and after 25 metres turn right down a short flight of steps to Widcombe Crescent.[1] Designed by Charles Harcourt Masters, this crescent is the only one in Bath which – if the Royal Crescent is taken as a template – is the wrong way round. The front of the crescent faces uphill, and it is the back which has the view. The internal layout of the houses is also reversed, with the main rooms at the back. If you look at the first-floor windows, you can see where the staircases have been fitted in. Not only that, but the central windows above the double doorways are bisected by party walls. Although the central windows above Nos 11 and 12 are clearly blind, those along the rest of the crescent are glazed to look like real windows. And then there are those floral bosses – or are they, as some have suggested, cabbages? No 5 also has the dubious distinction of being the birthplace, in 1811, of one of the nineteenth century's greatest religious rogues, Henry Prince, who founded the Agapemone – or Abode of Love – at Spaxton in Somerset.[2] In the 1830s, James Brooke, later to become the Rajah of Sarawak, lived for some time at No 1, which

---

1 To avoid the steps, turn right after crossing the road and left into Widcombe Crescent.

2 The story of Prince and the Agapemone is told in *The Year of the Pageant*, published by Akeman Press.

his father had retired to after returning from India. It is fascinating to think that these two characters, who both went on to achieve fame and notoriety, albeit for far different reasons, were once near neighbours in this out-of-the-way spot.

Although some purists decry the design of Widcombe Crescent, most people agree that, for all its faults, it has a charm all its own, very different from the impact of other crescents. From the back, however, it certainly does have impact, as you will see later.

Walk up the short flight of steps[1] beside the double-bayed house at the end of the crescent onto Widcombe Terrace for a prospect – more Tuscan than English – of luxuriant gardens and tree-clad hillsides. Although very different to the crescent, Widcombe Terrace is believed to have been built at the same time by Charles Harcourt Masters, possibly to a design by Thomas Baldwin.

Head back down the steps to Widcombe Crescent, turn right up the steps to Church Street and turn right.[2] Church Street leads to the heart of old Widcombe The first house on your left, with its second-floor mullion windows blocked, dates from the seventeenth-century. On your right is the back of Widcombe Terrace. A little further along is Somerset House, ostensibly early-nineteenth-century, but containing within it a much older building. Widcombe Villa, to the left of it, was added later. Further along on the left, Nos 11/12 date from the mid-sixteenth century, if not earlier. Further along on the right is Widcombe Lodge, once the home of Henry Fielding's sister, Sarah, who wrote *The Governess*, the first children's novel

---

1 Unless you are following a step-free route.

2 To avoid the steps, turn right out of the Crescent onto Widcombe Hill and turn right.

Opposite: Widcombe Terrace

Top: 'A view more Tuscan than English' from Widcombe Terrace

Above: A seventeenth-century house in Church Street

Below from left : St Thomas à Becket church in the mid-nineteenth century; the Italian fountain; a carving on Widcombe Manor

in English, in 1749. Fielding, who was a friend of Ralph Allen's and made many visits to Bath, is also believed to have stayed here.

Ahead is Widcombe old church, built in the 1490s and dedicated to St Thomas à Becket, but heavily restored by Major Davis.[1] If you **walk through the churchyard** – taking extreme care over the rough ground – to the left of the church and down to the railings overlooking the road, you will have a panoramic view not only of Widcombe Manor, but also of an ornamental lake and cascade across the valley. You will also see some curious gargoyles on the church. The building abutting the churchyard is known as the Garden House. It was originally a superior kind of gazebo, with a room above an open colonnade. The ground floor has now been enclosed and a circular extension added to create one of Bath's most unusual and charming houses.

On leaving the churchyard, turn left and carry on along Church Street (keeping a look out for Prior Park high on the hill ahead) **to the gates of Widcombe Manor.** This was built in the late seventeenth century, but the

---

1 The church is open on Sunday mornings for services and between 2.30pm and 5.30pm on Sunday afternoons from May to September.

magnificent Baroque façade, with fantastic grotesques – part lion, part Pan, part Green Man – carved on the keystones, dates from around 1727. The fountain, which bears the Medici coat of arms, is thought to have been made in Italy in the sixteenth century. When this vision of gracious living came on the market in 2011, the guide price was 'in excess of £10M'.

A mid-nineteenth century view of Widcombe Manor, St Thomas à Becket church and the dovecote

For a step-free route – or to avoid a footpath which may be muddy after heavy rain – carry on along Church Street to Ralph Allen Drive. Otherwise **head back to the church and turn right up Church Lane.** After passing Gothic Cottage on the left, you pass an iron gate on the right. Just past it look back over the wall on the right for a glimpse of one of Bath's most remarkable buildings – an octagonal dovecote with more than a passing resemblance to the Tower of the Winds in Athens. Engravings of the tower appeared in Stuart and Revett's *Antiquities of Athens*, published in 1762, and influenced, among others, James Wyatt, who incorporated an almost exact copy of it in the Radcliffe Observatory at Oxford. Nothing appears to be known about the origins or architect of the dovecote, but if it was indeed built during the first wave of enthusiasm for Athenian architecture, then it may be Bath's earliest Greek Revival building. **By the gate of a house called the Dell, go down a short flight of steps on the right.** As you continue along the path, you may catch another glimpse, through a gap in the hedge, of the dovecote. **At the end of the path, turn left along Church Street to Ralph Allen Drive.** This busy road was originally a wooden-railed tramway from Ralph Allen's stone quarries at Combe Down to a wharf on the river in Widcombe. Wagons laden with stone descended the hill by gravity, controlled only by a brakeman, and the empty wagons were hauled back up by horses. The lodge on the left-hand side of the road was designed by John Wood. There is a similar lodge at the top of the drive. Across the road is the Abbey Cemetery, opened in 1842, which is visited in Walk 8.

Turn right downhill past a splendid early-eighteenth-century doorway in the wall, until you come to a car showroom, incorporating an old mill. Upper Widcombe Mill, as it was known, was supplied with water from a chain of ponds in the grounds of Widcombe Manor. There has been a mill on this site since at least since the sixteenth century, but the Domesday Book recorded two mills in Widcombe and this may have been one of them. It ceased operation in 1927, when the owner of Widcombe Manor gave it to his chauffeur to open as a garage.

Upper Widcombe Mill, and the ponds that fed it, in the late nineteenth century

Cross the road, turn left uphill and take the first right along Lyncombe Vale. The house on the corner stands in the grounds of a spa-cum-pleasure garden known as the Bagatelle. It opened in 1769 but lasted for little more than a decade. By 1774, it had been renamed Cupid's Gardens, which suggests that its attractions were of a distinctly concupiscent variety.[1]

If you **keep to the left-hand pavement along Lyncombe Vale**, you will soon find yourself high above the road, with a millstream burbling along beside you and green fields beyond. Jane Austen came this way in May 1801 with a Mrs Chamberlayne, whom she had found it difficult to keep up with on a walk to Weston. This time, however, 'Mrs Chamberlayne's pace was not quite so magnificent … It was nothing more than I could keep up with, without effort, and for many, many yards together on a raised narrow footpath I led the way. The walk was very beautiful, as my companion agreed whenever I made the observation.'

After the road rises to meet the pavement, the millstream disappears into a culvert by Lyncombe Vale Farm – early eighteenth century and looking

---

1 The original Cupid's Gardens were in London. Opened in the 1680s, they were originally called Cuper's Gardens after the proprietor, Abraham Boydell Cuper. They became known – first unofficially and then officially – as Cupid's Gardens. One contemporary described them as 'a scene of lewdness' and they were immortalised in a folk song in which a sailor, on a visit to the gardens, takes up with two maidens. They were closed down in 1753.

as though it should be in the heart of the country. Beside it is Lyncombe House Lodge, built in the 1880s with a porch and veranda supported on rustic branches. Look up to the right for a glimpse, through trees, of Lyncombe Hall, constructed of rubble stone with Venetian windows, and the oldest surviving building – apart from the farm – in Lyncombe.

Carry on up the road until you come to a junction. You will shortly be heading up to the right, but first **turn left** to see Lyncombe House, half-hidden by later buildings. This was Lyncombe Spa, opened in 1742 after the discovery of a chalybeate spring. It later became a private house and is now a school. Up to the right, behind the ultra-modern coach-house conversion, there was a pleasure garden called King James's Palace because of a local legend that James II stayed hereabouts during a visit to Bath in 1687. It opened in the 1770s and closed around 1805, and seems to have been a lively place, with firework displays, concerts and public breakfasts.

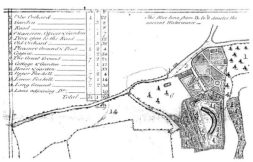

An early-nineteenth century plan of Lyncombe Spa

Head back up Lyncombe Vale Road, taking the left-hand fork at the junction. A stiff climb takes you past the back of Lyncombe Hall, its early-eighteenth-century façade largely hidden behind a late-Victorian extension. **At the crossroads, carry straight on down Lyncombe Hill.** Although little known, the late Georgian buildings on Lyncombe Hill are among the most attractive in the city, with detached and semi-detached villas on the left and a range of terraces on the right.

Turn right down Forefield Rise, past one of Bath's few red-brick terraces, with the cliff-like back of Widcombe Crescent ahead. Whereas the front of the crescent is secluded and demure, the back looms above the valley below like an ocean liner coming into port. That is not an analogy which would have occurred to Harcourt Masters, of course, but it is remarkable how Widcombe Crescent prefigures buildings such as the modernist Marine Court in St Leonards on Sea, designed in 1936 as 'a building embodying the beautiful curves of a great ship – a vertical liner on land', and inspired by seeing the Queen Mary in dock.[1]

At the bottom of Forefield Rise, you are back on Ralph Allen's tramway. Turn left for a few metres before turning up a path on the left, crossing

---

1 From directly below, Widcombe Crescent also bears an uncanny resemblance to a row of buildings photographed through a fish-eye lens, another analogy that would not have occurred to Harcourt Masters.

Widcombe Crescent from below
An Edwardian view of Prior Park Buildings

the stream running down from the mill and turning right to the central house in Prior Park Buildings. Built by John Pinch in the early 1820s, this is the last of the great Georgian terraces. As befits its date, it is not only set well back from the road but also behind a row of gardens. Most architects would have hidden the stream underground, but Pinch made a feature of it. It was an inspired touch, and an indication of how far ideas of the picturesque had taken hold even in Bath. Another innovation was the insertion of windows into the central pediment. Yet, despite the building's marks of modernity, it was essentially backward-looking. John Wood had designed the palatial north side of Queen Square almost 90 years earlier, but Pinch's debt to his great predecessor is unmistakable. Comparison with Queen Square only underlines how much had changed in the intervening period, however. The north side of Queen Square was designed like a palace because it looked out across an open and very public space. When John Palmer built the north side of St James's Square in the early 1790s he adopted a similar approach. Pinch, however, opted to hide his palatial front behind trees and gardens, reflecting and responding to the early nineteenth-century retreat from the public to the private. Following that trend, however, meant that it no longer made much sense to use an architectural language designed for public spaces. So Prior Park Buildings represents not the continuance of a tradition but its swansong. Magnificent though it is, after this there was nowhere left to go.

A new architectural language was needed, a language of detached and semi-detached villas rather than terraces and crescents, of shrubberies and hedges rather than public promenades, of the picturesque rather than the palatial. You can see how such a language was developed, if you **walk back along Prior Park Buildings and turn right along Prior Park Road.** On the other side of the road are five late-Regency semi-detached villas. Charming, unpretentious and resolutely suburban, they represented a radical departure from the Georgian ideal: although semi-detached, each is set in its own grounds, its own little kingdom.

A little further along, you can see how the early Victorians took things one step further. Nos 61 and 63, on either side of Bewdley Road, were built in Tudor-Gothic style in 1843, only a couple of years after Brunel's Tudor-style Bath station. Here Italianate proportion and decorum have given way to idiosyncratic asymmetry, evoking all manner of associations with the distant past. The gable end, anathematised by the Georgians, has also made a triumphant return.

The movement away from terraces to detached or semi-detached villas finds a curious echo in the changes that overtook dance forms in the early nineteenth century. At the beginning of the century, the standard form was the 'long set' in which two rows of couples faced each other – like terraced houses on either of a street – and progressed up or down the set, dancing with successive partners. As the century wore on, however, it was displaced by dances such as waltzes and polkas, in which couples moved around the room as a unit, eschewing contact with other couples. That this development paralleled the move from terraced to detached or semi-detached living is a curious instance of how correspondences can sometimes occur in the unlikeliest places.[1]

---

1 Although the move from terraces to detached or semi-detached villas occurred nationally, it seems to have happened earlier in Bath than in other fashionable towns and cities. This may have been because, by 1830, Bath had more than enough terraces for those who wanted to live in them. Terraces and crescents continued to be built in places such as Clifton, Cheltenham, Torquay and Brighton until the mid-nineteenth century and beyond, although villas gradually eclipsed them in popularity.

Turn and head back down Prior Park Road. Opposite Prior Park Buildings, monumental late-Victorian semi-detached houses represent a further evolution of domestic design. At the end of Prior Park Buildings look up to the left to see where Prior Park Cottages – built at the same time as Prior Park Buildings – climb steeply uphill. You will notice that No2 – once known as Good Hope Cottage – has picturesque Gothic-style windows. Those on the first floor are modern, but those on the ground floor probably date from when the house was built. The row of

The row of workmen's cottages built by John Wood for Ralph Allen around 1737

cottages on the left-hand side of Prior Park Road, however, are much earlier. John Wood built them around 1737 for Ralph Allen's stonemasons and they are among the earliest purpose-built workmen's cottages in existence.

The tramway continued across Claverton Street, where its route is now covered by buildings, to a wharf on the river of which no trace survives. The White Hart Inn, on the right, was also built for Ralph Allen; the walled garden at the back is one of the finest alfresco drinking and dining spots in the city. The statue of the white hart over the entrance came from the White Hart on Stall Street when it was demolished in 1867.

Turn left into Claverton Street, cross at the pedestrian lights, turn right and walk past the Baptist church. On the corner by the canal, the inscription, 'Instead of the thorn shall come up the fir tree', is a reference to the beerhouse that the church pulled down to build a schoolroom. **Turn left down a footpath to the canal towpath.** Up to your left is the original Gothic-style Ebenezer chapel of 1820. The canalside cottages to its right are all that survives of a once-thriving canalside community that was destroyed when the new road was built in 1975. **Continue under the road bridge and past the canal pound.** Thimble Mill, beside the next lock, was used to pump water up the flight of locks. **Walk up to the road and continue along it for 90 metres before crossing a metal footbridge over the river.** Part way across look back at the river bank, which, before the dual carriageway was built, was lined with houses. **Carry on under the railway station and head north along Manvers Street, turning left at the end to return to the starting point.**

7
BATH NEW TOWN
Over the River to Bathwick

Distance *3 miles*

Time *2-3 hours*

Accessibility *Mostly on pavements or paved surfaces, although with one country footpath and a canal towpath which may be muddy; several flights of steps, with step-free alternative available*

Public toilets *Henrietta Park (south-west corner); Sydney Gardens (near Bathwick Street entrance)*

Starting point *Kingston Parade (outside Visitor Information Centre)*

> *Long suburbs extend now on every side of the city, and the meads on the opposite side of the river, which, when the Parades were built, justified the motto upon one of the houses, 'Rus in Urbe', are now covered with another town.*
> Robert Southey, 1807

This walk explores 'Bath New Town' established across the river in Bathwick in the late eighteenth and early nineteenth centuries. **From the Visitor Information Centre, turn right along the south side of the abbey and carry on round into Orange Grove. Turn right past the row of shops on the south side, cross two sets of pedestrian lights, turn left and follow the balustrade round into Grand Parade.**

From here you have a good view across the river to Bathwick. In the early eighteenth century, there were no grand buildings on the far bank, just a mill with water meadows and market gardens beyond. In the distance, you might have glimpsed through the trees a few houses clustered around the ancient church of Bath Wick (as it was then known).

In 1726, William Pulteney, later Earl of Bath, acquired the Bathwick Estate from the Earl of Essex for £12,000, as part settlement of a debt. Around ten years later, Bath's first pleasure gardens opened on the site now covered by the northern part of the recreation ground. Known as Spring Gardens, they were reached by ferry from North Parade. There was no further development until 1767, when William's great niece, Frances, inherited the estate. Her husband, William Johnstone, changed his name to William Johnstone Pulteney and set about planning what became known as Bath New Town. His first step was to build the bridge

Opposite: Henrietta Park, laid out where Frances Square was to have been built

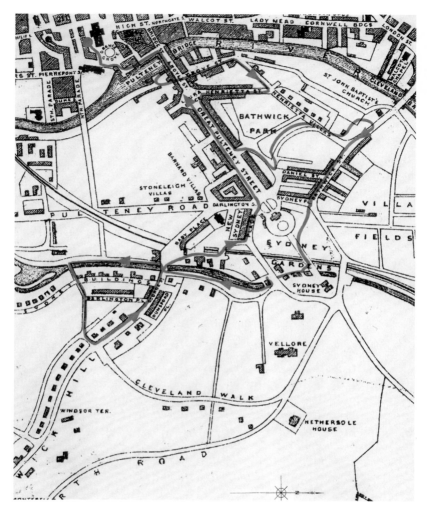

to your left. To provide access to it he had to build a new street to link up with Northgate Street. This meant knocking down several buildings, including the old church of St Mary by the Northgate. Although this had not been a church for almost 200 years, the tower was still in use as the city gaol. The corporation struck a deal with William Johnstone Pulteney: he could demolish the buildings as long as he provided the site for a new gaol in Bathwick and laid on a supply of water to the city from springs on his estate.

Robert Adam's design for the bridge was inspired by Palladio's unrealised design for the Rialto in Venice. It is one of the few bridges in the world to be lined with shops on either side. The first stone was laid in 1769 and it

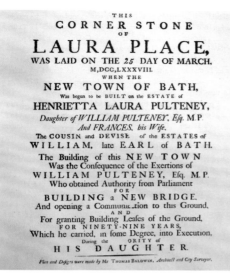

THIS
CORNER STONE
OF
LAURA PLACE,
WAS LAID ON THE 25 DAY OF MARCH,
M,DCC,LXXXVIII.
WHEN THE
NEW TOWN OF BATH,
Was begun to be BUILT on the ESTATE of
HENRIETTA LAURA PULTENEY,
Daughter of WILLIAM PULTENEY, Esq. M.P.
And FRANCES, his Wife.
The COUSIN and DEVISE of the ESTATES of
WILLIAM, late EARL of BATH.
The Building of this NEW TOWN
Was the Confequence of the Exertions of
WILLIAM PULTENEY, Esq. M.P.
Who obtained Authority from Parliament
FOR
BUILDING a NEW BRIDGE.
And opening a Communic tion to this Ground,
AND
For granting Building Leafes of the Ground,
FOR NINETY-NINE YEARS,
Which he carried, in fome Degree, into Execution,
During the ORITY of
HIS DAUGHTER.

Plan and Defigns were made by Mr THOMAS BALDWIN, Architect and City Surveyor.

A transcript of the inscription on the foundation stone of Laura Place

Laura Place and Great Pulteney Street in 1795, showing how much was built before the slump of 1793 brought work to a virtual standstill

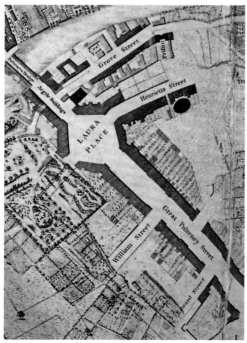

was completed five years later. The gaol – which you will see later – was completed at around the same time. Because of a major economic slump, however, little else was built in Bathwick for over a decade. Not until 1788 did Henrietta Laura Pulteney, William Johnstone Pulteney's daughter, lay the first stone of Laura Place, the centrepiece of the first stage of a development masterminded by Thomas Baldwin. Five boom years followed, during which Argyle and Great Pulteney Streets were built, together with the east side of Henrietta Street and the first part of Sydney Place. Then came an even greater slump, triggered by the outbreak of war with France. Although work continued sporadically, the initial momentum was never recovered. For decades, maps of the city continued to show projected streets and squares extending to the north, south and east of Great Pulteney Street, most of which were never built. Over two centuries later, much of the land earmarked for building remains undeveloped.

The view of Pulteney Bridge and weir from

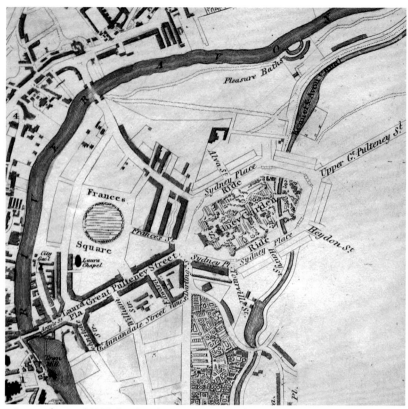

A map of around 1830 showing the many streets and squares that were never built

where you are standing is justly celebrated, but there is something odd about it – you are looking at the backs of the buildings across the river in all their rubble-stone disarray. Although largely screened by trees, it is curious that something most Georgian architects and developers would have tried to hide from public scrutiny forms part of one of the most familiar views of the city.

Walk to the end of Grand Parade and turn right across Pulteney Bridge. The left-hand side of the bridge suffered a partial collapse in 1800 and was rebuilt by John Pinch, Surveyor to the Bathwick Estate. You will be seeing more of his work later. More recently, worrying cracks have appeared in the bridge, leading to calls for traffic to be banned to protect it from further damage. At the end of the bridge, take a look at the vista ahead, with Sydney House (now the Holburne Museum) at the far end of Great Pulteney Street. The shopfront on the right at No 16 is especially fine; less impressive is the evidence of subsidence in the plat band with Argyle Buildings chiselled into it up to the

WALK 7: BATH NEW TOWN

The weir from below Pulteney Bridge

Fishing from the old weir in 1967

right. **Walk down the steps below it** for one of the most spectacular views in Bath.[1]

In the early 1970s, as part of a major flood-prevention scheme, the weir, which had always run diagonally across the river, was reprofiled to its current horseshoe shape. Although the river still floods after prolonged rain, the waters no longer rise almost to the top of the arches under Pulteney Bridge as they once did. On the other side of the river the colonnade under Grand Parade has been closed to the public for years – surely one of the most scandalously underutilised public spaces in the city. The archway with its gate firmly closed leads to Boatstall Lane and the East Gate, which you saw in Walk 1. Before Pulteney Bridge or the colonnade was built, the lane led down to a ferry across the river.

Carry on down the steps to the open space where Pulteney Cruisers leave for the trip upstream (an essential part of any visit to Bath). **Turn left and go through a tunnel under Great Pulteney Street.** Here you can see how the buildings were raised high above the flood plain. Starting at ground level, basements and sub-basements (and in some cases sub-sub-basements) were built first. The ground floor came next, with pavement and road built up in front of the house to the same level, and the other floors followed. Below the pavement and roadway, semi-circular vaults, where coal could be stored, extended under the street. The tunnel under Great Pulteney Street is, to all intents and purposes, a large open vault.

It emerges in Grove Street, which must have been a delightful spot when first laid out. The Rising Sun Inn on the other side of the road opened in 1788, with a view over the river. From here, visitors could hire boats to carry them upstream to the pleasure gardens at Grosvenor. Things soon changed. In 1792, John Eveleigh opened a large builder's yard beside the river. Although the building on your left as you walk up from the tunnel

1 For a step-free route, cross the road, walk to the end of Argyle Street and turn left down Grove Street.

is new, it incorporates a pediment from Eveleigh's yard bearing the date 5792. This is a Masonic date, with 4000 years added to the standard date to reflect the belief that the world was created in 4000BC. The buildings on the right beyond the Rising Sun date from the late nineteenth century. They replaced a row of buildings dating from around 1792 which were prone to flooding and had deteriorated to become some of the most notorious slums in the city. There is a charming datestone from 1887 on St Mary's Church House.

As you **continue along Grove Street**, a much grander building comes into view on the right. There is something very odd about it, though – the top three floors are impressive enough, but the ground floor

The old gaol in Grove Street

Henrietta Street

looks more like a basement – which is exactly what it was meant to be. Like the houses in Great Pulteney Street, it was built from the basement up, but the street was never built up to what should have been its ground floor. Not that the inmates would have been that concerned; far from being a desirable residence, this was the new gaol, whose external grandeur masked a grim and cramped interior. It was designed by Thomas Atwood in palatial style so that the elegant residents William Johnstone Pulteney hoped to attract to Bathwick would not be offended. It soon became apparent, however, that people did not want to live near a prison, however refined it looked from the outside. No grand mansions were built alongside it and the raised street in front of the gaol was never built. When it closed in 1842, it became a police barracks and has now been converted to apartments.

Carry on along Grove Street for a little way and, just after Henrietta Place, turn along a **footpath leading off to the right. This leads to Henrietta Street, where you turn right.** Look out for two archways on the left that led to Laura Chapel, the proprietary chapel for Bathwick's well-heeled residents. Opened in 1795, it was demolished in 1909. When you reach Laura Place, look across to Johnstone

Street, originally intended to lead to a grand crescent overlooking the river. Only the first few houses in Johnstone Street were built, and it now looks across the recreation ground to a sports centre.

Turn left along Great Pulteney Street, designed by Thomas Baldwin with an ingeniously asymmetrical arrangement – three rows of terraces on the south side and two on the north. It was designed like this so that, when you approached it from the streets on either side, you would not look across to another street but to a building with a grand pediment. It was the same trick Thomas Jelly used at Edgar Buildings. The impact of Jelly's grand design was destroyed when Edgar Buildings and Milsom Street were encumbered with shopfronts. Baldwin's scheme failed because the streets on either side were never built.

As you walk along, you can see how the first turning on the right – William Street – faces such a pediment. When you come to the first turning on the left – Sunderland Street – the pediment opposite, which incorporates the Pulteney coat of arms, is even grander.

Turn left along what there is of Sunderland Street, walk down the ramp and turn right. Across the road, Henrietta Park occupies a site originally intended for a grand square. **At the end of the road walk up to the right** and look along Daniel Street. There is no clearer demonstration of

Part of the Pulteney coat of arms

The ruined mortuary chapel

how suddenly the money ran out than this quiet street. Work on it started in 1792, but got no further than the first three buildings on the south side – including the Pulteney Arms – before the crash of the Bath Bank in March 1793 brought it to an abrupt halt. It was not until 1810 that John Pinch took up where Baldwin had left off – and, as you can see, the buildings he designed were very different.

Turn round, head into the park and turn right. When you reach Henrietta Road, cross over and turn right. Just before the end of the road, go through a **small gateway on the left into St Mary's churchyard,** dominated by the ruined shell of the mortuary chapel. The chapel was designed by John Pinch and built from the stones of the old Bathwick church, which was demolished in 1818. Pinch is

buried under the large tomb beneath the chapel's east window. **Head to the left of the chapel and walk round the churchyard.** A blocked-up Gothic archway in the far wall once led to the rectory, which has now been converted to flats. **Go through a pair of iron gates and then turn right** – but not before carrying on for a few metres to see, on the right, a tomb with a chilling message – 'This Grave is Full'. St John's church, over to the left, was consecrated in 1862.

When you reach Bathwick Street – once a secluded byway but now one of the most congested streets in the city – look across to where a small archway known as Pinch's Folly stands incongruously in front of an apartment block. It may once have stood at the entrance to long-lost pleasure gardens called

Rochfort Place and Pinch's Folly around 1910

Villa Fields, although it is also claimed, more prosaically, that it was the entrance to John Pinch the Younger's builder's yard. To its right is Rochfort Place, only four houses long, supremely elegant, with a couple of superb fanlights. The toothing stones on the left tell their own story of buildings projected but never built. Next to it, and dwarfed by its neighbours, is the oldest surviving house in Bathwick, dating from the seventeenth century and originally the manor house. The awkward spacing of the second-floor windows is due to the building having been gabled; a parapet was added in the eighteenth century to modernise it.

Turn right along Bathwick Street and cross Henrietta Road to what was, at the time of writing, the most recent bit of Bath's archaeological jigsaw to emerge into the light of day. In 2011, three small early twentieth-century houses on the site were demolished to make way for a neo-Georgian apartment block. When the site was cleared, archaeologists quickly established that they had been built on the site of a Roman road and a building dating from the early years of the Roman occupation.

As you carry on, the single-storey extension on the corner of Daniel Street, which now houses a launderette, was originally part of a pub. Although it closed in 1872, its elaborate sign bracket survives. On the north side of Daniel Street look out for an early bit of infilling – a two-storey building, dwarfed on all sides and tucked away behind a high wall.

As you continue on past the Barley Mow – one of Bath's friendliest pubs and open all day should you feel tempted to call in – look to the right to see Daniel Mews, still with its pennant-stone setts. The Crown Inn opposite dates from 1899; its claim to be the oldest pub in Bath is based on the age of the building it replaced.

At the end of Bathwick Street, look to the right along Sydney Place, designed by Baldwin and built between 1792 and 1796. Baldwin intended Sydney Place to consist of eight such terraces, encircling Sydney Gardens, but this is the only one built before the money ran out. Jane Austen lived at No 4 from 1801 to 1804. In 1804, work started on the second of the eight terraces, on the other side of the gardens, to a design by John Pinch, but the other six never materialised.

Cross two sets of traffic lights and go through the gateway into Sydney Gardens. These are the only pleasure gardens in Bath to have survived, albeit in much altered form.
Follow the wide path through the park as it swings first right then left and climbs gently uphill. Just before crossing the railway, you will see a Roman-style temple on the left. It was built to promote Bath in the Empire Exhibition at the Crystal Palace in 1911 and re-erected here two years later to commemorate the Bath Pageant of 1909.[1]

The Gorgon's Head on the 1911 temple in Sydney Gardens

Cross the railway line, brought through the gardens in grand style by Isambard Kingdom Brunel in 1841, **and carry on uphill. Just before a bridge over the canal, turn right and go through a gateway onto the towpath.**[2] This stretch of the canal was designed to harmonise with the pleasure gardens. The two Chinoiserie

A special train to mark the 165th anniversary of the first train from London to Bath steams through Sydney Gardens on 30 June 2006

1 Contrary to what the presence of the temple may suggest, the Pageant took place not here, but in Royal Victoria Park.

2 For a step-free route, carry on over the canal bridge and bear right. On leaving the park, turn right for a few metres before crossing the road and going along a footpath to the right of Sham Castle Lane, beside a large building that originally housed the canal company's offices, and carrying on down to the canal towpath.

bridges were cast at Coalbrookdale in Shropshire, and the tunnel portals beyond them were adorned with elaborate carvings. Over the eastern portal is the figure of Old Father Thames; looking westward, you can see Sabrina, spirit of the Severn. It was in this manner that the Kennet & Avon Canal, which opened in 1810, proclaimed its achievement of linking these two great rivers. The tunnels were necessary because there were still plans to continue the terraces of Sydney Place along the roads on either side of Sydney Gardens when the canal was built.

Turn right and head towards Sabrina's tunnel. The building on top of the tunnel, occupying land originally earmarked for part of Sydney Place, was designed by John Pinch to house the canal company's offices. As you walk through the tunnel, look out for mason's marks on the stones. Near the far end, look up to see a hole in the roof. This led up to a trap door in one of the offices and may have been designed so that instructions or information could be shouted up or down as boats passed underneath.

Once through the tunnel, follow the path over the canal and past the back of the offices before continuing along the left bank. Sydney Wharf, which you can see ahead on the right bank, was once a hive of activity, lined with warehouses, builders' yards, stables and blacksmiths. Very few of the original buildings survive, although some of the new ones mimic the style of those that once stood here. The large building behind Bath Narrowboats is a modern retirement complex.

Walk up the ramp to the road, cross the zebra crossing, turn right across the bridge and go down a flight of steps to continue along the towpath.[1] The houses on the left with their gardens coming down to the canal may seem idyllic today, but this too was once a busy commercial area. A little way along are two former industrial buildings – a malthouse,

1 For a step-free route, do not cross the zebra crossing but turn right downhill to Raby Place, turning right along Sydney Wharf and skipping the next four paragraphs.

still with 'Maltsters' faintly visible on its wall, and a coal wharf. Both are now offices.

Just past the first lock – complete with lock-keeper's cottage – cross an iron footbridge and walk up an alleyway to Sydney Buildings. The lamp post ahead of you is one of the oldest in the city, dating from around 1830 when gas lighting was introduced to Bathwick. **Cross the road and carry on up the steps.** After passing the turning to Darlington Place, views across National Trust-owned fields open up on the right. **Take the next turning on the left to emerge on Bathwick Hill** amidst some of the finest buildings in the city. Most are by John Pinch, although No 35 across the road, with a Greek Revival porch and superb ironwork, which dates from around 1835, was probably the work of his son, John Pinch the Younger. Nos 36 & 37 next door, however, with their shallow, double-storey bays, were designed by the elder Pinch and date from around 1827.

Turn left and walk downhill past more of Pinch's work from the 1820s. Devonshire Lodge has a particularly fine doorway, while No 3, next door, has a Gothick-style porch which sits uneasily with the Greek Revival decorations on the gateposts.

Sion Place, five houses long, was designed by Pinch in 1826. His trademark approach to building on hills was to make the cornices and plat bands flow down the hill. Here, because the houses are separated by pilasters, only the cornices flow down. Beyond Sion Place comes the obtrusive St Patrick's Court, built in 1966. Dunsford Place, across the road, was built by Pinch in the early 1820s. Here

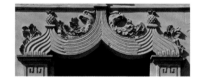

Above: George Street

Above right: Gothick decorations on 3 Sion Place

Right: Dunsford Place

Opposite: One of the tunnels on the Kennet & Avon Canal

Above:
Darlington Place

Above right: Seer's
coal office at the
top of Raby Place

Right: Raby Place
and St Mary's
church

Opposite:
New Sydney Place

neither platband nor cornice flows down the hill, yet it is very fine, with splendid wrought-iron balconies. Note too the understated way in which the terrace accommodates itself to the bend in the road not with a curved façade but by a subtle change of direction part way down.

After crossing Darlington Place, you come to George Street, more modest but still with Pinch's characteristic sense of proportion and attention to detail. As you cross Sydney Buildings, look up to the left to see the back of Darlington Place, commanding one of the finest views in the city.

Cross the zebra crossing and continue downhill over the canal to Raby Place, built by John Pinch between 1818 and 1825. The house at the top was demolished by Brunel to make way for his railway and later rebuilt. If you **turn right along Sydney Wharf** and peer over the wall at the back you will see the tunnel under the house. Notice also the faded lettering for Seer's Coal Office – another reminder that this was very much a working area at one time.

There is a good view of St Mary's church from here. It was designed by Pinch, and demonstrates how this supreme classicist could not only turn his hand to the Perpendicular Gothic but create a masterpiece in the process. The design was groundbreaking. It was the first true Gothic Revival church built in England – its foundation stone was laid in 1814 and it was consecrated six years later. The Gothic – or Gothick – style had been around for half a century or more but was inspired by fanciful notions of a semi-mythical past rather than a study of architectural styles. St Mary's marked a decisive break with such frippery. Among the architects who were influenced by St Mary's was James Savage, who designed the first Gothic Revival church in London – St Luke's, Chelsea – six years later, using Bath stone.

As you carry on along Sydney Wharf, the building ahead of you on the corner of Raby Mews – also sitting on top of the railway – was a pub called the Cleveland Arms (as you will see if you walk past it and look back at the faded lettering on the side wall). Unlike the house at the top of Raby Place, Brunel did not pull it down; he simply drove his railway underneath.

Carry on until you come to a gate with Raby Villa on the right. Turn left across the railway bridge – with splendid views of Brunel's line in both directions – **and turn right at the bottom of the slope.** Ahead lies the part of Sydney Place designed by John Pinch. Built between 1804 and 1808, it was originally known as New Sydney Place. The houses in it were numbered from 93 to 103, indicating that there was still every intention of completing the six other terraces in the fullness of time. The wall on your left has an orangery on the other side, while an exquisitely proportioned conservatory sits atop the porch at the end. It was in this house that Queen Charlotte, the wife of George III, stayed when she came to Bath to take the waters in 1817.

Turn left along Sydney Place. The *Pevsner Architectural Guide to Bath* describes this as 'the most beautiful of Bath's nineteenth-century

buildings'. It is a bold statement, and not one everybody will agree with, even though all the other candidates – Cavendish Place, Cavendish Crescent, Sion Hill Place – are also by Pinch. What can be said without fear of contradiction is that buildings do not come much finer than this. The way everything – cornices, mouldings, friezes and plat bands – flows up the hill, the way in which full-height rounded bays are placed at either end, the way the ironwork punctuates the largely unadorned façade, the design of the fanlights – all is masterly. Unlike Wood, with his alchemical imaginings and druidic fantasies, there is no hidden agenda with Pinch – what you see is what you get – but many have queried whether he is not the finer architect, and, perhaps, the finest of all those who practised in Bath.

Cross over before you reach the end of Sydney Place and carry on to the traffic lights. Few buildings have had such an eventful history as the one on your right. When Thomas Baldwin built Great Pulteney Street, he drew up plans for a neo-classical building called Sydney House at the end, forming the entrance to the pleasure gardens. However, the crash of 1793 forced him into bankruptcy, and his assistant, Charles Harcourt Masters, took over. He ditched Baldwin's plans for the building – probably because he or some of the shareholders considered them too modern – and drew up plans based on Baldwin's design for the Guildhall from two decades earlier. He made one major change, bringing forward the central tetrastyle portico to create a porte cochère, but otherwise the west front of the building was virtually identical to that of the Guildhall – or at least it was until John Pinch the Younger added an extra storey in 1836. What Harcourt Masters did was to make a design from the 1770s the centrepiece of a development conceived in the 1790s. Had Baldwin's original design been realised, we would have had a unified and superbly impressive piece of urban design. As it is, Sydney House and Great Pulteney Street, impressive though they are, do not cohere in the way great architecture should.

Above: The Holburne Museum, once the entrance to pleasure gardens frequented by Jane Austen

Opposite: Trompe l'oeil window in Grove Street

That was not the end of Sydney House's tribulations, however. The declining fortunes of the gardens led to their closure in the 1850s. The building became a school but by the early twentieth century it was derelict. Threatened with demolition, it was saved by the trustees of the Holburne of Menstrie Museum, who decided it would be a good place to display their collection. Sir Reginald Blomfield refurbished the building, demolishing everything but the façade, and the museum opened in 1916. In 2008 it closed for another refurbishment, including the addition of an extension to the rear, and reopened in May 2011.

Cross at the traffic lights and head straight on along Great Pulteney Street. Here Baldwin's genius for urban design moved beyond the built environment to forge a link with the natural world. Don't cross over, but stand on the right-hand side of the pavement and look along the street and you will see, rising above the buildings beyond Pulteney Bridge, a hill crowned with trees. This is Twerton Round Hill, and the alignment of the street towards it was no accident. In February 1799, a correspondent wrote to the *Bath Chronicle* expressing 'admiration at the pleasing and

happy effect of the hill that terminates the view directly in a line with Great Pulteney Street in approaching Bath' and suggesting that an obelisk celebrating Nelson's victory at the Battle of the Nile be built on it.

Twerton Round Hill soon disappears behind the late-Victorian extension to the Guildhall as you continue along Great Pulteney Street. Early visitors would have had it in view for longer as they approached the city; they would also have looked, as they passed the streets leading off to left and right, over land earmarked for development, building sites destined never to be built on. The new town on the east bank of the Avon, had it been built as Baldwin intended, would have been the grandest neoclassical development in the world. It is hard to believe that anyone really thought it would all come to pass, sustained solely by an ever-increasing number of wealthy visitors. Such are the delusions formed in years of economic boom. But even though only a small part of the plan was realised – and then in a modified form – it remains one of the classic pieces of urban design. We can also be grateful that John Pinch, who was brought in to take the development forward in the early nineteenth century, was an even greater architect than Baldwin.

Carry on across Laura Place and along Argyle Street. Keeping a look out for the trompe l'oeil window on the corner of Grove Street, dating from when there was a second-hand bookshop here, **carry on across Pulteney Bridge and head back to the starting point.**

8

A GLIMPSE OF TIVOLI
Combe Down & Prior Park

Distance *Full walk, 6.5 miles; two shorter options available*

Time *4-5 hours (full walk)*

Accessibility *The walk up to Combe Down and the circuit of Prior Park Gardens both include sections which may be muddy. The walk around Combe Down includes two short flights of steps.*

Public toilets *Prior Park Gardens*

Starting point *Kingston Parade (outside Visitor Information Centre)*

Prior Park Gardens are administered by the National Trust and are open daily from early spring to the end of October and on Saturdays and Sundays in the winter. An entry charge is payable for non-National Trust members. For further details see www.nationaltrust.org.uk/priorpark/.

> *There, where the long street roars, hath been*
> *The stillness of the central sea.*
> Alfred Lord Tennyson, *In Memoriam*

> *It is a glimpse of Tivoli in a Somerset valley. What other English city has such a bit of Italy at its gates?*
> Frederic Harrison, 1914

In the Jurassic Period – 195 to 135 million years ago – the area around Bath lay under a warm, shallow sea. Over time, sediment built up on the sea bed, individual grains became coated with lime, and these compacted, forming layers which bonded together to form the sedimentary limestone known as Bath stone. Although Bath stone is layered, it is, unlike many other stones, a 'freestone' which can be cut or sawn in any direction. When used in buildings, however, it needs to be 'laid on its bed, as nature laid it down in the quarry', otherwise the layers eventually start to flake or peel away. The quality and versatility of Bath stone as a building material has been known since Roman times, but it was only with Ralph Allen's takeover of the quarries at Combe Down in the early eighteenth century that its extraction was ratcheted up to industrial level, with it reaching a national and eventually an international market.

   In this walk, we head up to Combe Down, the village that grew up around Ralph Allen's quarries, before continuing down to Prior Park,

Opposite: The Palladian Bridge at Prior Park

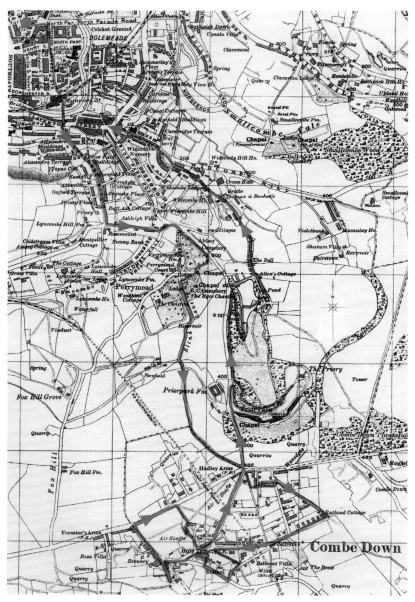

which he built with the proceeds. Combe Down is just over a mile south of Bath, but is 140 metres higher, so getting there entails a stiff climb. For a less strenuous option, First Bus No 1 runs every half hour from Dorchester Street to the Hadley Arms in Combe Down, from where you can set off round the village before heading down to Prior Park and back

WALK 8: A GLIMPSE OF TIVOLI

to Bath. A third option, for those who are pressed for time, is to miss out Combe Down, walking up to Prior Park along the suggested route, and heading back to Bath from there.

Until the early eighteenth century, Combe Down was a high and lonely plateau, populated by shepherds and a few quarrymen living in makeshift huts. Ralph Allen changed all that. He was from Cornwall, the most technologically advanced mining district in the world, where fortunes were being made from tin and copper. Although Allen had made his fortune from reforming the postal service, he saw the stone quarries' potential, and, by ploughing his money into them, transformed Combe Down into a major industrial complex, with the infrastructure to support it. His quarries soon became a tourist attraction in their own right. A visitor to Bath in 1743 described how he

took a walk to Mr Allen's house and his quarry of stone ... The quarry is a surprising place where he digs the stones, which is done with great ease ... They drive in iron wedges and then loosen it with iron crows, which often breaks off pieces of a prodigious size, then they fix a large chain round it and crane it up – it goes by a horse, when at the top of the pit it is placed upon a carriage of wood which

An early twentieth-century view of a quarry at Combe Down

A mid-eighteenth century view of Prior Park, with the tramway running down what is now Ralph Allen Drive

has iron wheels about it 18 inches high. This goes on a groove fixed in the earth and when it comes to the descent of the hill, it is managed by one man … [He] has also built a long row of houses near the quarry where many of his workmen live. He has also all his iron work for the making his instruments of all kinds for the use of the quarry and also carpenters.

Ralph Allen died in 1764, and, after the death of his widow two years later, the estate was inherited by Gertrude Warburton, Allen's niece, who was married to the Bishop of Gloucester. The bishop dismantled Ralph Allen's tramway, although the quarries remained in operation and continued to attract visitors. In 1788, the Rev S Shaw described how he had entered

> a cavern of near 300 yards long, which, from the vast quantity that has been got out for many years to supply the city with its beautiful free-stone, we saw wrought out into various lofty and spacious rooms, and regularly supported by able pillars, left for that purpose, that add a pleasing idea of safety to the observing eye. The whole appears neat and agreeable, not much unlike the vaulted apartments in the rustic of a nobleman's mansion. The gentle weepings of the rock in some parts form petrefactions, which, together with a few spars interspersed, reflect the lights of the candles very brilliantly. The former mode of conveying the large blocks directly down the hill to Bath, by machines running on grooves or frames of wood, such as we see in the collieries about Newcastle, is now no more; they carry them in common wagons, to the great detriment of the roads, and inconvenience of travellers.

In 1796, the estate passed to the Earl de Montalt, whose lack of interest in the quarries was matched by a desire to develop Combe Down as a fashionable country retreat. He converted the quarrymen's cottages to lodgings, built an elegant terrace and promoted Combe Down's bracing climate – perfect for convalescents and those with respiratory problems anxious to escape the smoke and dust of Bath.

De Montalt died in 1803 and was succeeded by his son, whose death four years later heralded the break-up of the estate. New quarry owners moved in and new quarries were opened. Rows of quarrymen's cottages were built – some of them in worked-out quarries – but alongside them grand villas started appearing – a juxtaposition that still defines Combe Down's unique character today.

If you are walking to Combe Down, head south from the Visitor Information Centre along Church Street, turn left along Lilliput Alley (North Parade Passage) and carry on along North Parade. Turn right along Pierrepont Street at the traffic lights. After crossing the end of Henry Street, cross at the pedestrian lights and continue along to the railway station. Cross at the pedestrian lights ahead and go through the tunnel to the left of the station. Carry on over a footbridge and two sets of traffic lights before turning right and then left up Lyncombe Hill. Just past the first row of three houses, turn left along an alleyway to see,

Architectural variety on Lyncombe Hill: Clockwise from top left: Minimalist elegance from 1817; the picturesque Gothicism of Abbey Lodge; Tudor-style Priory Lodge

through locked gates, a Baptist Burial Ground, opened in 1807. Most of Bath's Georgian burial grounds have either been built on or redeveloped. This is one of the few that survive. Back on Lyncombe Hill, the rubble-stone building on the right, once known as Pope's Villa, dates from the early eighteenth century and may originally have been a mill. Southcot Place, a little way up on the left, dates from 1817.

Early-nineteenth-century villas tower above you on the right as you continue up Lyncombe Hill. Southcot House – No 37 – on the left dates from the eighteenth century, but was substantially altered in the nineteenth, when the crenellated parapet was added. The minimalist elegance of No 45, dating from 1817, is set off superbly by box hedging. By contrast, Abbey Lodge – No 30 – high up on the right is a full-blown example of picturesque Gothicism.

Next to Abbey Villa, largely hidden by trees, is Oxford Terrace, seven buildings long and dating from the 1820s. Pediments grace the central house as well as those at either end, and, while the central house has three storeys, the rest of the row is two storeys high. Beyond it is Priory Place, two pairs of semi-detached houses, the first with full-height segmental bays, and both with blind central windows. Finally comes Priory Lodge, a Tudor-style villa dating from around 1830.[1]

---

1 The similarity between Priory Lodge and a group of Tudor-style villas designed by Edward Davis on Entry Hill suggests that he may have been the architect.

Turn left down Rosemount Lane, originally known as Rough Lane and renamed when the road surface was improved. As you head steeply downhill, superb views open up – over to the Abbey Cemetery and Perrymead on the right, and across fields to Widcombe Crescent and Terrace on the left.

Turn left at the end and right up Ralph Allen Drive. After crossing the bottom of Perrymead, go through the gates of the Abbey Cemetery and walk up the main path. After passing the city's Crimean War memorial, the path curves round to a Norman-style chapel designed by GP Manners in 1844. **Head to the right of the chapel and bear right, following a rough path alongside a wall.** On the other side of the wall is the Catholic cemetery, opened in 1859. The main chapel is in the centre; the French Gothic-style building on the right was a private chapel for the Eyre family of Hassop in Derbyshire.

Go through a kissing gate and turn left uphill. The road soon turns into a rough lane, climbing ever more steeply through a tunnel of trees. This was the old road from Bath to Combe Down, which fell into disuse when the new road up Ralph Allen Drive was opened. Visitors to Bath as far back as the early sixteenth century complained about the steep and stony roads, with streams trickling down them, which led down into the city. They were centuries old even then. Most have been transformed beyond recognition; this is one of the few to survive, yet its existence is hardly noted. It seems curious, in a World Heritage city, that something which predates most, if not all, of its buildings, and which speaks so eloquently about the countless generations who have trudged into that

Hanging Land Lane leading up through Pope's Arch

city for business or pleasure should be accorded so little recognition or protection. Although in the nineteenth century, it became the fashion to call it Pope's Walk – because of the legend that the poet Alexander Pope walked up it to visit his friend Ralph Allen – it was formerly known as Hanging Land Lane or Blind Lane.

Eventually you pass under a grotto-like archway, built by Ralph Allen to carry one of the drives on his estate over the lane.[1] After this the lane levels out, with houses on the left and a Ministry of Defence site – soon to be decommissioned – on the right.

Carry on along the path until you emerge at the top of Ralph Allen Drive. Cross over to the Hadley Arms (where, if you caught the bus up from town, you will be joining the walk).[2] Turn left across the Avenue and then right down the drungway (the local name for an alley) to the right of the telephone box. After 50 metres, turn left along another drungway. Turn right at the end and after 25 metres go through a wrought-iron gate on the left into Tyning Place (taking care to close the gate behind you). This is typical of the rows of quarrymen's cottages built in the nineteenth century. It was built on firm ground but the gardens – on the right – sit over an underground quarry. The old quarrymen knew where the quarries were and did not build on them. Only later, when the quarries fell into disuse and knowledge of their whereabouts faded (or was ignored), were houses built over them – with far-reaching consequences.

At the end of Tyning Place, go through another gate, turn left and then right along Gladstone Road. After 200 metres, when the road ends, continue along a drungway. At the end, look to the right where Glenburnie, built in the 1840s, boasts some of the finest ironwork in Bath. Over to your left, beyond the allotments, is Upper Lawn, the only working quarry left in Combe Down.

Turn right along Church Road, past more villas from around the 1840s. The old school, further along on the left, was founded in 1830 and extended in the late nineteenth century. Orchard House, on the right, is a modern take on mid-nineteenth-century

Ironwork on Glenburnie

1 If you want to head straight to Prior Park, missing out Combe Down, turn left along a footpath shortly after going under the archway and turn right along a road. After 100 metres turn left downhill. At the bottom, cross over and turn left down Ralph Allen Drive. The entrance to the gardens is 50 metres along on the right.

2 As this is a busy road, you may wish to avail yourself of the zebra crossing 50 metres to the right.

Italianate design. You can see the real thing if you look to the left, just past the school, at Ashlands.

Carry on along Church Road. Hope Cote Lodge on the right dates from the early nineteenth century but had a French-style mansard roof with dormer windows added

Dial House

in the late nineteenth century. After a modern house comes a row of three buildings from around 1820, two of which have had an extra storey added. Opposite is the old vicarage, designed by HE Goodridge and built in 1838 at a cost of £2,000. The Union Chapel, on the right, was established in 1815 by Baptists and Congregationalists and was the first public place of worship in the village. Claremont House, next door, dates from around the same time and, by the look of it, originally only had two storeys. The cast-iron balustrade on top of the building is particularly striking. The church, designed, like the vicarage, by Goodridge, opened in 1837. The churchyard has never been used for burials; its landscaped grounds are formed from old quarry spoil heaps.

The row of cottages on the right, known as the Old Rank, was built by John Wood for Ralph Allen's workmen in 1729. They are the oldest buildings in Combe Down. Dial House, in the centre, was occupied by the Clerk of Works and contained a room which was used for divine worship. The Rev John Collinson, in his *History and Antiquities of the County of Somerset*, published in 1791, painted a vivid picture of what this area looked like 220 years ago:

> On the summit of Combe Down ... among many immense quarries of free-stone, are large groves of firs, planted by the late Ralph Allen Esq for the laudable purpose of ornamenting this (at that time rough and barren) hill. Among these groves is a neat range of buildings ... It consists of eleven houses, built of wrought stone, raised on the spot; each of which has a small garden in front. These were originally built for the workmen employed in the quarries, but are now chiefly let to invalids from Bath, who retire hither for the sake of a very fine air (probably rendered more salubrious by the plantation of firs) from which many have received essential benefit. The surrounding beautiful and extensive prospects; the wild, but pleasing irregularities of the surface and scenery, diversified with immense quarries, fine open cultivated fields, and extensive plantations of firs, which throw a solemn gloominess of shade, impervious to the sun and winds, over a fine soft turf free from underwood; all serve to render this a delightful summer retreat.

At the far end of the row, Lonsdale, unashamedly late Victorian, is followed by a neo-Georgian bank of roughly the same date. Beyond that is Isabella Place, built by the Earl de Montalt and named after his wife.

Turn left along a drungway opposite the old bank and walk through to Belmont Road. The mid-nineteenth-century villas opposite may look unexciting, but you are looking at their backs – their front elevations, with views over the valley, are much grander. **Turn right and walk down to the end of the road**, where you can see the front of the end house – West Brow – with unusual triangular windows projecting on either side. Looking ahead along Beechwood Road, the large Arts & Crafts house on the left – Beechwoods – dates from 1930.

Turn right up Summer Lane. Quarry Vale Cottages, beyond the school, were built against the face of a worked-out quarry in the early nineteenth century. More quarrymen's cottages can be seen above them, creating an evocative panorama of early industrial housing. A drungway separates the earlier cottages – on the left – from the later ones. **Turn right along it, walk up a flight of steps and turn left along Church Road.** The buildings ahead, on the left-hand side of the road, once looked very different. The shop on the corner was William Colmer's bootmaker's and there was a post office in the single-storey extension on the left; after it closed a Miss Ponting ran a stationer's there. Bath Crockhire, on your left as you pass the top of Summer Lane, occupies the old Jupiter beerhouse. Just past it, a drungway beside the hairdresser's gives access to Byfield Buildings. These caught Pierce Egan's eye when he passed this way in 1819:

> Byfield Buildings is … pleasantly situated, and a few paces forwards the visitor, if inclination permit him, may descend into the stone quarries at Combe Down, opened and worked by Mr Allen. This sudden contrast is

Church Road in the 1920s, when this section was known as Westbury Avenue extremely pleasing: the vast depth of freestone which has been excavated from the earth; the lofty arches, or pillars, remaining in a craggy state, left by the excavators to let in light to the subterranean passages and caverns which extend for a considerable way under the earth, most interestingly claim the attention of the explorer. The appearance altogether has an effect difficult to convey to the reader anything like an adequate representation: several men are employed in breaking up the freestone into different sizes, and which, it seems, yields with much placency to the tools used upon it; and carriages and horses are also seen among the openings, loading for the buildings of Bath. From its yellow appearance, it has a very clean and pleasing look. On regaining the daylight ... several shafts are seen in the fields, raised about three feet from the ground, to let light into different parts of the quarry, to give facility to the excavators in proceeding with their work.

Sadly, it is no longer possible to take up Egan's suggestion. Over the last decade, one of the key components of the World Heritage Site, the quarries which provided the stone for Georgian Bath, have been effectively obliterated, with hardly a murmur of protest. Whether future generations will appreciate the enormity of the loss remains to be seen. They will, however, be able to gain some idea of what they have lost – as can we – by heading to another World Heritage Site, 70 miles south-west, where the stone quarries at Beer welcome visitors, as Combe Down's once did.

Take the next left down Rock Hall Lane. On your left – at the time of writing – stood the malthouse of the old Combe Down Brewery. Despite being an important part of Combe Down's heritage and standing in a sensitive site at the heart of the old village, developers have been given the go ahead to redevelop the site. They have undertaken to incorporate a small heritage centre in the development so that future generations can see what Combe Down used to be like.

Combe Road in the early twentieth century, with the malthouse now scheduled for demolition on the left

On the right is the King William IV Inn, built around 1830 by Philip Nowell, Combe Down's most important nineteenth-century quarry owner, as a place to entertain – and impress – potential clients. It paid off – among the buildings he provided stone for were Longleat House, Windsor Castle and Buckingham Palace; he was eventually knighted by the king he had named the inn after. The old stone yard on the left – where there are now plans to build up to eight houses – stood at the entrance to the Byfield Quarry.

A little further along is Philip Nowell's house – Rock Hall. The original early nineteenth-century house, with full-height canted bays flanking a tower, is on the right. In the late nineteenth century it was extended, in Jacobethan style, to create a Magdalen Hospital. Later it became a home for mentally handicapped children, but since 1988 it has provided sheltered accommodation and further extensions have been added.

An eighteenth-century map of Combe Down, showing the workmen's cottages, with another row of buildings, including the Carriage Inn, at an oblique angle above them. The dotted lines indicate the tramway, which divided into two branches outside the inn, with one branch terminating in Davidge's Bottom, on the left.

The Avenue in the early twentieth century. The Carriage Inn occupied the row of cottages on the right

Walk back up Rock Hall Lane and carry on along Combe Road. Notice how the entrance to Brunswick Place, built around 1815, is at first-floor level, suggesting it was built in an old quarry. The nursery opposite occupies a telephone exchange built in 1939. The Bath Turnpike Trust boundary post at the end of Combe Road marks the old boundary of Monkton Combe and Lyncombe & Widcombe.

Turn right along Bradford Road. Just past the zebra crossing, turn right into The Firs, and immediately turn right again along a grass-grown drungway. When it forks, carry straight on and go down winding steps into another old quarry. Opened by Ralph Allen, this was known as Davidge's Bottom. To your left, beyond No 6, is a former beerhouse called the Rock or Davidge's. The entrance to the underground workings was in the ivy-covered rockface behind it.

Carry straight on along the road out of the old quarry. At the end turn left past Isabella Place and left again into The Avenue. On the right, the cottage to the left of the newsagent's formed part of Combe Down's first inn. Built by Ralph Allen around 1731, it stood beside the tramway that took stone down to Bath, and was known, appropriately enough, as the Carriage. The tramway, whose course you will be following for the next 700 metres, had wooden rails with a gauge of three feet nine inches. The wagons, which were about 13 feet long, sat between cast-iron wheels and were hauled – if they needed to be hauled – by two horses. For most of the way down to Bath, however, gravity – controlled by a brakeman – was more than adequate.

A little way along on the left is Park Place, a short but elegant row built in the 1820s and looking across to the equally elegant Park Villa. Firs Field, on the left, sits over a large underground quarry opened by Ralph Allen in 1729. When the war memorial was erected in 1921 it was positioned over a column of stone to prevent it collapsing. The field was named after the firs that Ralph Allen planted here. Although early writers saw this as a sign of his benevolence in creating a picturesque landscape, it was no less hard-nosed than his development of the quarries. Pine plantations were as profitable in the eighteenth century as they are today.

The Firs Field was the base for the Combe Down Stone Mines Stabilisation Project, completed, after eight years work, in November 2009. Nine miles of tunnels – covering an area greater than the walled city of Bath – were filled with 600,000 cubic metres of bubbly concrete at a cost of £160,000,000, so that houses built over the old workings would not sink into them.

You may be wondering why, since the underground stone workings have so far been referred to as quarries, this project was concerned with stone mines. As this requires some explanation, you may wish to avail yourself of one of the seats in Firs Field to take it in at your leisure.

Although it is now fashionable to describe the old quarries as mines, there is no historical sanction for this. There were underground workings on Combe Down long before Ralph Allen arrived. John Wood described a quarry at Horsecombe Vale which was 'not only the most westward, but the oldest of all the penetrations that have been made into the bowels of the hill in search of free stone', and was 'of great note in the days of Leland', who lived in the early sixteenth century. Wood also explained how, because of 'accidents frequently happening in the old subterraneous quarries, Mr Allen began to dig for stone in a new quarry, open from the top'.

Later writers such as Mowbray Green, in his 1904 study of *The Eighteenth-Century Architecture of Bath*, continued to talk in terms of stone quarries rather than mines. When Benjamin Boyce published a biography of Ralph Allen in 1967, he followed suit, explaining that Allen's quarries 'were open from the top rather than being cut in horizontally like a mine as the dangerous older ones were'. So, as recently as 1967, although the quarries could be described as 'like mines', they were still most definitely quarries. The men who worked in them were quite clear as well; there were never any miners in Combe Down, only quarrymen. As in any other craft industry, job titles were supremely important. It would have been as much of an insult to call a quarryman a miner as it would have been to call a coal miner a quarryman. It would have been a brave man – or a foolish one – who talked of stone mines in Combe Down's beerhouses a century ago. If you look at the 1984 autobiography of Frank 'Tanky' Elms, a lifelong Bath stone quarryman, you will find that, although he refers to dozens of underground workings, he never calls them mines. And Peter Addison, whose 1998 book, *Around Combe Down*, includes a comprehensive guide to the underground workings, explains that 'in the Bath stone area all sites of stone extraction were traditionally known as quarries, whether surface or underground workings.' It is also worth noting that the underground stone workings at Beer, in the Jurassic Coast World Heritage Site, are always referred to as quarries. It could be argued that, now that Combe Down's quarries have effectively been lost to posterity, it does not matter too much what they are called, but it is as well to get these things right.

As a codicil, it is gratifying to report that, late in 2011, after the preceding paragraph had been written, what will surely become the definitive study of the subject was published. *Bath Stone Quarries* by Derek Hawkins covers not only the quarries at Combe Down, but also those in the Avon valley and at Box and Corsham. Illustrated with stunning colour photographs and including detailed maps of the underground workings, this is an essential addition to the library of anyone even remotely interested in Bath's history – and, as you'll have guessed from the title, 'mines' don't even get a mention. He even refers to the Combe Down project as a 'quarry stabilisation' programme.

A little way along on the right is Williamstowe, a striking example of late-Victorian philanthropy. If you turn off along the lane, you come to Livingstone Lodge, with a poem celebrating the great explorer:

He lived to clear a way and carry light
To far-off kindred lost in darkest night;
An ardent soul that was content to die
For peace – for progress – for humanity.

Beyond it is a House of Rest for 'sickly children', with a foundation stone laid in 1884. A little further along on the left is a wooden Mission House, while on the right is a row of 'comfortable homes for Combe Down working men'. Williamstowe was the brainchild of a Mrs Williamson, the widow of a Yorkshire vicar, who also set up 'orphan homes on the family system' at Claverton Down and Macaulay Buildings. The idea was that the rents from the 'comfortable homes' would pay for the upkeep of the House of Rest and the orphanages.

At the end of The Avenue is the Hadley Arms, built in the 1840s by a quarrymaster called Charles Spence, with an entrance to the Firs Quarry at the back.

Cross over to the top of Ralph Allen Drive. To the right of the two large pillars is a lodge built by John Wood, matching the one near the bottom of the drive. As you **walk along Ralph Allen Drive**, the road suddenly falls away down a 1 in 10 incline. This is where the horses that hauled the stone from the quarries were taken off and the wagons were given a gentle shove. It was a sight that inspired a poetess called Mary Chandler to write in 1734:

Hence is seen
The new made road, and wonderful machine,
Self-moving downward from the mountain's height,
A rock its burden of a mountain's weight.

Continue down Ralph Allen Drive to the main entrance to Prior Park.[1] There is some graffiti dating from 1769 – only five years after Ralph Allen's death – on the right-hand pillar. Whoever carved it must have been extremely brave – or extremely foolhardy – at a time when such audacity was likely to be rewarded with a whipping or transportation. The pillars on the opposite side of the road stood at the entrance to Prior Park Farm, built in 1747 and demolished in 1964 to make way for housing.

Carry on downhill for 80 metres to the entrance to Prior Park Landscape Gardens. You will be handed a map and guide to the gardens at the gate, which renders a detailed description here somewhat superfluous. A suggested itinerary, though, is as follows: From the entrance, walk up to the ruins of the grotto, encrusted with minerals from Ralph Allen's native

---

1 This is the private entrance to the school; the public entrance to the gardens is 80 metres further down the road.

Cornwall, now encased within a shed and slowly being restored. In front of the grotto, you will see a bark-chipping path. Follow it as it winds downhill and turn left along the serpentine lake at the bottom. When you reach the path at the end of the lake, turn right along it. As you walk

Prior Park in the mid-nineteenth century

alongside the lake towards a sham bridge, however, Prior Park mansion appears high above you embowered in trees, sublimely incongruous in this sylvan setting. But if you are thinking that the view of the house from here might just possibly be the most spectacular in Bath, it is a mere prelude to what comes next – and for that you need to carry on through a gate.

Suddenly, the curtain of trees disappears, spirited away by the genius of landscape design. Above you, the house appears uncluttered and monumental; it would have appeared even more uncluttered before Henry Edmund Goodridge built the flights of steps below it in the 1830s. Far below, a Palladian bridge is mirrored in the still waters of a pond dug in the middle ages to provide fish for the monks of Bath Abbey. Beyond it lies the city of Bath, with the green roofs of Snow Hill to the fore – and, although you can see Walcot church and Camden Crescent from here, all the city's other major sights are hidden from view. The view

The view from Prior Park

Prior Park on fire in 1991

from here is never less than spectacular, and, on a quiet, frosty morning, with the valley below you deep in shadow, you may – if you don't let the gate bang too loudly behind you – see deer scuttling across the silent slopes.

This is a good place to consider the origins and significance of the extraordinary building above you. Philip Thicknesse, one of Allen's contemporaries, described it as 'a noble seat, which sees all Bath, and which was built, probably, for all Bath to see'. Although it looks like a country house, it is no such thing. Allen's wealth came not from the land but from industry. Stone from his quarries trundled down the tramway past Prior Park to build the city below. From here he could look down and survey work in progress, in the same way that northern industrialists would, in the following century, look down from their mansions high in the hills on the smoky mill towns they had created in the valleys below.

Prior Park served another function. Builders in London and elsewhere did not have a high opinion of Bath stone: according to John Wood, they thought it was like 'Cheshire Cheese ... a material unable to bear any weight, of a coarse texture [and] bad colour'. Accordingly, Ralph Allen resolved to 'exhibit it in a seat which he had determined to build for himself near his works, to much greater advantage, and in much greater variety of uses than it had ever appeared in any other structure'. Prior Park was, in other words, a show house, built to demonstrate the suitability of Bath stone for the grandest buildings in the land.

Work on it started in 1733. John Wood drew up plans for the house to be flanked on either side by pavilions and outbuildings, with the whole ensemble linked by galleries. In 1748, however, with work still far from complete, Wood argued with Allen over proposed changes to the design and was dismissed. Richard Jones, Ralph Allen's clerk of works, took over, changing much that had already been built and drawing up radically different plans for the remaining buildings.

That was by no means the end of the building's tribulations. In 1829, it became a Catholic seminary. Henry Edmund Goodridge, fresh from his work on Beckford's Tower, was engaged to remodel it. He added the flights of steps and drew up plans for an immense domed basilica – a Basilique du Sacre Coeur de Montmartre avant la lettre. It was never built. In 1836, Prior Park suffered a major fire and was largely rebuilt. The seminary closed in 1856 and in 1867 the building was bought by the Bishop of Clifton to become a Catholic boarding school. It was damaged by bombing in 1942 and suffered a second major fire in 1991, but is still a Catholic boarding school today.

The gardens below the house evolved over a period of 30 years, between 1734 and Ralph Allen's death in 1764. Among those who contributed to their design were Alexander Pope and Lancelot 'Capability' Brown, arguably the two greatest landscape theorists of the early eighteenth century. Had Allen done nothing more than turn the slopes below his house over to grazing sheep, he would still have had one of the most dramatic prospects in the West Country. It was the sensitive arrangement of elements within that prospect that transformed something remarkable into something truly unforgettable.

Although they became justly famous, after Allen's death the gardens went into decline. His successors took little interest in them, and visitors – whom Allen had encouraged – were no longer welcome. Despite their proximity to Bath, however, the gardens were not sold for development, nor were any major changes made. They were, to all intents and purposes, abandoned – lost gardens at the edge of the city. In 1993, they were taken over by the National Trust, who set about restoring them to their former glory. Since then, an astonishing amount of work has been done, revealing and restoring features forgotten for over two centuries.

Eighteenth-century landscape gardening broke with the earlier tradition of formal gardens, based on a single axial view from a grand house, creating instead a series of oblique views which visitors came upon as they strolled along a network of winding paths. Two and half centuries after Ralph Allen's death, the lost landscape gardens of Prior Park have been reclaimed and we can once again walk the paths and encounter the surprise views designed for our edification by one of the eighteenth century's greatest entrepreneurs.

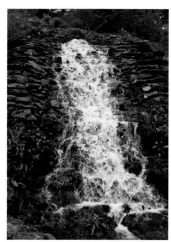

The Cascade

Carry on through another gate, past a sign warning of steep and slippery paths and turn right along the Priory Path. Just before a summerhouse turn right up steps, go through a kissing gate and walk up to a bench with another, very different panorama of Bath. Below you lies the heart of the World Heritage city – the Abbey, Pulteney Bridge and the great crescents to the north – framed by Prior Park's wooded slopes. It is, quite simply, one of the finest urban panoramas in the world.

From here retrace your steps through the kissing gate and back to the main path. Carry on uphill, but, just after going through the gate, turn right down a flight of steps. This leads to the Cabinet, the open space where Ralph Allen's guests would have gathered to admire the magnificent cascade, now newly restored. Take the path leading out of the Cabinet, but almost immediately turn right down a steep path to view the site of the Gothic Temple, with yet another cascade alongside it.

As you turn to head back up the path, look across the grass to the right to see a bark-chipping path leading up through the trees. Head up it and, at the top, turn right through another gate and follow a path leading gently downhill with magnificent views across the combe.

After arriving at a rock gate which once opened onto the carriage drive, the path doubles back on itself, with a sheer drop on the left. The views from here, of the Palladian Bridge below and of the mansion high above, are superb. When you reach the meadow, the path doubles back on itself again, heading down a flight of steps and past the Palladian Bridge. This – perhaps more than anywhere else in Bath – is a place to linger. Cross the Palladian bridge, scarred by time-worn graffiti, look up to the mansion, stroll up to the ice-house and take tea at the tea-house. The chances are you will be in no hurry to drag yourself away, but, when you do, **leave the gardens by the lower gate and turn left along Church Lane.**

After passing the Dell, look out for the octagonal dovecote on the left. **Carry on past the church along Church Street and at the end turn left down Widcombe Hill,** passing Cambridge Place – a row of four detached and two semi-detached villas designed by John Pinch – on the right. The old church hall on the left is now home to the Natural Theatre Company. Founded in Walcot Street in 1969, the Nats, as they are familiarly known, are Bath's greatest cultural ambassadors and the driving force behind Widcombe Rising, a biennial street party celebrating the cultural diversity and community spirit of this part of the city.[1] The sculptures which adorn the building, representing some of the company's best-loved characters, were carved by trainee masons from the City of Bath College in 1995. The jacket and hands of the Flowerpot Man were modelled on a photograph of Prince Charles. Opposite is Widcombe new church – St Matthew's –

---

1 One of the aims of Widcombe Rising was to demonstrate that Claverton Street could be closed to through traffic. As a result of the campaign, the council agreed in June 2012 to make Rossiter Road two-way and restore some semblance of peace to the heart of Widcombe.

Above: The Natural Theatre Company's Flowerpot Man, with Widcombe Rising in full swing in the background

Below: An eighteenth-century map of Widcombe, showing the tramway running between the White Hart and the workmen's cottages before terminating at a quay on the Avon

Bottom: North Parade Bridge, before its ironwork was encased in stone

which opened in 1847, when the bells were transferred here from Widcombe old church.

Cross the bottom of Prior Park Road by the White Hart Inn, carry on to the pedestrian lights, cross and turn right past the Baptist church. Turn left down a path to the canal and walk along the towpath. After passing a lock, turn right across the canal and carry on alongside the river. All trace of Ralph Allen's wharf has disappeared – even the course of the river has been altered as part of flood-prevention measures – but it stood roughly where a horse chestnut now shades a bench and a rubbish bin. **Carry on under St James's Railway Bridge**, its Bath stone sadly patched with brick. There is a dramatic view of St John's church, framed by the archway, as you pass under it. **Carry on to North Parade Bridge** – built of iron in 1835-6 and encased in stone in 1936-7 – **and, after passing underneath it, climb the spiral stairs, cross the river and carry on back to the starting point.**

9
THE CALIPHATE OF LANSDOWN
A Visit to Beckford's Tower

Distance *6.5 miles*

Time *4-5 hours*

Accessibility *Some of this walk is across fields and footpaths which can be muddy in places. It also includes some steep climbs and several stiles.*

No public toilets

Starting point *Kingston Parade (outside Visitor Information Centre)*

Beckford's Tower is open from Easter until the end of October on Saturdays, Sundays and Bank Holiday Mondays from 10.30am to 5pm. An admission charge is payable. For further details see www.bath-preservation-trust.org. uk.

> *'One of my new estates in Jamaica brought me home seven thousand pounds last year more than usual. So I am growing rich, and mean to build towers, and sing hymns to the powers of heaven on their summits.'*
> William Beckford, *Letter to Lady Craven*, 1790

> *'To what purpose,' asked they, 'have we been brought hither? Hath our Caliph another tower to build?'*
> William Beckford, *Vathek*

Most visitors to Bath never so much as glimpse its most extraordinary building, while most residents – although they will almost certainly have seen it from a distance – have never climbed its 154 steps to see what its creator called 'the finest prospect in Europe'. Beckford's Tower was a folly on the grand scale built by the eccentric and charismatic William Beckford. Lord Byron hailed him as 'England's wealthiest son' and he was widely believed to be the richest commoner in England. His wealth came from slavery. Beckford's great-grandfather had sailed from London to Jamaica at the age of 18 to seek his fortune. By the time he died in 1710, aged 66, he was not only governor of the island but 'in possession of the largest property real and personal of any subject in Europe'.

Under his son and grandson the estates continued to prosper. His grandson – William's father – also had a high-profile political career in England, championing the cause of the plantation owners. William,

Opposite: Beckford's Tower at night

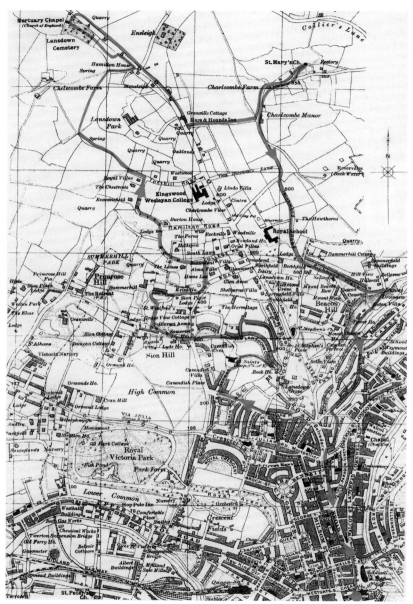

however, was only interested in developing what today would be called his 'creative side'. He inherited the plantations at the age of ten in 1770, but made only one half-hearted attempt to visit them, getting no further than Portugal, where he hob-nobbed with royalty and acquired a country estate before making his way home.

As well as being an avid – if somewhat indiscriminate – art collector, he had a passion for tall buildings. His first major project was Fonthill Abbey in Wiltshire, a Gothic fantasy designed by James Wyatt with a tower higher than Salisbury Cathedral. To emphasise the vastness of its baronial hall, it was fitted with 35-foot-high doors which were opened and closed by a dwarf Beckford brought back from Italy. Not only did he squander much of his wealth on Fonthill; the income from his plantations was fast dwindling due to lack of supervision. He was forced to sell Fonthill to settle his debts, but this proved to be a blessing in disguise, for two years later the tower collapsed, taking much of the abbey with it.

In 1822 Beckford moved to Bath, where after inspecting – and rejecting – Prior Park as a possible residence, he settled in Lansdown Crescent, bringing his dwarf with him. Despite being in his early sixties, his passion for tall buildings was soon rekindled. This time, it was not an abbey he had in mind, but something more exotic. In 1782, he had written a lurid fantasy called *Vathek*, about an oriental potentate who indulged in random acts of savagery and murder, many of them involving young boys. Vathek spent much of his time in a tower surveying his domain and it was such a tower that Beckford now set about building high above Bath. Rather than the lair of a sadistic despot, however, it was to be a treasure house crammed with *objets d'art*, its rooms hung with damask curtains lined with scarlet serge, a marble statue of Beckford's patron saint, St Anthony of Padua, in a dimly-lit sanctuary, and cabinets of curiosities to enrapture privileged guests. Beckford commissioned Henry Edmund Goodridge to build the 37-metre tower in 1824. It represented a clear break with the Gothicism of Fonthill, but was something of a hybrid, built in a 'Greco-Italian' style which, according to Goodridge's son, combined 'the purity of the Greek and the freedom of the Romanesque'.

Beckford then set about buying or leasing land between his house in Lansdown Crescent and the tower – over a mile away – to create a ride, so that he could travel between the two in privacy. He landscaped the ride, planting trees and shrubs, building gateways, walls, archways and even a tunnel under a road. Sadly, most of it has disappeared, lost to development or reclaimed by nature; the only part to survive in anything like its original state – behind Lansdown Crescent – is on private land.

Although you cannot follow in Beckford's footsteps, you can emulate his example and walk up to the tower. It is no mean climb: the plateau on which it stands is 225 metres above sea level – some 65 metres higher than Combe Down – and then there is the small matter of the 154 steps up the tower. But for the finest prospect in Europe that does not seem too arduous – and there is plenty to see along the way.

Starting from the Visitor Information Centre, walk to the left of the Abbey and head towards the High Street. Continue along Northgate Street and up Broad Street. At the top, turn left along York Buildings.

Cross at the pedestrian lights and carry straight on up Bartlett Street. The ornate ironwork across the street was a sign bracket for Evans & Owen's department store, which occupied the buildings on either side.

Cross Alfred Street and carry on along Saville Row, past the back of the Assembly Rooms. Cross Bennet Street, turn left and then right up Russel Street, built in the 1770s, with some fine fanlights on the left-hand side. **At the top turn left along Rivers Street and then first right up Gloucester Street,** looking up to see the faded lettering over the shop on the right-hand corner.

At the top of Gloucester Street, cross Julian Road and carry on up Burlington Street. This part of Bath suffered badly during two nights of bombing in April 1942, and many other buildings were demolished in the 1970s. Among those that survive are Nos 6-13, on the right-hand side of Burlington Street, with curious pediments over their first-floor windows. The architect is unknown, although the similarity of the pediments to

Portland Place

the one that once graced John Eveleigh's offices in Grove Street suggests it may have been him. At the top is Portland Place, built – possibly by Eveleigh – around 1786. The delightful double ramp, flanked by obelisks, gave sedan chairmen access to the high pavement. Less appealing is the attic storey Major Davis added to the three houses to the right of the central pediment. To the east of Portland Place are the monolithic Ballance Street flats, built by the council between 1969 and 1973.

Turn left along Portland Place and carry on past twentieth-century buildings. The layout of Northampton Street, which you pass on the left, is particularly appealing – wide at the top before narrowing as the terraces on either side step down the hillside. The bottom of the street dates from the early 1790s; the upper part was built in the 1820s.

Carry on as the road swings left downhill past Garden Cottage, and turn right into Park Street Mews. Ahead are the backs of the houses in Park Street – note the use of brick in the building with the full-height bay up to the right. Brick was used extensively for internal and party walls in Bath's late-Georgian buildings, but it is unusual to catch a glimpse of it like this.

Turn right up Park Street, described by Dickens in *The Pickwick Papers* as 'very much like the perpendicular streets a man sees in a dream, which he cannot get up for the life of him'. **At the top, carry on up a footpath to the right,** past a wall embellished with crosses and shields. The blocked-

Clockwise from top left:
All Saint's Chapel;
An aluminium aspidistra;
A map of 1810 showing the projected Lansdown Square;
The embattled gateway;
'Rus in urbe' in Lansdown Crescent

up Gothic archway led to the vaults of All Saints proprietary chapel, built for the residents of Lansdown Crescent in 1794. It closed in 1937 and, after being badly damaged by bombing in 1942, was demolished. Some of the material was reclaimed to construct the house that now stands on the site.

After passing two posts at the top of the path turn right. Above you is Lansdown Crescent, with the grass in front nibbled by sheep, a perfect realisation of *rus in urbe*. The archway topped by four urns links Lansdown Place West to Lansdown Crescent and was built by William Beckford, who owned the houses on either side. The plants in the urns are made of aluminium, which was very new – and very expensive – at the time.

When the path emerges on Lansdown Place East, turn left uphill. Take the first right at the end of Lansdown Place East and then turn left along Upper Lansdown Mews. When Lansdown Crescent was built there were plans for a large square, called Lansdown Square, behind it. Like other projected developments, this appeared on maps of the city for a few years before the scheme was quietly dropped.

After passing Beckford's Stables on the right – modern buildings set around an old yard – you come to Dixon Gardens, a modern development set in a walled garden once owned by Beckford. Above the houses you will see a Norman-style embattled gateway. This was the entrance to Beckford's Ride; the path leading up to it ran behind the wall on the right.

Just before the end of Upper Lansdown Mews, look out for a small dome topped with a weathervane in the garden of No 20. It belongs to an Islamic-style summer house and, as this was one of the houses owned by Beckford, it was long assumed, given his predilection for all things oriental, that he built it. It is now known, however, that it was installed by Captain Frederick Huth, an Oriental scholar who lived at No 20 around 1900.

Follow the road as it turns left and go under Beckford's archway. The buildings on either side are not at the same level, and the archway, which you might reasonably expect to connect them, does not. It is entered from a room in 20 Lansdown Crescent, but only goes as far as the wall of 1 Lansdown Place West, which Beckford fitted with a mirror to give the illusion that it carried on. One visitor who was taken in by this was Beckford's friend Henry Venn Lansdown, who admitted that 'the effect is most illusive, nor should I have guessed the truth had I not seen the reflection of my own figure in the glass.'

The view of Lansdown Crescent as you emerge from under the archway is one of the most dramatic prospects in the city, and serves as a taster of the delights to come. **Turn right down Lansdown Place West and continue down to the crossroads. Continue straight on up Sion Hill, taking the pavement on the left-hand side.** As you climb, look out for a gateway with Doric columns on your left. This was the entrance to Lyde House, a late eighteenth-century mansion which by 1800 had become a school. It was still being used as a school in 1942 when it was badly damaged by incendiary bombs. It was later demolished and modern houses now cover the site. Ahead is Sion House, probably built around 1790.[1] To the left, an archway leads into the former grounds of Lyde House.

---

1 Although Sion House is generally attributed to John Pinch with a date of around 1820, it is similar to other late eighteenth-century buildings on Sion Hill. It also appears in a Bath Directory for 1800 with a Mr Charles Arthur in residence.

Sion Hill Place
The façade saved by Ernest Cook

Turn right into Sion Road and then left into Sion Hill Place. The road curves between trees to emerge in front of one of Bath's finest buildings, Sion Hill Place, designed by John Pinch and built between 1818 and 1820. The end houses have full-height segmental bays, superb porches and fanlights, while the centre house, set slightly forward, has an undemonstrative pediment. Although reminiscent of New Sydney Place, here Pinch did not have a sloping site to worry about, nor did he have to fit in with an established streetscape. Like a mansion or palace, Sion Hill Place stands alone, relating to nothing but the grass and trees around it, yet is unequivocally urban and triumphantly urbane. It represents a pinnacle of classical design; architecturally, as far as the nineteenth century was concerned, it was – with a few honourable exceptions – all downhill from here. But, for all its harmonious proportions, Sion Hill Place holds a marvellous secret.

If you look at the west end, you will see that a blank-windowed building, now largely hidden by trees, has been tacked onto the end house. It dates from the mid-1930s and was added by Ernest Cook. Round the corner, and sadly out of view, is the façade of a building by John Wood which originally stood in Chippenham High Street and was rescued by Cook when it was demolished to make way for a Woolworth's. The end house is now part of Kingswood School.

At the far end of Sion Hill Place carry straight on into Sion Road. The church you can see over to the right is St Stephen's on Lansdown Road. **When you reach Winifred's Lane, follow the road up to the left and bear left up Waldegrave Road. At the top of Waldegrave Road**

turn left. By the gates of Kingswood Preparatory School, carry on uphill as the road swings to the left. The tower you can glimpse through the trees on the left is known as Blaine's Folly. It was commissioned around 1880 by Sir Robert Stickney Blaine, MP and Mayor of Bath, as an unemployment relief measure. Its design was based on that of Beckford's Tower. The belvedere at the top was at one time used by the prefects of Kingswood School as a den, but deterioration of the building has led to it being sealed off.

At the top of the road, turn left by Fonthill House. A few metres along at the end of the road is the entrance to

Blaine's Folly

the Primrose Hill Community Woodland. Established in 2000 on 24 acres of meadowland, over 20,000 native trees have been planted here in what has become an important wildlife habitat. It is an inspirational project and Beckford – a great planter of trees – would undoubtedly have approved – although just as certainly he would have wanted it all to himself. Our route lies not through the woodland, but **through the gateway ahead leading to Chelscombe Farm. After 300 metres, just after the track starts to descend and the high hedge on the left comes to an end, turn right up a grassy but well-worn path over rough ground.**

The view from above Chelscombe Farm

The path soon levels out, running parallel to a high hedge on the right. When you reach the far corner of the field, cross a stile beside a six-bar gate on the right (don't be tempted to go through the shiny new kissing gate in the direction of the tower). Carry on along a track, and, after about 15 metres, look out for an archway hidden in the undergrowth on the right. Beckford's Ride – here threading its way through old quarries planted with flower beds and fruit trees – lay on the other side, and it is through this arch that Beckford, on his way up from Lansdown Crescent, would have had his first glimpse of the tower.

Carry on along the track and, just before you reach the road, look for a depression – choked with weeds – on the other side of the wall on the left. It was here that Beckford's Ride emerged from a tunnel under the lane. As Henry Venn Lansdown's account of his visit to the tower makes clear, this was no ordinary tunnel:

> We observed before us a grotto, into which we entered. On the right is a pond of gold and silver fish, which are fed every morning by the hands of the gifted possessor of this charming place. On the opposite side 30 or 40 birds assemble at the same time to hail the appearance of St. Anthony's devotee, and chirrup a song of gratitude for their morning meal. The grotto is formed under a road, and is so ingeniously contrived that hundreds have walked over it without ever dreaming of the subterranean passage beneath. The grotto-like arch winds underground for perhaps 60 or 70 feet. When coming to its termination we are presented with a flight of rustic steps, which leads us again directly on to the down. Looking back you cannot but admire the natural appearance of this work of art. The ground over the grotto is covered with tangled shrubs and brambles. There is nothing formed, nothing apparently artificial, and a young ash springs as if accidentally from between the stones.

In the early 1900s the grotto was home to a tramp called Long Horn Jack who habitually wandered around Bath wearing a huntsman's long green coat and black cap. It was filled in when the houses were built on the right.

When you reach the main road, cross over and turn left along the pavement. After 200 metres, cross back to the second lay-by, go through a small metal gate and turn right. You may be a little surprised, as you approach the climax of the walk, to find yourself in a cemetery. Beckford would have been somewhat surprised as well, for he laid these grounds out as ornamental gardens, with no expense spared. What you cannot see is the tower, and this at least is in keeping with his original intentions. Here is Henry Venn Lansdown again, describing his arrival in the gardens:

> Venerable bushes of lavender, great plants of rosemary, and large rose trees perfume the air, all growing as if indigenous to the smooth turf. In one place clusters of rare and deeply crimsoned snapdragons, in another patches of aromatic thyme and wild strawberries keep up the charm of the place. As we draw nearer to the tower the ground is laid out in a wilder and more picturesque manner, the walks are more serpentine. We turned a corner, and

Mr Beckford stood before us, attended by an aged servant, whose hairs have whitened in his employment, and whose skill has laid out these grounds in this beautiful manner. Mr Beckford welcomed me in the kindest way, and immediately began pointing out the various curious plants and shrubs. How on this happy spot specimens of the productions of every country in the world unite! Shrubs and trees, whose natural climates are as opposite as the Antipodes, here flourish in the most astonishing manner. We were shown a rose tree brought from Pekin and a fir tree brought from the highest part of the Himalaya Mountains ... Here are pine trees of every species and variety – a tree that once vegetated at Larissa in Greece, Italian pines, Siberian pines, Scotch firs, a lovely specimen of Irish yew, and other trees which it is impossible to describe. My astonishment was great at witnessing the size of the trees, and I could scarcely believe my ears when told that the whole of this wood had been raised on the bare down within the last 13 years. The ground is broken and diversified in the most agreeable manner: here a flight of easy and water-worn steps leads to an eminence, whence you have a view of the building and an old ruin overgrown with shrubs, which looks as if it had seen 500 summers, but is in reality no older than the rest of this creation. On ascending the easy though ruined steps of this building, passing under an archway, the view of the tower burst upon us, and a long, straight walk led us directly to the entrance. From this point the view is most imposing. On your right is a continuation of the shrubberies I spoke of, at the end of which is a lovely pine, most beautiful in form and colour, which by hiding some of the lower buildings thus makes a picture of the whole.

The ruin has long gone, but a pair of venerable yews now fulfil the role once performed by the archway, hiding the tower until, passing between them, it suddenly appears, with the boughs of a cedar of Lebanon lying picturesquely athwart the path in the foreground.

After passing some imposing gates on the right, turn left along a grassy path for 50 metres to find a large pink granite sarcophagus. Two years before his death, Beckford designed this tomb for himself and had it erected in the shadow of the tower. It was set on a mound surrounded by a trench in accordance with the way Saxon kings – whom Beckford claimed to be descended from – were buried. After his death in 1844, the authorities would not permit his burial in unconsecrated ground. The tomb was moved to the newly-opened Abbey Cemetery in Widcombe and he was buried there. When his estate was

A mid-Victorian view of the cemetery

sold, the tower and its grounds were bought by the landlord of a local inn who planned to open them as pleasure gardens. Beckford's daughter was so horrified that she bought them back and presented them to the Rector of Walcot for use as a cemetery, on condition that her father's tomb was transferred there. It duly returned in 1848, although the grave of Beckford's dog Tiny, which he had also designed and which stood nearby, was considered by the ecclesiastical authorities as unfit for consecrated ground, and it was removed. The fate of Tiny's body is unknown, although his ghost is said to haunt the churchyard, along

Spiral staircase in Beckford's Tower

with that of his master. Near Beckford's tomb are the graves of his friend, Sir William Holburne, and Henry Edmund Goodridge, who designed the tower.

The cemetery closed in 1992, but long before that the tower, which had been converted to a mortuary chapel, had become a serious liability. The interior was gutted by fire in 1931 and in 1969 the Rector of Walcot described it as having 'neither ancient value nor contemporary interest; it's not even a good folly'. If Elizabeth and Leslie Hilliard had not stepped in and spent a fortune converting it to a home-cum-museum, it would almost certainly have been demolished. In 1977 they established the Beckford Tower Trust to safeguard its future and in 1993 it was taken over by the Bath Preservation Trust. Two years later a structural survey revealed that the wooden frame supporting the lantern was rotten and the ironwork corroded. A public appeal was launched and, with the support of a grant from the Heritage Lottery Fund, the lantern was rebuilt and the tower refurbished.

So, while you can no longer walk up Beckford's Ride nor look over the gardens laid out at such cost, you can still climb the spiral staircase of this glorious folly. 'The height is so great that everything looks quite diminutive,' wrote Henry Venn Lansdown of the view from the top; 'the road running in a straight line across the down reminds one of a Roman work, and the whole expanse of country surrounding recalls the Campagna.' Whether or not the view will remind you of ancient Rome, a visit to Beckford's Tower is still one of the high points – in more ways than one – of a visit to Bath. And for total immersion in the Beckford experience, you can stay in a holiday let run by the Landmark Trust on the ground floor of the tower, decorated as it would have been in Beckford's

The Gates of Death

day.

When you leave the tower, head back to those imposing gates you saw earlier. Known as the Gates of Death, they were built after the gardens became a cemetery, to a design by Goodridge. **Go through the gates, cross the road and turn right.** The Hare & Hounds pub, 700 metres along on the left, started life as a small seventeenth-century beerhouse, but has been extended many times since. As you walk past, look for the faded names of old licensees over the window at the far end – once the entrance to the beerhouse.

The resited holy well at Charlcombe

Carry on for 25 metres until you come to a driveway on the left to Littledown Farm and Northlew. Here you have a choice. The next part of the walk involves a steep descent with steps and a stile. To avoid it, carry on down Lansdown Road to return to the city centre. Otherwise, **turn left down the drive, go down a footpath to the right of Northlew, at the bottom of which a stile leads into a meadow.** The view from here over the Charlcombe valley, with the land shelving gently away, can have changed little since May 1799, when Jane Austen 'took a charming walk ... across some fields to the village of Charlcombe, which is sweetly situated in a little green valley, as a village with such a name ought to be'.

Carry on down the field. At the bottom go through a kissing gate and turn left along a lane. After 350 metres you will come to Charlcombe church and holy well. According to tradition a church was established on this site by the Abbess Bertana in AD675. Parts of the present building, including the doorway and font, date from the eleventh century. The well, which was a holy place long before Christianity came to these shores, originally stood in the gardens of the rectory, which was sold by the church in 1986. A bearded hermit took up residence by the well to try to save it, but, after he was evicted, the water was piped to a new well, which was rededicated by George Carey, Bishop of Bath & Wells, in 1989. It lies at the end of a tranquil garden shaded by trees, and is still used for baptisms today.

Head back along Charlcombe Lane, and carry straight on along Richmond Road at the junction. After passing the Royal High School – founded in 1865 for the daughters of army officers – **turn left into Richmond Place**, where you will find, a few doors along, the Richmond Arms, an excellent local hostelry with a sheltered garden in front.

Richmond Place is one of the longest continuous Georgian terraces in Bath; it must also be the one with the greatest variety of building styles. It is a delightful small-scale development, much of it looking across a large green. **At the end, carry on past No 57** – its Italianate lines set off by a Rococo-Gothic pergola – **and turn left along Summerfield Road. When this swings to the left, turn right down a short flight of steps by a house called Ridgeway. Bear right down a longer flight of steps and continue down a path. At the bottom of another flight of slippery steps, turn right along a footpath. After 125 metres, bear left down a narrower path between a Bath stone wall and a wooden fence.** After passing an end-of-terrace house on your right, look up to see a pediment with the Pratt coat of arms over the central house in the terrace. This is Camden Terrace, built around the same time as Camden Crescent. When you reach Camden Road, cross over and look back to see how Camden Terrace has been largely hidden by later buildings.

Carry on down Gay's Hill. After passing the end of Belgrave Crescent, look up on the wall of Gay's House to see a sign dating from when it was an 'asylum for teaching young females household work'. This was

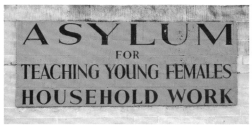

Gay's Hill Asylum

founded in 1819 for 'the rception of such destitute female children who are of an age to leave school but not yet old enough for household service.' **Just before the road swings to the left, bear right along Alpine Gardens. At the top of Lower Hedgemead Road** (from where there is a good view up to Camden Crescent) **go through a gate down to the left into Hedgemead Park. Walk down the steps and carry straight on. Go through the gate ahead, across the path and through another gate before heading to the right past a bandstand. Keep to the right of a children's playground, passing the walls of old buildings. Once past the playground, turn right, walk up to Belvedere and turn left downhill. Continue on down Lansdown Road and Broad Street, and along Northgate Street and High Street to return to the starting point.**

10

RIVER, RAIL & INDUSTRY
Westwards to Twerton

Distance *7 miles*

Time *4-5 hours*

Accessibility *This walk includes footpaths through woods and fields and alongside the river, which may be muddy, along with several flights of steps.*

Public toilets *Dominion Road, Twerton (off High Street midway between Old Crown and Full Moon pubs); Royal Victoria Park Play Area, Upper Bristol Road.*

Starting point *Kingston Parade (outside Visitor Information Centre).*

> *TWIVERTON (provincially called TWERTON) is a neat, interesting looking village, and is rather conspicuous for its large broad-cloth manufactory.*
>
> Pierce Egan, *Walks Through Bath*, 1819

In April 1805, Jane Austen wrote to her sister that she had had 'a very pleasant walk to Twerton'. Unfortunately, she gave no further details and most books on Jane Austen in Bath gloss over this passing reference. This is hardly surprising. Although part of the World Heritage Site, Twerton is a world away from the genteel charms of those areas more usually associated with Jane's sojourn in the city. When she walked there, Twerton was still a village, although the changes that were to transform it into an industrial powerhouse were already under way. It was far from being the only industrial area in Bath, however. Industry may not be readily associated with the city, but it is as much a part of its heritage as the Georgian squares and crescents that feature on every visitor's itinerary.

Opposite: Dredge's Bridge, arguably Bath's most important industrial monument

In the middle ages, Bath was a major weaving centre – Chaucer's flamboyant Wife of Bath is a fictional representative of a class that grew rich from the trade. Milling and brewing were also important industries, as was coal mining, with the closest pit only three miles west of the city. The opening of the Avon Navigation between Bath and Bristol in 1727 was a major boost to Bath's industrial growth, as was the arrival of the railway in the mid-nineteenth century. The Great Western (GWR) opened its line through Bath in 1840-41, the Midland Railway arrived 25 years later and in 1870 the Somerset & Dorset linked Bath with Bournemouth. Large goods yards were built on the west side of the city, and factories soon sprang up around them.

From the Visitor Information Centre, head south along Church Street, turn left along Lilliput Alley (North Parade Passage), continue along North Parade and turn right at the traffic lights by Good Buy Books. After crossing the end of Henry Street, cross at the pedestrian lights and continue along to the railway station. Opened in 1840, this was designed

One of the oldest railway stations in the world, designed by Brunel and opened in 1840

by Isambard Kingdom Brunel in Jacobethan style. It sits on a curved viaduct at first-floor level and is wedged between two river bridges. Its constricted site explains why – apart from a lengthening of the two platforms – it has hardly changed in the intervening years. The GWR was one of the earliest railways to be built and many of its structures in the Bath area were designed for maximum impact. Considering how rail travel has developed in the last 170 years they have survived remarkably well and are regarded as a major element of the World Heritage Site – which makes it even more of a pity that the ramp to the right of the station, built by Brunel, was wantonly demolished, despite strenuous efforts to save it, early in 2012, leaving the London-bound platform without any means of level access.

Go through the archway to the left of the station and cross the pedestrian bridge over the river. Called Halfpenny Bridge, this replaced an earlier wooden bridge which cost a halfpenny to cross. In 1877, the Bath & West Show was held at the top of the hill you can see in front of you. An excursion train pulled into the station, disgorging hundreds of people who swarmed onto the bridge, which was soon full from end to end as the tollkeeper on the far side struggled to cope. The bridge collapsed under the weight, ten people lost their lives and many more were injured. When the bridge was replaced it was decided that tolls would be dispensed with, although the old tollhouse still survives.

Turn left along the road for 90 metres, before turning left and doubling back alongside the river. As you go under Halfpenny Bridge look up to see the flood-level markers on the wall. The railway bridge ahead is known as Skew Bridge because it crosses the river at such an oblique angle. Originally this too was made of wood but was hurriedly replaced after the Halfpenny Bridge disaster.

As you walk up steps to the road, take a look at the viaduct on your left, which Brunel designed to look like a city wall or fortress. Originally, the

The original Skew Bridge, built of wood

two wide archways had flattened Tudor-style arches; these were replaced with steel girders in 1911 when heavier locomotives were introduced. Roads once ran through both archways, but the road layout was altered in the 1960s. The smaller arches were put to a variety of uses. The door between the two turrets led to a police station, while another arch was used as a mortuary for bodies taken from the river.

Until Pulteney Bridge was built in the 1770s, the only way across the river – except by ferry – was the Old Bridge, which stood midway between the footbridge and the road bridge on your right. It dated from 1340 and originally had a chapel on it dedicated to St Lawrence. It was rebuilt in 1754, but, after being widened several times, was demolished in 1966.

Continue alongside the river, crossing two busy roads (you may find it easier to cross the road bridge and use the two zebra crossings before crossing back, rather than running the gauntlet of the traffic). Carry on along the Lower Bristol Road and, after 100 metres, cross at the traffic lights and continue in the same direction. The left-hand side of the road was once lined with houses, but only one survives, on the corner of what was Angel Place. On the right-hand side of the road is the most impressive collection of former industrial buildings in the city. First comes the Camden Malthouse & Silo, built in the early nineteenth century and later extended.

Turn left just before the petrol station, walk along to the viaduct and turn right. If you go through the fifth archway (with a Pathways sign on it) and look up you will see where the original viaduct has been widened.

The Bayer Corset factory

If you carry on through the archway, you will see, on your right, half a Morris Minor stuck in the wall.

Carry on along the road beside the viaduct, passing offices built on columns to keep them clear of the floods that were once a regular feature here. **Turn right into Oak Street**, built around 1820 and cut in two by the railway less than 20 years later. Modest but elegant, it originally stood in semi-rural isolation, with a view of the river. Facing you, the red-brick Bayer Corset Factory dates from around 1890. To its right is Camden Mill, built as a steam-powered flour mill in 1879-80, extended in 1892 and converted to offices in 1974-5.

Turn left and continue along the Lower Bristol Road. The next factory was Stothert & Pitt's Newark Works. The company moved here from Newark Street, on the other side of the river, in 1857. The original factory, nearest to you, was designed by a 34-year-old local architect called Thomas Fuller. Shortly afterwards, he left for Canada, where he won a competition to design the new parliament buildings in Ottawa and went on to become one of the most famous architects in North America. Despite its current dereliction, the quality of the building shines through. It represents an attempt to adapt Palladian principles – in the city where they had been so successfully redefined a century earlier – to nineteenth-century industrial use. Ironically, it is closer to the monumental, heavily-rusticated style of many of Palladio's urban palazzos – such as the Palazzo Thiene – than anything by John Wood. It also looks distinctly un-English, for the very good reason that Fuller, instead of staying in Britain, moved to Canada, developing his distinctive style and influencing other architects there. Newark Works is, therefore, a rare – possibly unique – bridge between British and North American architectural traditions, while at the same time indicating their common pedigree.

The oldest part of Stothert & Pitt's works, designed by Thomas Fuller in 1857

Stothert & Pitt's eventually became Bath's biggest employer. Although the company made a range of products, it was its cranes that brought it international renown. The four cranes alongside the M Shed in Bristol were built by Stothert & Pitt in 1951; many others can be found on docksides around the world. In 1980, the director of the Science Museum in South Kensington said that the work of Stothert & Pitt was Bath's greatest contribution to world history. In the mid-twentieth century, over 2,000 people worked for the company and when the works closed in 1989 – having been taken over by Robert Maxwell's Hollis Group three years earlier – 580 people lost their jobs. Although many of the later buildings have been demolished, the original factory survives as a reminder of Bath's best-known company. Several suggestions have been put forward as to what it could be used for – a Museum of Bath, a heritage and archive centre, workshops, performance spaces, galleries, a creative hub. Given the size and adaptability of the buildings on the site, there is no reason why it could not fulfil most if not all of these functions. Hopefully, the imaginative uses to which so many of Bristol's former industrial buildings have been put will inspire the powers that be to breathe new life into this iconic building and help regenerate this part of the city.

As you carry on, look up to the left after passing Pickford's to see the GWR Goods Shed, built in 1877 and now converted to offices. On the next corner is the Green Park Tavern, built around 1813 as a private house. It is hard to imagine what a delightful spot this must have been, with open fields at the back and a view across the river to Green Park. Even after the railway opened and it became a pub, this area was still a leafy suburb. Large and very desirable riverside villas were built across the road, only to disappear as Stothert & Pitt's continued its relentless advance westward.

Turn left beside the Green Park Tavern along Westmoreland Road, go under the railway bridge and turn right along Westmoreland Station Road, which served the GWR goods yard. Just after passing a range of low buildings on the right, you need to **turn down an alleyway guarded by two posts made from old rails** – but first carry on to the gates at the end, which give a good view of the line and the old goods yard. The only traffic that now uses the yard is rubbish – 50,000 tons a year sent from Bath to a landfill site in Buckinghamshire.

After going under the railway, walk past a terrace with Bath-stone ground floors and brick first floors; the brick was presumably intended to be covered with render so that it looked like stone, as indeed some has been. **At the end turn left along the Lower Bristol Road.** The modern office buildings with black windows across the road stand on the site of the Midland Railway goods yard.

On the left is St James's Cemetery, opened in 1861 and closed in 1937. The chapels and lodge were designed by Major Davis in French

Gothic style. A fleche on the chapels was repaired after bomb damage in 1942 but taken down in 1978 because of fears that it could collapse. The stones were numbered and stored in the chapels in the hope that it would be restored. One of the most unusual graves in Bath – in the form of an ammonite – can be seen on the far left-hand side of the cemetery.

Take the next left up Brougham Hayes. The terrace on the right was built around 1831. Hayesfield Girls' School, further up on the left, started life as a barracks in 1864, before becoming the Somerset Certified Industrial School a few years later. It has also housed a Domestic Science College and the City of Bath Technical School.

The Industrial School on Brougham Hayes, now part of Hayesfield Girls' School

Cross the zebra crossing and carry on uphill. Just before the railway bridge, go down a flight of steps on the right and walk along a path beside the line. Ahead is Oldfield Park station, opened in 1929 and scheduled for closure in 1968. Although it won a reprieve, the service remained abysmal. In 1970, there were only five weekday trains to Bristol – at 7.15, 7.37, 8.38, 17.03 and 18.38. Today it has a far better service and is used by almost 217,000 passengers a year. Notice how the rubble-stone bridge beyond the station has a flattened Tudor-style arch similar to those in the viaduct you saw earlier. Most of the bridges between Bath and Bristol are of this design, which is found almost nowhere else on the rail network.

When you reach the road, cross and continue along a footpath beside the line. After swinging to the right, the footpath emerges at the top of Bellotts Road. The pillar on your right stood at the entrance to the Bath Cabinet Makers Factory, which occupied the site on the right-hand side of the road. **Head straight on along a footpath beside the cemetery. When you reach the road, carry on alongside the cemetery.** After passing the last house on the right, you need to cross over and turn down a path on the right – but before you do that carry on along the road for a short distance. If you look over the wall when you reach the end of the cemetery, you will see the graves of the Carr family – more on them shortly. When you reach the railway bridge, there is a splendid view back down the line. Looking the other way, the view is blocked by another bridge, which carried the Somerset & Dorset Railway over the GWR on a punishing gradient of 1 in 50.

Fielding's Lodge

Head back and turn left down the path across the old Somerset & Dorset line, which closed in 1966. To the right, the line is now a linear park, and this continues on the other side of the bridge. Carry on along the street ahead, turn right and then left along the Lower Bristol Road. The building opposite – currently disused but scheduled to be converted to a supermarket – was built in 1966-67 for Bath Cabinet Makers. It is now officially part of Bath's heritage, having been Grade II listed. Several early eighteenth-century buildings were demolished to make for it, including one called Fielding's Lodge, where Henry Fielding wrote part of Tom Jones.

As you cross the end of Jew's Lane, look to the left to see a remarkably low bridge. The reason for the lane's name is unknown. The Golden Fleece, across the road, has been a pub since the 1840s. Next to it was another pub, the Seven Stars, which closed in the 1990s. A little further on, look out for Dillon's butcher's, still advertising its wares decades after closing. Beyond it is a building from the 1820s which is now part of McDonalds. Beyond the traffic lights are two villas – Hollies and Twerton Villa – from around 1842, with a former maltings beyond them. Opposite them is Twerton station, which opened in 1840. After electric trams started running to Twerton in 1904 the number of people using the station fell sharply. It closed as a wartime economy measure in 1917 and never reopened. The buildings are still largely intact, however – a rare survival of a virtually unchanged station designed by Brunel.

The Twerton McDonald's

Before the railway was built, the Lower Bristol Road swung to the left here, but, because the railway blocked the road at the far end of the

Twerton High Street from the station c1910

village, it was rerouted along a new road built alongside the viaduct. **Turn left under the skew bridge, following the old road and carry on along the High Street.** The Zion Chapel on your right was built in 1853 and is now a photographic studio. A couple of doors past the Twerton Chippy is a row of three Bath stone cottages with faded writing on their platband – a now almost illegible testimony to their extraordinary history. This was once the White Hart Inn, which opened some time before 1767. After it closed in 1899, it was acquired by the Twerton Lodge of Good Templars, who turned it into a Temperance Institute and Restaurant. At the opening ceremony, they burst the old vats and broke 'other things connected with alcohol'. It lasted only eight years, however, before being converted to cottages. The words 'WHITE HART TEMPLAR INSTITUTE AND RESTAURANT ... TWERTON LODGE' can still be made out, with some of the words they covered up – 'WINES & SPIRITS' – showing through underneath.

Nelson House, across the road, was the home of the Bence family who owned the maltings on the main road. Next to it is a rubble-stone building – also with three-storeys but nowhere near as high – dating from the late seventeenth or early eighteenth century. Further along, the three-storey rubble-stone building at right-angles to the road on the left was the George Inn, which closed around 1880. Next to it is the Old Crown, open by 1760 and still in business

Weavers' cottages in Twerton High Street

today. Facing it, on the other side of the road, is an impressive row of old weavers' cottages.

Turn right along Mill Lane, where the Baptist church, built in 1808 and hidden behind a later extension, was converted to flats in 2006. Go under the railway and turn left along a rough pavement. The monumental gateway with green metal gates across the road was the entrance to Twerton Upper Mills. The words ISAAC CARR & CO LTD, WOOLLEN MANUFACTURERS can still be made out on the wall of the building to the right of the gates.[1] A little further on, at Rackfield Close, is another row of old weavers' cottages.

Further along, you come to an archway under the viaduct with a row of numbered units beyond it. These were originally intended as homes for the people whose cottages were demolished to make way for the railway. They consisted of two rooms with a single window by the front door. Even by the standards of the 1840s, they were so grim that the occupants did not put up with them for long.

Turn left through the archway, and on the other side of the viaduct look to the right to see one of the chimneys attached to these undesirable residences. Carry on up the path, cross the road leading downhill and turn right up the road leading uphill past the Full Moon,

weavers' cottages which only became a beerhouse in 1876. Continue past the Sunday School of 1816 and through the churchyard. The church was rebuilt (except for the tower) in the 1830s, although traces of Norman work, including the font and a doorway, can still be seen.

Workers' cottages in the arches of the viaduct

Once through the churchyard, carry on along the road for 200 metres, before turning right along Walwyn Close. At the end go down a flight of steps and turn left alongside the railway. A little way along, look out for the castellated portal to the first of two tunnels. Just beyond it, if you turn off the path and walk down to stand on top of the tunnel, you can look ahead to see the mouth of the next tunnel along the line. Back on the path, look to the left to see a flight of abandoned steps leading up into the woods. The expanse of level

1 In May 2012, plans were announced to demolish this building to build student accommodation.

An old photograph of the west tunnel at Twerton

Looking westward from above the tunnel

ground to the left of it was the site of Wood House, built by Edward Davis for Charles Wilkins, the local mill owner, in 1838.

Carry on along the path, passing the entrance to the second tunnel. Go through a kissing gate and carry on through the field ahead, passing a row of trees to your right. After 100 metres bear right towards an interpretation panel above the western portal of the tunnel. Although you cannot see it, the tunnel mouth has the same kind of flattened Tudor arch as the bridge further along the line. What you can see are the embattled turrets and parapet and the stunning view down the Avon valley to Kelston Park, built by John Wood the Younger in the 1760s for Sir Caesar Hawkins, sergeant-surgeon to the king.

This delightful spot is an appropriate place to consider the history of the village you have just walked through. It was originally known as Twiverton, but this was usually shortened to Twerton. The abbreviated version was officially adopted in the nineteenth century. At the time of the Domesday Book it had four mills, two of which were converted to cloth or fulling mills by the late fifteenth century.

The opening of the Avon Navigation in 1727 heralded the start of a new era. A new cut, 500 metres long, was constructed to avoid the two weirs which Twerton's millowners had built across the river. Although the new cut was designed by John Hore, an experienced canal engineer, the contract for building it was awarded to John Wood, newly-arrived in Bath from Yorkshire. Wood explained that,

> for the better execution of the work I forthwith procured labourers that had been employed on the Chelsea water works, and sent them down to Bath to dig the canal I had undertaken; till which time the real use of the spade was

unknown in, or about the city, and the removal of earth was then reduced to a third part of what it formerly cost.

Brass mills were established on the island created between the new cut and the river. Although officially called Weston Island, it soon became known as Dutch Island because of the number of skilled metalworkers from the Low Countries who came over to work in the mills. On the Twerton side of the river were two long-established mills, known as the Upper and Lower Mills. In the 1730s, Isaac Sperin took over the Upper Mills to produce cloth. He embarked on a programme of expansion and by the 1780s the Upper Mills were among the largest and most up-to-date in the West Country. Although Sperin made a fortune from the Upper Mills and established Twerton as a major weaving centre, the process was not without its difficulties. The growth of the mills was accompanied by the introduction of new technology. This put skilled men out of work, and, in the absence of officially-recognised trade unions, they took direct action, smashing machines, torching mills and threatening mill owners. It was not just local men who were involved. On several occasions, millworkers from Bradford on Avon, Trowbridge and other weaving towns marched on Twerton to smash machines.

A visitor in 1801 reported that around 80 boys and girls – some as young as eight – were employed at the Upper Mills because their small, soft fingers were suited to certain intricate – and hazardous – operations. Even though child labour was commonplace, conditions must have been bad, for Twerton vestry committee expressed concern about the welfare of children working at the mills on several occasions.

Around 1800, the Lower Mills were also converted to cloth production. In 1807, they were taken over by the man who was to oversee the greatest expansion of the cloth trade in Twerton – Charles Wilkins. By the 1820s he had also acquired the Upper Mills, as well as most of the property in the village. He replaced the old water-powered mills with multi-storey factories; by the 1830s the Upper Mills contained 67 power looms driven by two steam engines. Wilkins employed over 700 people at the two mills, with another 300 outworkers in cottages around the village. Perhaps mindful of earlier attacks on the mills, he also became captain of the local militia. He is best remembered, however, for docking a shilling from the wages of female workers who were caught in any of the local pubs, a practice commemorated today by a local women's clog morris side called Mr Wilkins' Shilling.

Production peaked in 1838, the year Wilkins moved into Wood House. By then he had already sold land to the GWR and been awarded the contract to build the railway through the village. The opening of the railway, however, signalled the start of a catastrophic decline in his – and Twerton's – fortunes. In 1841, he was forced to mortgage the land and effects he had not already sold to the GWR. Things did not improve. In

1844, Wood House suffered a major fire. The following year, he went into partnership with Thomas Carr from Cumberland. Two years later, Carr bought him out, moved into the rebuilt Wood House and set to work turning the business around. It was an uphill struggle. The *Bath Postal Directory* for the following year noted that although Twerton 'was formerly noted for its extensive manufacture of superfine woollen cloth ... at present there is only one mill, the productions from which are very limited'. Despite this inauspicious start, Thomas Carr established a mill-owning dynasty that lasted over a century. In 1855, the business was

The Lower Mills in the early twentieth century

taken over by his son Isaac – whose name you saw earlier on the Upper Mills. The Carrs never resumed production at the Lower Mills, which after lying empty for a while became a carpet factory. When Isaac Carr wanted to expand the business, he built a new five-storey mill on Dutch Island equipped with machines for carding, scribbling and spinning.

Although the business continued to operate successfully well into the twentieth century, the trade depression of the 1920s and 1930s was followed by extensive damage to the mills in the Bath Blitz, and in 1954 the company went into receivership. Stothert & Pitt acquired the Dutch Island site and the Upper Mills became a shoe factory. Bath Council placed a compulsory purchase order on the Carr estate, which the family contested unsuccessfully. The surviving members of the Carr family were paid £15,000 for the estate and allowed to spend the rest of their days in Wood House. It was eventually demolished in 1965 and much of the land was used for housing.

The Lower Mills, which had been taken over by W&R Cook in 1891 to produce ready-made suits, continued in operation until the 1960s, but were demolished in 1965. The mill Isaac Carr had built on Dutch Island burnt down in 1981; many of the buildings at the Upper Mills had already

Weston Island on an Ordnance Survey map of 1886

gone in the late 1960s when the river was realigned. So, despite Twerton's extraordinarily rich industrial heritage, there is precious little to show for it.

Retrace your steps back into Twerton, go down the footpath under the railway opposite the Full Moon, cross the main road and turn right and then left over the bridge onto Weston – or Dutch – Island. The large sluice gates downstream to your left are part of the Avon flood prevention scheme. Until the mid-1960s there was a weir here, running diagonally across the river. The Lower Mills stood on the left bank just beyond it. There was another weir upstream, on the other side of the bridge.

Weston Island is now occupied by a bus depot and there is no trace of the mills that operated here for over 250 years. **Follow the footpath through the bus depot and cross a bridge over the new cut.** The Dolphin Inn on the far bank dates from the same time as the Avon Navigation. **Turn left along the towpath and walk along to the lock** where the new cut rejoins the river. If you walk a little way past the lock and look over to the far bank of the river you can see the site of the Lower Mills. Don't run with the idea that this part of Bath is little more than a graveyard of vanished industries, however. The mills may have gone, but on this side of the river many new factories, large and small, have taken their place. If you carry on along the river bank for about 150 metres, you will come to Rotork, a world leader in the design and manufacture of electric, pneumatic and hydraulic valve actuators and gearboxes, which employs over 2,000 people.

Walk back along the towpath, but, before you reach the Dolphin, turn left up Osborne Road. The large industrial units on the left near the top of the road stand on the site of the Bath Brewery, a massive state-of-the-art complex built in 1896. It was taken over by George's of Bristol a mere 27 years later and closed down. It later became maltings before being demolished in the 1970s. Before turning right down Avondale Road, walk on to the narrow bridge which crossed the Midland Railway. To right and left, sidings once flanked the line. More recently, the trackbed was earmarked to form part of an expensive, disruptive and unwelcome Rapid Transit scheme, which has – for the moment at least – been shelved. Congestion is one of Bath's abiding problems, but most people failed to comprehend how conversion of this bit of old railway line would have helped to ease it.

 As you **walk down Avondale Road**, exuberant brickwork turns an otherwise unremarkable street into something memorable. The decorative flowers on the side walls of Nos 23 and 24 are a particularly cheerful touch. The use of yellow brick – rare in Bath – along with rusticated dressings and some fine bonded brickwork are among other features to look out for.

At the bottom of the road turn left along the towpath past the Dolphin. This is not only one of the oldest stretches of canal in the country, but, upstream from the Dolphin, one of the loveliest. **Continue past the junction of the new cut and the river and, just before a pedestrian bridge, turn left.** The Herman Miller factory, on your right, was designed in 1975 by Nicholas Grimshaw (who later designed Thermae Bath Spa) and Terry Farrell. After passing a veterinary surgery, you cross the old railway line. The house on the right – No 16 – was the stationmaster's house.

The New Cut near Weston Lock

Looking east towards Weston station around 1910

To find the old station, **turn right along Ashley Avenue** and look for a single-storey building just before the road swings up to the left at the end. It closed in 1953.

At the top, turn left past the Weston Hotel (opened around 1897), right across two sets of pedestrian lights and right downhill past the closed public toilets. Locksbrook Cemetery, opened in 1864 and closed in 1937, it is now a Nature Conservation Site. If you **turn left as you enter the cemetery,** you will come to a First World War cross of

Locksbrook Cemetery around 1870

remembrance surrounded by lines of war graves. There are 132 military graves in the cemetery, most dating from the First World War when a large military hospital was established nearby on the site now occupied by the Royal United Hospital.

Turn left out of the cemetery and just past it you will see a group of rubble-stone buildings on the left, once a farm. Next to them is Locksbrook Place, a modest but extremely attractive row of cottages built in the early nineteenth century. A little further on, look across the road to see the façade of the old Windsor Castle Inn, with modern residential units now installed behind it.

Continue along the Upper Bristol Road past St John's church, built in 1836-8 and extended by Major Davis in 1871, with the gloomy text 'Abide with us for it is toward evening' over the porch. Across the road is the site of the old gasworks, established in 1818. **Turn left up St Michael's Road.** St Michael's Cemetery, on the left, has two chapels. The farther one, built for nonconformist funerals and now converted to a forge, has an unusual octagonal design. **Go along the road opposite the cemetery gates, with Baytree House on the corner. At the end, cross the zebra crossing and turn right downhill.** The eclectic and charming collection of buildings on the right includes the early nineteenth-century Paradice Place and the former Park Tavern, opened in the eighteenth century as the Blue Lodge and recently closed. At the bottom of Park Lane, look over to the right to see the old gasworks offices across the road. Beyond a late-nineteenth-century red-brick range is a Bath stone building, dating from 1858, with 'Bath Gas Light and Coke Company' chiselled into its cornice.

Turn left along the Upper Bristol Road with the Royal Victoria Park Play Area on your left. The Hop Pole Inn, 175 metres along on the right,

Down House

opened in the 1820s, and is well known for the quality of its ales and home-cooked food. A few doors along from the Hop Pole, set back from the road, is a villa also dating from the 1820s. Originally known as Down House, it once stood in splendid isolation. At some stage, it was divided into two, with an extra front door added and the central window on the first-floor lengthened, destroying its symmetry. At the end of the next row is Sterling House, built at the same time and originally known as Albion House. Beyond it, the left-hand side of the Territorial Army building was once the Albion Cabinet Works, whose name can still be seen on the façade. The rows of buildings to its left have an unusual design feature – Bath stone with red-brick banding.

Cross at the pedestrian lights, turn right to the end of Albion Terrace and left along Victoria Bridge Road. Built in 1836 to an innovatory design by a local brewer called James Dredge, Victoria Bridge is as important to Bath as the Clifton Suspension Bridge is to Bristol. Some civil engineers regard it as even more important than Brunel's iconic structure, because it pioneered a new method of cantilevered bridge construction which later became standard. Although it is arguably Bath's most important industrial monument, it has suffered years of neglect. In October 2010 it was declared unsafe and closed. Eventually, temporary repairs were carried out and it reopened in May 2012. A month later, councillors voted in favour of a £2.5M project to build a faithful replica of the bridge in steel, incorporating as much of the original wrought-iron structure as possible.

Go down the steps to the right of the bridge and turn left along the towpath. This leads past Norfolk Crescent and Norfolk Buildings – both largely hidden behind trees and undergrowth – and under a pair of bridges. The farther one carried trains into the Midland station; cars now use it to get to the supermarket you can see on the left. The other bridge, for pedestrians, rests on the abutments of a

Norfolk Crescent from the river

railway bridge that was dismantled after the line closed. A little further along you go under an early-twentieth-century road bridge.

Further along on the left are Green Park Buildings West, work on which started in the 1790s. There was a matching range, called Green Park Buildings East, where Jane Austen lived in 1804-05, on the other side of the park. It was demolished after much of it was burnt out by incendiary bombs in April 1942. A busy road, lined with modern buildings scheduled for demolition, now runs through the site. As at Norfolk Crescent and Norfolk Buildings, the buildings here are almost invisible from the river – and vice-versa. The river here is not just underutilised; it is treated as though it is not there. When factories, foundries and railway yards occupied the far bank, this was understandable; now that they have gone, a reappraisal of the relationship between the river and the community through which it passes seems long overdue. Like Norfolk Crescent and Norfolk Buildings, Green Park was built to take advantage of a riverside location; Green Park Tavern, on the Lower Bristol Road, was so called because the view of Green

Park across the river was something to celebrate. One day, perhaps, we will be able to celebrate it again.[1]

Just past Green Park the path drops down to the riverside. The view ahead is one that has changed beyond all recognition in the last century. Across the river, you can see the old factories and mills you passed on your way out to Twerton. Of the industrial buildings and warehouses that once stood on this side of the river, however, not a trace remains. The densely-packed streets of terraces and tenements, the courts lined with workshops, foundries, stables and yards, the street-corner beerhouses, and the brothels that made this area – depending on your point of view – irretrievably depraved or irresistibly attractive – all are gone. Whether this loss of heritage is to be lamented or not is debatable. Although many of those who once lived here were hard-working, clean-living and eminently respectable, many were not, and this was just about the roughest part of town. George Sanger, who had first-hand experience of Bath in the mid-nineteenth century, wrote that it 'had at that time a very unenviable reputation as regarding its lower classes [and] had in its slums what was considered to be the most brutish and criminal mob in England'.

As you pass Camden Mill – across the river – you are walking where Narrow Quay once stood. As you climb a slope to emerge beside the road you come to what was Broad Quay. Although the Avon Navigation continued to the weir below Pulteney Bridge, few vessels, apart from those bound for the canal or for Ralph Allen's stone wharf in Widcombe, went

Floods at Broad Quay around 1920

beyond the old bridge. Most docked here, in what was the heart of Bath's mercantile quarter. A century ago there were dockside cranes here, offloading cargoes into wagons or loading goods onto boats moored alongside the quay. On the far side of the quay were rows of warehouses, with a malthouse towering over them. In its shadow was an old inn called the Waterman's Arms. Nothing whatsoever is left – and all that remains, to get back to the starting point, is to **carry on alongside the river, cross two zebra crossings, follow the road round to the left of the bus station and continue up Southgate and Stall Streets.**

---

1 And maybe sooner rather than later. In June 2012, the Bath Avon River Corridor Group unveiled ambitious proposals to make the river a focal point for redevelopment and regeneration. Although independent, it has been charged with advising councillors, council officers and departments on a river-led regeneration strategy.

11

A PASTORAL IDYLL
Over the Fields to Weston

Distance *5.5miles*

Time *3.5 hours*

Accessibility *This walk includes steps and footpaths which may be muddy*

Public toilets *Weston High Street (west of Crown & Anchor); Royal Victoria Park Play Area; Royal Victoria Park Pavilion, Royal Avenue*

Starting point *Kingston Parade (outside Visitor Information Centre)*

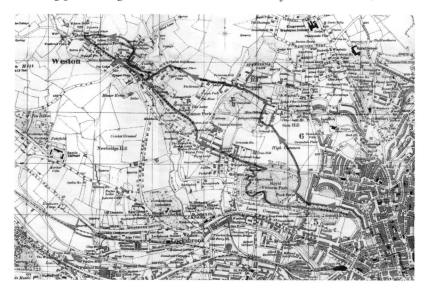

We walked to Weston one evening last week, and liked it very much. Liked what very much? Weston? No, walking to Weston.

Jane Austen, to her sister Cassandra, 11 June 1799

Like the last walk, this one heads west, but, instead of seeking out industrial heritage, follows the footsteps of Jane Austen to the village of Weston. Jane Austen walked to Weston several times during her stay in Bath. On 21 May 1801, almost two years after the evening walk described above,

Opposite: Looking west from Primrose Hill

she wrote to her sister about another excursion, this time in the company of an early fan of speed walking:

> Our grand walk to Weston was again fixed for yesterday, and was accomplished in a very striking manner. Every one of the party declined it under some pretence or other except our two selves, and we had therefore a *tête-à-tête*, but *that* we should equally have had after the first two yards had half the inhabitants of Bath set off with us.
>
> It would have amused you to see our progress. We went up by Sion Hill, and returned across the fields. In climbing a hill Mrs Chamberlayne is very capital; I could with difficulty keep pace with her, yet would not flinch for the world. On plain ground I was quite her equal. And so we posted away under a fine hot sun, *she* without any parasol or any shade to her hat, stopping for nothing, and crossing the churchyard at Weston with as much expedition as if we were afraid of being buried alive. After seeing what she is equal to, I cannot help feeling a regard for her. As to agreeableness, she is much like other people.

Walking to Weston was a popular pastime. In *Walks Through Bath*, published in 1819, Pierce Egan wrote:

> When the weather invites, a walk to the neat and pretty village of Weston cannot fail in affording gratification and delight to every visitor of Bath; and in the spring part of the season, it may be viewed as a grand promenade, and is well frequented by most of the fashionable company in the city.

Although much has changed in the intervening two centuries, not only can you follow the route Jane Austen and Pierce Egan took; part of it still lies across fields, while Weston village, although much knocked about in the 1960s and 1970s, remains a delight.

Starting from outside the Visitor Information Centre, walk over to the left of the Abbey, head diagonally across the Abbey Church Yard, go to the left of the Roman Baths Kitchen and under an archway into Cheap Street. Here you are following in the footsteps not of Jane Austen but of Catherine Morland and Isabella Thorpe in *Northanger Abbey*, hot on the heels of two young men they had espied in the Pump Room:

> They set off immediately as fast as they could walk, in pursuit of the two young men. Half a minute conducted them through the pump-yard to the archway, opposite Union Passage; but here they were stopped. Everybody acquainted with Bath may remember the difficulties of crossing Cheap Street at this point; it is indeed a street of so impertinent a nature, so unfortunately connected with the great London and Oxford roads, and the principal inn of the city, that a day never passes in which parties of ladies, however important their business, whether in quest of pastry, millinery, or even (as in the present case) of young men, are not detained on one side or other by carriages, horsemen, or carts. This evil had been felt and lamented, at least three times a day, by Isabella since her residence in Bath; and she was now fated to feel and lament it once more, for at the very moment of coming opposite to Union Passage, and within view of the two gentlemen who were proceeding through the crowds, and threading the gutters of that

interesting alley, they were prevented crossing by the approach of a gig, driven along on bad pavement by a most knowing-looking coachman with all the vehemence that could most fitly endanger the lives of himself, his companion, and his horse.

When it is clear, cross Cheap Street and head up Union Passage. At the end, walk up the steps to Upper Borough Walls and turn left. After passing the old city wall, **turn right along Trim Bridge, carry on through St John's Archway, along Queen Street and into John Street.** As befits a country walk, we start by looking at an old farmhouse, albeit one that has not been a farmhouse for a very long time. Near the end of John Street, on the right, you will see a shoddy Victorian pastiche of an Elizabethan building, with leaded lights, a broad gable end and the upper floors jettied out over the street. It should come as no surprise to learn that it is by Major Davis. Beyond it, however, is a building which dates from the seventeenth century if not earlier. Known as Barton Farmhouse, it stood at the centre of a working farm until the early eighteenth century, when it was incorporated into the newly-built John Street. Unfortunately, it received a makeover from Major Davis in 1867, when he turned it into part of Jolly's department store.

As you **turn left along Old King Street**, take a look, on the right, up Barton Buildings, built in 1768 by John Wood the Younger. The street slopes gently uphill and the cornices and plat bands sweep up between the buildings. Surprisingly, Wood the Younger did not employ this elegant device elsewhere, leaving John Pinch to adopt it as one of his trademarks in the early nineteenth century.

Carry on to the end of Old King Street, cross at the traffic lights, turn right up Gay Street and left into Queen's Parade Place. Cross over and walk up the steps by the telephone box to the 'quiet and retired gravel walk' along which Anne Elliot and Captain Wentworth stroll at the end of Jane Austen's *Persuasion*.

Above: Barton Buildings

Right: The back of the Circus from the Gravel Walk

Keep a look out, 100 metres along, for the entrance to the Georgian garden at the back of No 4 The Circus. It was laid out shortly after the house was built in 1761, with flower beds set amid a parterre of clay and gravel. In 1836, the house was extended and the excavated soil was spread over the garden, which was then redesigned. For 150 years the Georgian garden lay buried and forgotten until, in 1985, Bath Archaeological Trust dug down to reveal it and restore it to its former glory.

At the end of the Gravel Walk carry straight on towards Marlborough Buildings, with a magnificent view of the Royal Crescent on your right. **When you reach Marlborough Buildings, cross over, walk a couple of metres down to the left and turn right up a narrow lane between old stone walls.** This is Cow Lane, its name indicating the sort of traffic that used it long before there were any grand buildings here. The greenhouses on the left, which belong to the Parks Department, are where the plants used in Bath's superb floral displays are grown.

At the end of the lane, turn right along the road skirting the park. On the right, the back of Marlborough Buildings displays an astonishing variety of extensions and modifications – and who says the Georgians didn't go in for high rises?

At the top, go through the gateway straight ahead, cross the zebra crossing and follow the Cotswold Way signpost up a footpath beside a metal fence. As you follow the path uphill, look over to the right for distant views of Lansdown and Cavendish Crescents. **When you reach Sion Hill, turn left.** Gothic Cottage, which you pass on the right, dates from 1797 – two years before Jane Austen's first Weston walk. Built of brick, it would originally have been covered in render. As you **follow the**

The back of Marlborough Buildings

WALK 11: A PASTORAL IDYLL

Gothic Cottage

Footpath across High Common

road round as it curves uphill, you may catch a glimpse, behind a high wall on the right, of a much larger, gothic-style building called Sion Cottage.

At the T junction, turn left along Summerfield Road. At the end, carry on along a footpath (following a Cotswold Way signpost) between stone walls. At the top of a flight of steps, you pass the entrance to one of Bath's most sadly missed pubs – the Retreat – which closed in 1975. Its sign bracket can still be seen over the gate. The pastoral view that suddenly opens up ahead, as you carry on down and turn a corner, is one of the loveliest and most unexpected in the city.

At the bottom of the path, cross Primrose Hill, passing an old farmhouse on the right, **and carry on down another footpath. This runs down to a kissing gate, before crossing a brook and continuing through a meadow. After you pass a kissing gate on the left, the path starts to climb between a canopy of trees. Carry on past another kissing gate and continue uphill, following signs for the Cotswold Way. Go through a kissing gate beside a seven-bar gate into a meadow. After 50 metres, the Cotswold Way branches off to the left. Follow it across the meadow and through another kissing gate. Follow the path downhill, continue down an access road, across another road and on down a path.**

After passing the churchyard on your right, look out for the figure of a boy clutching a sheaf of barley on a house on the left. Some claim it represents St Alphege as a child. Alphege was born in Weston in 954 and, after becoming a monk, rose quickly through the ranks, becoming Prior of Glastonbury, Abbot of Bath and Archbishop of Canterbury, before being stoned to death at Greenwich by marauding Vikings in 1012. The provenance of the figure is unknown, however, and the sheaf of barley suggests it may have come from one of Weston's two breweries, which you will be seeing later.

Turn up to the right through the churchyard. If you look over to the right, you will see a large urn surrounded by railings. This marks the grave of the architect Thomas Warr Atwood, John Wood the Younger's bitter rival. He died in 1775 when the floor of a building in the High Street, the demolition of which he was superintending, gave way. The tower of the church is fifteenth century, but the rest was rebuilt by John Pinch the Younger in 1830-2. Further additions were made in 1893.

Carry on past the church and bear left downhill when the path forks. This leads down to Church Street, one of Weston's most delightful corners. The pavement is not only high above the road, but screened from it by a row of gardens, with steps diving down between them. The first building on your right – rubble stone covered in render, with a double-storey window above the entrance – dates from 1739. As you **carry on past the library**, flanked

Church Street c1910

by modern buildings, you will notice an old advertisement for Wills's cigarettes on the wall at the end. This was once a pub called the Queen's Head. When it closed in 1914 it became a shop.

Opposite the old Queen's Head is the King's Head, still very much in business. It has long been one of Weston's principal inns, but for details of its early history and of an extraordinary ceremony that took place there in 1834, you will need to look in *Bath Pubs*.

Turn right up Trafalgar Road. Early-eighteenth-century rubble-stone cottages soon give way to grander houses built in the early nineteenth century after the street was named in honour of Nelson's victory. The Countess of Huntingdon's Chapel on the left also dates from this time. Unlike the Countess of Huntingdon's Chapel on the Paragon in Bath, this is still used by for worship by the evangelical sect founded by the Countess.

A few doors up from the chapel, look out for some faded lettering on the side wall of No 9. This was Pointing's Brewery, which extended back a considerable way along Wellington

Countess of Huntingdon's Chapel

Buildings. There was an even larger brewery – Edgecumbe's – on the right-hand side of the road – hence the high windowless wall. If you go

Trafalgar Road c1910

up the lane beside it, you can still see the brewery yard with the maltings beyond it.

Carry on along Trafalgar Road, passing Wellington Buildings on the left. Follow the road as it curves left along Brookfield Park. At the crossroads carry straight on. When the road swings to the right by the United Services Club, carry on along a footpath and bear left downhill. After 50 metres, you come to Nelson Cottages, on the right, dating from the same time as Trafalgar Road. **Turn left, cross the road to Weston Free Church and turn left along the High Street.** Look for a narrow building on your right – No 82 – built in the gap between the houses on either side. This was a beerhouse called the Globe, the smallest for miles around, which closed in 1966. A little further along, go through the archway of an apartment block to see Belton House, elegant and Italianate with a superb fanlight, but with its garden cut away to create a car park.

Old buildings in Weston High Street

A little further along the High Street on the left is a fascinating row of buildings, with a superbly-preserved seventeenth-century Cotswold-style cottage at the end, its large gable facing the road. Opposite are Westbrook Villas, semi-detached and dating from around

1840, with false windows straddling the party wall. Further along on the right is a row of early eighteenth-century cottages at right-angles to the road. Opposite, hidden behind trees, is Southbank, a large, mid-eighteenth-century house with a seventeenth-century east wing. Also dating from the seventeenth century is the large, grey rubble-stone building on the right (just past the Mazda garage), which was originally Penn Hill Farm.

When you reach the Crown & Anchor – opened around 1833 and with the finest inn sign in the city – **cross the zebra crossing and turn right along the High Street. At the bottom of Trafalgar Road, cross over to the King's Arms and continue along the High Street.** Look out for the chiselled lettering above the single-storey schoolroom (now a scout hall) on the left. As you walk along you get a good view of the buildings on the raised terrace on the left, as well as the steps leading up to them.

At the end of the High Street, cross and head up to the left of the war memorial. The fittingly named Prospect House high up on the left probably dates from around 1740. To the right of it, Prospect Cottage is considerably earlier. Set

The Crown & Anchor

back behind trees on the other side of the lane leading up to the church, Vine House and Lansdown House date from the early eighteenth century – Vine House is dated 1706 – but were substantially altered in the early nineteenth century. Together with Lansdown Terrace, built in the early nineteenth century, they form a delightful group at the heart of the village. All, though, were earmarked for demolition by the council to make way for road widening, and were only saved when one of the residents refused to move.

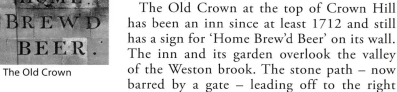

The Old Crown

The Old Crown at the top of Crown Hill has been an inn since at least 1712 and still has a sign for 'Home Brew'd Beer' on its wall. The inn and its garden overlook the valley of the Weston brook. The stone path – now barred by a gate – leading off to the right is an old packhorse road, which probably followed the course of a Roman Road. It leads past a row of houses known as the Grove, whose multi-coloured backs can be seen as you **continue along the main road into Weston Park.**

Today, the old packhorse road goes no further than the end of the Grove, its course obliterated by large villas built in the mid-nineteenth century. The road you are walking along was built around 1845; shortly afterwards the land on either side was divided into large building plots.

These are among the most desirable residences in Bath, although most are hidden from view behind hedges, shrubs and trees. When you reach an open field on the left, Weston Hill, a large, asymmetrical, Dutch-gabled house built in 1852, comes into view ahead. Nowhere in Bath does the early-Victorian ideal of the picturesque semi-rural retreat survive as evocatively as here.

Further along on the right is Weston Lea, with some splendid Gothic-style French windows. Thomas De Quincey's mother lived here with his sister Jane from around 1841 until her death in 1846. His sister continued to live here until her death in 1872. Next door is Glenfield, built around 1850. Then comes Richmond House, probably dating from around 1820. At the end of the road is a pair of early nineteenth-century semi-detached villas with a striking ironwork verandah on the first floor.

Cross over, turn right and walk along to Weston Road. Straight ahead is Snapdragons Nursery, a massive Italianate villa of around 1850. To its right is a Gothic-style villa – now a school – built around 1835. As you **turn left along Weston Road** (keeping to the left-hand pavement), you are back on the course of the Roman road. The Gothic-style Bath Priory Hotel, on the right, dates from around 1835. It is worth taking your time along this stretch, for nineteenth-century eclecticism and opulence has ensured that each house has some felicitous detail to set it apart from its neighbours. The oldest buildings are a pair of cottages dating from the 1780s. Shortly after they were built, the Moravian church bought them to establish a cemetery on land at the back. The cemetery closed around 1904, but, although the cottages were sold, they are still known as Moravian Cottages today.

On the left, a little further along, is a delightful early-nineteenth-century survival – the old Bath Nursery shop. The nursery covered 15 acres and supplied plants to the grand villas round about. With its single storey topped by a pediment, it is reminiscent of Kensington Nurseries on the London Road. The nurseryman's cottage can be seen behind it.

An 1850 advertisement for Bath Nursery

Just past a mini-roundabout, cross the zebra crossing and continue along Weston Road. On your right is an old quarry known as the Great Dell, where woodland walks wind between tall trees and a memorial to Shakespeare stands at the centre of a clearing. **After 100 metres, turn right along a footpath following a signpost to the Botanical Gardens.** Look out on the right for the back of an enormous carved head. **At the end of the railings, take the path to the right to find the entrance to the Great Dell.**

Go through it and head up to the right for a closer look at that enormous head. It depicts Jupiter and was the work of a local sculptor called John Osborne. He was a farm labourer who was encouraged in his artistic endeavours by a wealthy patron. Although it aroused a great deal of interest when it was exhibited in 1831, nobody bought it. Osborne died young, leaving a wife and children, and a subscription was launched to buy the head and relieve their distress. It was erected here in 1839. Walter Savage Landor, who was at the unveiling ceremony, declared that 'nothing of Michelangelo is nobler'.

Jupiter

As you **head down to the bottom of the old quarry**, you pass the Shakespeare Memorial. When it was unveiled in 1864 to mark the 300th anniversary of the Bard's birth, the ceremony was interrupted by the collapse of the stand in which local dignitaries were seated. 'Happily,' an unsympathetic eyewitness recorded, 'none were hurt, and the public around, on recovering from their surprise at the sudden disappearance of the minor officials from their elevated position, were the better able to appreciate the ludicrous figure which some of the sprawling forms presented.'

When you leave the Great Dell, cross the road and go through a gate into the Botanical Gardens, which were established in another old quarry in 1887. They contain one of the finest collection of plants on limestone in the West Country, as well as an extensive rock garden, with

The Botanical Gardens

a large pool surrounded by Japanese maples at its heart. The gardens have an understated charm, which means that they are often overlooked by visitors to the city. For plantsmen and garden-lovers, however, they are one of Bath's major attractions. A classical-style temple, built to promote Bath at the Wembley Exhibition in 1925, and later re-erected here, is now an interpretation centre. There were once two cottages in the gardens, one of which was a photographic studio in the nineteenth century. The foundations of the buildings, cunningly reworked to look like outcrops of stone, can be seen as you walk through the rock garden.

After looking round the gardens, **go through the main gate on the south side and bear left downhill across the grass. After crossing a path, you will see a lake ahead. Head to the right of it and, when you reach a path, turn left along the north side of the lake. When you reach the road, turn left along it and continue past the Victoria Obelisk.** The Dairy Farm to the left of it was built as a cottage orné in 1831. Beside it is a small aviary. **Carry on through the gates, cross the road (with care) and carry on through the gateway guarded by two sphinxes into the Royal Avenue.** To your left is the Royal Crescent, to your right a rather fine bandstand, with superb acoustics, designed by Major Davis. A little further along, the large urn filled with plants and surrounded by one of the most vibrant floral displays in Bath was the work of Stefano Pieroni, who had a studio in Bath Street and also made the fountain on Terrace Walk.

On the right-hand side of the road is a vase, embellished with writhing snakes, whose origins are far more murky. It was once claimed that it belonged to an eighteenth-century celebrity called Lady Miller who hosted parties at her villa in Batheaston. At these parties, aspiring poets would be invited to drop odes into a vase which had been found in Cicero's garden near Rome in 1769 and shipped back to England. The poems were read out and the best of them were published. After Lady Miller's death, the vase – or so the story went – ended up here. Not until someone pointed out that this vase had nowhere for odes to be dropped into – and, moreover, looked nothing like the pictures of Lady Miller's vase – was the story discredited.

Continue on along the Avenue and leave the park through a gateway guarded by lions. Carry on down to Queen Square, turn left along the north side, cross at the lights and retrace your steps to the starting point.

One of the lions at the entrance to Royal Victoria Park

12

HIDDEN VALES & UNTRODDEN WAYS
Sham Castle & Smallcombe

Distance *4.5 miles*

Time *2.5-3 hours*

Accessibility *This walk includes footpaths which may be muddy, as well as stiles and several flights of steps*

No public toilets

Starting point *Kingston Parade (outside Visitor Information Centre)*

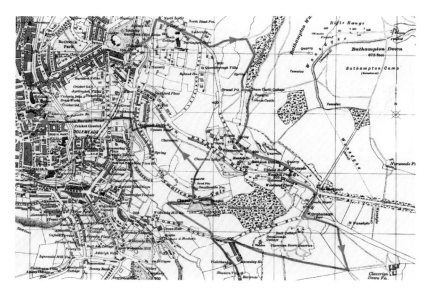

The elevation of these hills is such, that their summits command a country so exceeding beautiful and of such vast extent, that the eye that views it, and the mind that considers it with attention, can never be enough satisfied: nor is the air upon them to be less admired for its salubrity.

John Wood, 1742

Sham Castle can be seen from many parts of Bath. This walk takes a closer look at it, along with some other little-known delights in the hills and valleys south-east of the city. There is a fair amount of off-road walking,

Opposite: Bath from Sham Castle

across fields and through woodland, so the going may be muddy, but, if you're hankering for the country without leaving the city too far behind, it is ideal.

From the Visitor Information Centre, turn right along the south side of the abbey and continue round into Orange Grove. Turn right past a row of shops, cross two sets of traffic lights, turn left and carry on along Grand Parade. Turn right across Pulteney Bridge and carry on along Argyle Street and Great Pulteney Street. Cross at the pedestrian lights at the end and carry on up Sydney Place and Sydney Road. Turn right at the traffic lights at the junction with Warminster Road and right again up North Road.

On your right, as you walk uphill, is the Bath Spa Hotel, originally built in 1835 as a Greek-Revival-style mansion for a retired Indian army officer. Extended several times since, it has also, in its time, been a school and a nurses' home. On your left is King Edward's School. As you climb, you will see an old house beyond the modern buildings. Originally called Nethersole, it also dates from around 1835, and now forms part of the school.

Just past it, cross the road, go through a kissing gate on the left and walk up a grass-grown track. A little way up you will see water flowing into a cistern, with a stone inscribed BCW. This formed part of Bath's eighteenth-century water supply. The path leading up the hill is an old quarryman's track, worn into deep ruts by countless carts carrying stone down to Bathwick. As you climb, the views open up before the track enters woodland. When you come to a parting of the ways, take the right-hand fork. After a few metres the path swings sharply to the right, levels out and goes through a kissing gate. Stone was quarried here from Roman times through to the nineteenth century and evidence of large-scale quarrying is all around in the uneven ground.

The path leads to an open area with a bench, an ideal place to catch your breath while taking in the view of the city. Cross a tarmaced drive and follow a path uphill to the left of an imposing gatepost. This winds past a curious stone structure, which turns out, on closer inspection, to form part of a vault. The thickness of its walls and its proximity to the quarries suggests it may have been a gunpowder store.

The path bears right towards Sham Castle, built in 1762 by Richard Jones, Ralph Allen's clerk of works, and originally known as the Castle on the Warren. Seen from a distance, it looks for all the world like a four-square building. It is only when you get close that you realise it is no more substantial than a stage set, its sham secret safe from all but those who take the trouble to climb up to it. There are superb views from here, as well as another marker stone with the weathered legend 'BCW No 15'.

There are plenty of inscriptions on Sham Castle as well, courtesy of those who have trekked up here over the centuries to carve their initials

Sham Castle in 1890

into the stone.[1] If you go round to the back, you can see where archways and doorways have been filled in, with a locked door leading into one of the turrets. If you return to the front, however, you will see that there are no archways – blocked or otherwise – corresponding to the blocked archways at the back.

Nineteenth-century prints show the central gatehouse looking much as it does today, but with ruinous and broken-down curtain walls and turrets on either side. However, a sketch made by Thomas Robins the Elder at around the time the folly was built suggests that it originally looked much as it does today.

The reason for its construction has long been the subject of debate. It was commissioned by Ralph Allen, but curiously it is not visible from Prior Park. It has been suggested that Allen could have seen it from his town house behind Lilliput Alley, but he left there before Sham Castle was built. It has also been suggested that it was designed to show off the superior qualities of the stone from Allen's quarries – but, if that was the case, he chose a seriously unimpressive consignment for the job.[2] It also seems that Sham Castle was originally painted white, which rather discounts the theory that it was a showcase for Bath stone. And, after all, if anyone wanted to know what Bath stone looked like, there was more than enough of it lining the streets of the city below. The arguments and the theorising will no doubt long continue – which, given the fanciful and deceptive nature of the building, seems very appropriate.

1 You are requested not to emulate their example.

2 Although the stone for Sham Castle may have come from Combe Down, evidence of quarrying just below Sham Castle suggests it came from here.

Carry on past Sham Castle (keeping close to the hedge on your right rather than veering off to the left) until you reach a five-barred metal gate. Go through it and follow a path past a house with a massive cat-slide roof. Just past it you may catch a glimpse through the trees on the left of one of Bath's most extraordinary buildings – Kilowatt House, built in 1935-8 by Mollie Taylor, where Agatha Christie's Poirot would undoubtedly have felt at home.

When you reach North Road, cross over and turn left uphill. After 200 metres, turn right down a side road by Northwick House. Although less than 100 metres long, this road, known as North Lane, has a few surprises in store. The first is the view along the driveway on the left towards Wood Hill Place, a pair of semi-detached villas. As you continue downhill, a squat Italianate tower with a pyramidal roof and ship-shape weathervane appears to the right. If you turn round and look back uphill, meanwhile, a totally different and very dramatic view of Northwick House – which looks unremarkable enough from the top – appears – another instance of grand frontages being at the back to take in the view.

Facing the bottom of North Lane is one of a set of six Greek Revival houses built in the late 1820s by HE Goodridge. All are impressive, but the one straight ahead stands out by reason of its colouring – the result of being exposed to heat or of paint being unwisely applied at some time, perhaps. Its pink hue – a blush of subdued colour amidst the beige uniformity of Bath stone – suits it perfectly. There is another, and even more unexpected, surprise in store, however.

Cross over and turn left up Bathwick Hill to take a look at the front of Wood Hill Place, which Goodridge built around 1820. Recently restored

Wood Hill Place

gateposts flank steps up to a wall topped by a pediment bearing the building's name. Semi-detached living does not come much grander than this – look how the centre of the building is recessed with a Doric loggia on the first-floor. What makes Wood Hill Place stand out, though, is over to the right, where the head of Apollo appears amid a sunburst in an explosion of pagan energy that is all the more startling because of the restraint of the rest of the building.[1]

As you carry on up Bathwick Hill, look out on the right for Bath's newest crescent – Combe Royal – below you on the right. Built in 2002, it consists of three terraced houses, making it, by a considerable margin, the shortest crescent in Bath.

Take the first right along Copseland, but not before looking over to the left to see the delightfully whimsical Round House (even though there

is nothing round about it) at the end of the Avenue. Dating from the early nineteenth century, it is often mistaken for a tollhouse, but, as far as is known, it has always been a private house. The magnificent set of chimneys on the right as you walk along Copseland belongs to a nineteenth-century mansion called Combe Royal.

At the end of Copseland, cross over and turn left along Claverton Down Road. Look out for Claverton Down

The Round House

Gospel Hall on the left, an Arts and Crafts gem built by Silcock & Reay in 1897 and recently converted to a house. The angels on the gable end are a particularly inspired touch.

Carry on to the junction with the main road and, just after passing Claverton Down Community Hall, go through a kissing gate on the right and head diagonally across the field. On the far side, turn right before reaching the gate and cross a stone stile. Follow another clearly-marked path straight ahead and, where this forks, bear right, going to the right-hand side of a fence. Go over a stile and head towards a long, low concrete building. As the path curves to the right, look for a metal kissing-gate on the left, by a modern house with a pond. Go through it and head down a path between two stone walls. Carry on down the path – which is steep and slippery in places – **to Widcombe Hill.** Take care at

the bottom, as the footpath leads directly onto the road. Across the road is a Bath Turnpike Trust boundary post, while the towers and turrets of Bathwick Hill's mid-nineteenth-century villas can be seen across the valley.

On your left is Macaulay Buildings, a semi-rural outcrop of Georgian Bath dating from the 1820s. Although a dead end, it is worth walking up to see how the seven semi-detached villas, joined together by

1 Originally, there was a matching feature at the other end of the building, but the insensitive addition of a ground-floor bay has concealed it.

their entrance lobbies with toilets above, step up the hill. Notice how three blank windows straddle the party walls in each set of buildings. The two villas at the top – Rood House and Macaulay House – with their castellations and gothic arches, look forward to the full-blown Gothicism of the Victorians.

Macaulay Buildings

Head back down to Widcombe Hill and **turn left**. Macaulay Buildings continues downhill; here, though, the three semi-detached villas, with their shallow full-height bays, are spaced well apart. No 2 was once an Orphans' Home, established by the Mrs Williamson who built Williamstowe at Combe Down. The words 'Orphans' Home' can just be made out under the cornice.

Prospect Road, the next turning on the left, is, like Macaulay Buildings, a dead end, but is well worth a detour. Apart from the prospect, which gets better as you ascend, there is the eighteenth-century splendour of Violet Bank Farm, and, at the end, a mid-Victorian mansion called Fairstowe and a white-stucco Regency house called Beechwood. From here you can survey the fields below, with winding paths cut through them as they would have been in the eighteenth century.

Head back down Prospect Road, cross Widcombe Hill and go through a kissing gate into the National Trust's Smallcombe Estate. Up to the right, diagonally across the field, a kissing gate leads into Smallcombe Wood, a hidden enclave of ancient woodland high above the city, cross-crossed by a maze of muddy paths, and carpeted in late spring with wild garlic. A diversion into it is highly recommended, although **the way ahead lies through the kissing gate on your left. Head across the field and, when**

Smallcombe Wood

you reach the far corner, go through a kissing gate by a water trough and turn sharp right down to a gate in the far right-hand corner. Go through the gate and turn right along the lane to two cemeteries. Ahead is St Mary's Cemetery, opened in 1856, which replaced the cemetery in Bathwick Street. On the right is Smallcombe Cemetery, opened in 1861 for nonconformist burials. Its tepee-like octagonal chapel was designed by AS Goodridge (the son of HE Goodridge). The chapel in St Mary's Cemetery is by Thomas Fuller, who designed Newark Works on the Lower Bristol Road and the Canadian Parliament Buildings.

St Mary's Cemetery

Both cemeteries closed in 1989, and this sylvan spot, surrounded by National Trust land, is one of Bath's hidden oases.

If you walk up the steep slopes behind Fuller's chapel you will find, amid the angels and crosses, something rather more exotic – a barley-twist colonette with patterned bands of bright enamel swirling upwards. At the base of the column a moss-grown, weather-worn inscription marks this as the last resting place of Mary Eleanor, daughter of the late William Kerr of Nassau in the West Indies, who died in Bath in 1888. The years have taken their toll of this vibrant splash of colour in a world of grey and green, but how brightly would it have shone when new.

Further along is a sundial dedicated to members of the Housman family, including AE Housman, author of *A Shropshire Lad*. Although it is sometimes claimed he is buried here, the inscription makes clear his grave is in Shropshire.

Head down the lane out of the churchyard and turn right up a drive between two gateposts to Smallcombe Farm. Just past the farm, go up a flight of waymarked steps. Carry on up the path before crossing a small bridge over the ditch on the left and going over a stile. Walk straight across the field, and go through a pair of metal kissing gates. The views across the city from here are superb, and you also have a good view of the houses on Bathwick Hill, to your right.

Once through another kissing gate, take the path bearing right. When you reach the corner of the field, go down a flight of steps to Sydney Buildings. Cross over, go down another flight of steps and cross the canal. To get back to the city centre, turn right, then left down a flight of steps and under the railway to Pulteney Road. Cross at the traffic lights, head along North Parade Road, cross another set of lights and carry on along York Street to the Visitor Information Centre.

Smallcombe Farm

13

DREAMING OF SUBURBIA
Bear Flat, Oldfield Park & East Twerton

Distance *4 miles*

Time *2-3 hours*

Accessibility *Step-free on pavements or footpaths*

Public toilets *Shaftesbury Road, Oldfield Park (by Co-op store) (Charge payable)*

Starting point *Kingston Parade (outside Visitor Information Centre)*

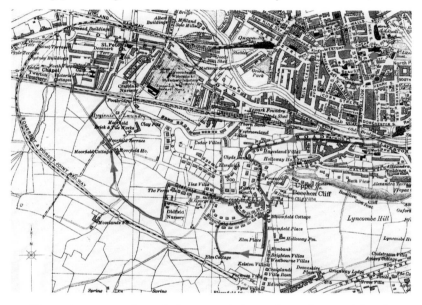

Thorough sanitary and remedial action in the houses that we have; and then the building of more, strongly, beautifully, and in groups of limited extent, kept in proportion to their streams and walled round, so that there may be no festering and wretched suburb anywhere, but clean and busy street within and the open country without, with a belt of beautiful garden and orchard round the walls, so that from any part of the city perfectly fresh air and grass and sight of far horizon might be reachable in a few minutes' walk. This the final aim.

John Ruskin, *Sesame and Lilies*, 1865

Opposite: St Mary's Buildings, Wells Road

Eighteenth-century Bath was defiantly urban. Although the *rus in urbe* ideal was one that developers pursued increasingly as the century wore on, the basis of urban design remained the terrace with its front doors opening directly onto a public promenade or pavement. Bath was designed as a paradigm of the polite society whose virtues were extolled by writers and philosophers. The word 'polite' came from the word 'polished'. In 1709, the Earl of Shaftesbury declared that 'all politeness is owing to liberty. We polish one another, and rub off our corners and rough sides by a sort of amicable collision.' The aim was conversation without constraint between people of different ranks, religion, occupation or politics.

At the beginning of the eighteenth century, this was a revolutionary idea. The barriers between different groups and classes of people were enormous. Within living memory, society had been torn apart by religious and political strife. Men still wore swords as a matter of course and were only too ready to challenge each other to duels. Nash's ban on the wearing of swords in Bath was only part of his campaign to make Bath the epitome of polite society – a template for what could be done elsewhere. In 1755, Lady Luxborough summed up Nash's aims succinctly: 'To promote society, good manners, and a coalition of parties and ranks; to suppress scandal and late hours, are his views.' He did not transform Bath overnight, however. Nash's biographer, Oliver Goldsmith, recalled that, at the start of his reign, 'general society among people of rank was by no means established. The nobility still preserved a structure of Gothic haughtiness, and refused to keep company with the gentry at any of the public entertainments of the place. But when proper walks were made for exercise and a house built for assembling in, rank began to be laid aside, and all degrees of people, from the private gentleman upwards, were soon united in society with one another.'

Nash actively discouraged private parties. Bath's success relied on a rigorously enforced regime of social gatherings – in the pump or assembly rooms, on the public walks or in pleasure gardens and coffee houses. By the end of the eighteenth century, however, many of Nash's aims had been achieved; society was much civil and the imperatives that had sustained this enforced sociability no longer applied. Increasingly, visitors to the city shunned the social round. Jane Austen's two Bath novels, *Northanger Abbey* and *Persuasion*, written in 1797-8 and 1815-16 respectively, chronicle the change in attitude in the intervening years. *Persuasion* features the Elliots, for whom 'the theatre or the rooms ... were not fashionable enough' and 'whose evening amusements were solely in the elegant stupidity of private parties'. Jane Austen obviously disapproved, but the Elliots were typical of many in the Regency period. Such attitudes would have been unusual 20 years earlier; in the mid-eighteenth century they would have been unthinkable.

One of the unforeseen consequences of creating a polite – or at least a politer – society was that people no longer wanted to live in the middle of a noisy, dusty and crowded city. Out-of-town or suburban developments, increasingly made up of detached or semi-detached villas set back behind gardens, became the new desideratum. As the upper classes moved out of the city, the lower classes moved in. Many once fashionable lodging houses became tenements, initiating a downward spiral that led to swathes of Georgian buildings being demolished in twentieth-century slum clearances. Meanwhile, the exodus from the city accelerated as the dream of suburban living filtered down from the upper to the middle and eventually to the working classes. It is that process which forms the subject of this walk.

From the Visitor Information Centre, head west along York Street and turn left into Stall Street. At the end, turn right along Lower Borough Walls, left along the footpath beside the former St James's cemetery and then left along St James's Parade. Originally known as Thomas Street,

St James's Parade

this was built in 1768 by Thomas Jelly to provide lodgings for wealthy visitors. Its Venetian windows and finely-moulded door frames looked across a broad parade from which traffic was excluded. Like many eighteenth-century developments, St James's Parade did not stay genteel for very long. The problem was the intermittent flooding this area was prone to. John Wood built his Parades high above the river, so that when it flooded only their basements got wet. When it flooded down here, everyone got wet – with the result that St James's Parade, along with the streets round about, soon acquired an unenviable reputation as a place not to stay. As soon as the wealthy visitors moved out, their places were taken by less wealthy visitors, and a process of decline rapidly set in. The indignities and adaptations this street has been subject to over the centuries are witness to that.

Walk to the end of St James's Parade and carry on, crossing the traffic lights to the bus station. Walk to the right of the bus station and cross a footbridge over the river. Carry on under the railway, take the pedestrian subway under the road and turn right. Follow the path uphill, bearing right when it forks to follow the Wells Road.

The row of buildings further along on the other side of the road dates from the 1830s, although part of it was rebuilt after being damaged by bombing in 1942.

Ahead on the left is St Mary's Buildings, designed by John Pinch around 1820, and one of Bath's least-known Georgian terraces. As you approach the bottom house, you can divert up a short flight of steps for a closer look. Superbly proportioned, with cornices sweeping elegantly uphill, the seclusion of St Mary's Buildings is only compromised by the noise of traffic on the main road. The bottom three houses were rebuilt after bombing in 1942.

The large building ahead on the right, as you **continue up the Wells Road**, is a former school, recently converted to apartments. Beyond it, recently rescued from near dereliction, is South Hayes House, which, despite its nineteenth century façade, dates from the early eighteenth century. Raglan Villa, next door, dates from around 1850. Higher up is an ornate gateway leading to South Hayes, an old row of gabled cottages altered and extended in the mid-nineteenth century.

As you round the corner, the villas become ever grander. **Turn left into Hayesfield Park**, where modern houses sit alongside nineteenth-century villas. The drungway crossing the road preserves the line of an old footpath through the fields that disappeared when the area was developed. Just beyond it on the left is one of the most spectacular end-of-terrace properties in the city, dating from 1904-6, with a half-timbered gable commanding a superb view down the Avon valley.

Turn left at the end of Hayesfield Park and carry on – with care – across a side road to Rolfey's antique shop. Bear right past the Co-op, cross the bottom of Bruton Avenue and cross the main road at the pedestrian lights to the Bear Inn. Although nothing you can see from here is earlier than the last decade of the nineteenth century, there have been buildings around here for centuries. The Bear stands on the site of an old inn, which once had a large brewery alongside. The inn was damaged by bombing in April 1942 and later rebuilt. Its name has nothing to do with bear baiting or heraldry. This area was known as Bear Flat because it was a flattish piece of land where barley – originally known as bere – was grown. There are many other places in Somerset and further afield with Bere or Bear in their names for the same reason.

Although the main road from Bath to the south ran through Bear Flat, the area remained predominantly agricultural until the late nineteenth century. There was an orchard at the back of the Bear, which disappeared in 1893 when Bloomfield Avenue was built. Across the road were more orchards, along with a villa and some cottages. A little further along was Holloway Farm, where Holloway Fair was held during the first week in May. It was also the venue for the Bath & West Show in 1877.

The development of the land on the opposite side of the road began in earnest just before 1900 and was largely completed before the First World War. As the roads were named after poets, the development was known as Poets' Corner. It was the work of four brothers, Elisha, Francis, John and Samuel Hallett – carpenters by trade – who moved to Bath from Witham Friary in the late nineteenth century. Between them, they built around 1,700 houses in Bath, with John being responsible for over three-quarters of them.

Hayesfield Terrace, opposite the pub, was built in 1895.[1] Work on Poet's Corner got under way in 1899 when the first houses in Shakespeare Avenue – to the right of Hayesfield Terrace – were built. The Hallett family were staunch Methodists, and so it was natural that the new development should have a Methodist church. Its foundation stones were laid in 1906 and the church opened a year later. Its spire can be seen rising above the houses across the road. Not surprisingly, there were no pubs in Poets' Corner. The Bear and another coaching inn called the Devonshire Arms, further up the main road, were the only places you could get a drink.

Poets' Corner was not the first suburban development in this area, however. If you **carry on across Bloomfield Avenue and head south along the main road**, just after passing a couple of shops you will come to Bloomfield Place, a row of cottages built around 1820 for traders and craftsmen working in the city. Beyond it is Elm Place, started around ten years later. Although much of Elm Place consists of two-storey buildings, there are three-storey pavilions

Elm Place

with rusticated ground floors and Doric pilasters in the centre and at the north end. There should have been a similar pavilion at the south end, but the terrace was never completed. Work on it was sporadic, as money kept running out, and it took almost 50 years to build. An electricity sub-station now stands at the southern end, with a short row of modern buildings beyond it.

Although this was a semi-rural retreat, to all intents and purposes Elm Place looks like a city street set down in the middle of the country – more *urbs in rure* than *rus in urbe*. It would be some time before a different style of architecture for suburban developments started to evolve. The grand villas opposite Elm Place date from the later nineteenth century and display a range of different styles.

At the end of Elm Place, turn right down a tarmaced path. From here you can see the back of Elm Place – a storey higher than the front because of the lie of the land – which at the time it was built would have enjoyed an uninterrupted view over the fields. If you look to the left, you can see

---

1 The northern end of the terrace was destroyed by bombing in 1942, along with the buildings that stood where the Co-op is today.

the backs of the houses further up Bloomfield Road – including another unfinished Georgian terrace. At the top of the hill is Bloomfield Crescent – originally known as Cottage Crescent – which dates from 1799 and was designed by Charles Harcourt Masters.

Carry on down the path and turn right into Maple Grove. To your left is a bridge over the former Somerset & Dorset Railway, which opened in 1874 and closed in 1966. Maple Grove itself – an eclectic mix of coursed rubble stone, pennant stone, brick, pebbledash and ashlar – was mostly built between 1905 and 1912. Worthy of special mention is the superb, art nouveau-inspired ironwork on No 19.

At the end, turn right into Bloomfield Avenue, developed in the 1890s, although with later infills. The infills as you turn the corner date from the 1950s and were by Cyril Beazer, who built hundreds of detached and semi-detached homes around the city in reconstituted Bath stone. Further along on the right is a much more recent infill, built of gleaming ashlar in Edwardian style. There is much to look out for here – note especially the superb horseshoe arch and intricate carvings on Nos 64-65. As you continue up the road, look how ashlar dressings have been used with red brick at Nos 16-17. This combination was very popular for a short time around the beginning of the twentieth century.

The houses on the left give way to tennis courts. Originally there were allotments here, creating an Edwardian version of a Georgian square. As you **round the top of Bloomfield Avenue and continue down the other side**, look out for the lack of symmetry in the gables of Nos 57-58, the triangular-headed windows of No 56, and the chunky Jacobethan pillars of Nos 51-53. On the left, past the tennis courts, is a house

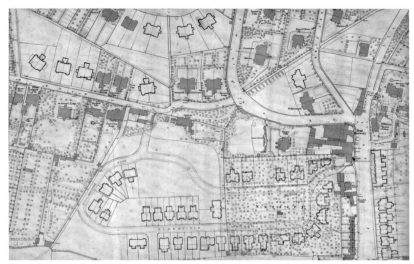

An 1886 Ordnance Survey map of Bear Flat with new roads and houses added in green

The allotments in Bloomfield Avenue

with a date of 1893. Fir Lodge, next to it, dates from 1909, as do the two semi-detached villas beyond it.

Cross over, turn right, walk along to Oldfield Road and turn left. The Old Cottage on the corner dates from the eighteenth century but was remodelled in picturesque style in the late nineteenth century. The Italianate villas you pass on the left date from the 1840s and are among the oldest buildings in the area. The modern St George's Lodge replaces a grand Victorian villa demolished after the Second World War, not because of bomb damage but allegedly as a result of depredations inflicted on it by soldiers billeted there. Most of the buildings on the right-hand side of the road are later,

Ordnance Survey maps of 1888 and 1904 showing how the area west of Oldfield Road was developed

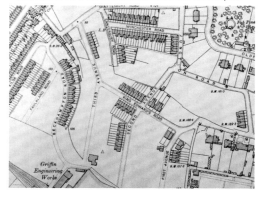

although the two pairs of semis (7-10) date from around the late 1850s. Curiously, their frontages are obscured by the sort of extensions you would normally expect to find at the back. Clearly the architect wanted the north side of the houses, with spectacular views and large gardens, to be free of encumbrances.

For the best part of 50 years, Oldfield Road was to all intents and purposes a cul de sac. Junction Road, leading off to the right, follows the course of a farm track that led across the fields. Oldfield Road ended at Cedar Park, with a view across open country to Moor Farm in the valley below.

Turn left along Oldfield Lane, following the course of another old farm track between stone walls. Nurseries were established on the left-hand side of the lane in the 1860s. The buildings associated with the nurseries are still there, but the land was built on in the 1970s. As you continue downhill, there is a good view of Bloomfield Crescent on the skyline ahead. **At the bottom of the lane turn right.** On your left is a new Catholic school, while an old gatepost in a wall on the right recalls the area's rural past. The church of Our Lady & St Alphege is by Sir Giles Gilbert Scott (also responsible for red telephone boxes and the Anglican cathedral in Liverpool). Designed in 1927-9, it was consecrated in 1954, a thousand years after St Alphege's birth in Weston. Modelled on Santa Maria in Cosmedin, Rome, an early Christian basilica, it gives the lie to those who believe that any building employing old styles is simply pastiche. The campanile should have been much taller, but there were fears that the foundations were too weak to support it. If you look back you can see how the new school echoes the design of the church without slavishly copying it – another instance of how buildings can take their lead from earlier buildings without being pastiches of them.

You have now reached the borders of Oldfield Park, originally known as South Twerton and developed from the 1890s onwards as a working-class suburb of high-quality terraced housing. Over a century on, with demand for affordable housing every bit as great as when the first residents moved in, house prices in Oldfield Park have risen steeply, fuelled by the buy-to-let boom; a high proportion of the houses now provide accommodation not for people who work in Bath but for students at the city's two universities.

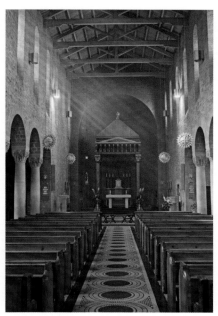

St Alphege's

Unlike Poets' Corner, Oldfield Park was provided with three pubs. When the Moorfields Inn on the corner opened in 1901, the houses around it had yet to be built. **Carry on past the turning to Third Avenue and continue on into Beckhampton Road.** The red-brick factory on your left was built in the 1890s as the Griffin Engineering Works and, like the Moorfields Inn, originally stood in splendid isolation.

The Griffin Engineering Works around 1900

The Scala in 1961

The Maypole Dairy on Moorland Road is now Oldfield Park Bookshop

After passing the turning on the left to Melcombe Road, a short diversion will take you to Moor Farm. **Turn right down a narrow alleyway between 18 and 19 Beckhampton Road, before turning left** past a range of old buildings that were once part of the farm. Until recently they were in industrial use, but in 2002 they were converted to houses and are now known as Shaftesbury Mews.

When you emerge onto the road, turn right and walk along to the zebra crossing. The Co-op you can see ahead was built in 1921 as the Scala picture house, which closed in 1961. Opposite the old cinema is a memorial garden dedicated to 16 people who were killed when an air-raid shelter on the site received a direct hit at 4am on 26 April 1942.

Cross the zebra crossing and turn left and right into Moorland Road. The buildings on the southeast corner – originally known as Moorland

Cottages – were there by the early 1880s, and are the earliest buildings along here. The row on the right was the last to be built, sometime after 1904. Past the Oldfield Park Bookshop – well worth stepping into, to inspect its range of local titles – you come to the site of another pub – the Livingstone, on the far corner of Livingstone Road. When it was destroyed by bombing in 1942, the licence was transferred to a former post office a few doors along. The site of the original pub is now occupied by a tile shop, but the Livingstone is still doing a roaring trade in its new premises.

Continue along Moorland Road and take the third right along the Triangle past the Baptist church, whose foundation stone was laid in 1902. **Turn left and then right.** Across the road is the former Methodist church, opened in 1892. **Carry on across the railway and turn right down the footpath along Highland Terrace.** This area, to the north of the railway, was originally known as East Twerton and was developed much earlier than the one you have just walked through. The earliest buildings date from the 1830s, although Highland Terrace was not built till the 1890s.

Turn left down Stuart Place. If you look up at the second block of three-storey buildings on the right you will see some odd-looking blocked windows at the side. These belonged to a prison block that once extended across the road and for some distance to the west. After the prison closed in 1878, a street was driven through the site and the walls on the right were incorporated into the buildings that stand there today. The rest of the block, on the left-hand side of the road, was converted to a sweet factory

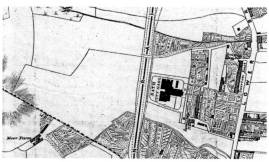

and later became part of Bath Technical College, before being demolished and replaced by the buildings you see today. If you **turn left at the end into Caledonian Road** you will find a more tangible reminder of the prison in the shape of the Governor's House, one of Bath's

A mid-nineteenth century map showing the prison with the railway running past it. Moor Farm is in the bottom left-hand corner

least-celebrated classical buildings. The prison opened in 1842 as a replacement for the gaol in Grove Street, which was overcrowded and insanitary. The committee appointed by the council to build it chose this site because it offered 'quiet seclusion, open, but not bleak or unprotected, with no obstruction to the free circulation of air'. It was, in other words,

The prison after conversion to a factory

a *rus in urbe* for the prisoners. Although hidden away in a back street today, there was little around it when it was built, and it was visible from the Royal Crescent, which is why – at least from a distance – it had to look like a grand suburban villa. The Governor's House now provides sheltered accommodation.

Walk past the front of the Governor's House, turn right towards Denmark Road and right again past Hedley Hall, originally East Twerton Congregational Chapel. The right-hand side of Denmark Street was built in the 1830s as East Twerton Terrace and was one of the earliest developments in the area. Some of the houses still have their original – and rather attractive – window frames.

At the end of Denmark Road, turn left and follow the road round towards Oldfield Park Infants' School. This started out in 1878 as East Twerton Schools. The playground to the right of it stands on the site of a row of buildings destroyed by bombing in April 1942. On your left as you walk along to the Lower Bristol Road is the old Bath Press building. Established in 1889 as a Phonetic Institute, it was extended several times to become one of the largest employers in the city. In 1934 it was renamed the Pitman Press. After changing its name to Bath Press, it closed in 2007 with the loss of 263 jobs. Tesco has submitted plans to redevelop the site.

Turn right along the Lower Bristol Road. St Peter's church on the right was designed by Major Davis and consecrated in 1880. It has now been converted to apartments. The church originally had a belfry which was removed after it became unsafe.

Cross at the pedestrian lights and continue along the Lower Bristol Road. The Victoria Works pub – until recently the Belvoir Castle – opened around 1850. Its new name commemorates Stothert & Pitt's Victoria Works which once stood nearby. The terrace of two-storey houses beyond the pub, called Victoria Buildings, dates from the early years of Queen Victoria's reign. Longmead Buildings – the six three-storey houses at the end of the row – are earlier, although their original grandeur has been somewhat compromised by ground-floor extensions. They stand on the border between Twerton and Widcombe – a Bath Turnpike Trust post, erected in 1827, marks the boundary.

Carry on past the petrol station and follow the road as it curves left. As you continue over two sets of pedestrian lights (following the road as it swings right), look to the left towards Western Riverside, a new residential development on the site of Victoria Works. The crane in front

The Stothert & Pitt crane back on home ground

of it was built at the works around 1904 and returned to the city in 2011 as the result of a campaign led by Bryan Chalker.

Continue along the main road and follow the pavement as it curves left into Ivo Peters Way. You are now at the heart of what was, until the mid-1960s, a major railway complex. Ivo Peters was a photographer who lived in the Royal Crescent and made a unique photographic and cinematic record of the railway in its heyday.

A major redevelopment of the area you are now entering is planned, and this will almost certainly make the directions that follow obsolete. The basic route should remain unchanged, however, so if you head east across the river and carry straight on into the old station, you will be on the right track (if you'll forgive the pun). If the changes have not yet taken place, go through a gap in the railings on your left and turn right, following the signpost to Sainsbury's. After crossing two zebra crossings, cross a footbridge over the river. The bridge to your right once carried trains into the Midland Railway station; the pedestrian bridge is a replacement for a similar bridge which was dismantled after the railway closed.

A Somerset & Dorset train standing in the Midland station c1910

Turn right across another zebra crossing and walk past the supermarket. Ahead is the imposing overall roof of the station built in 1870, a scaled-down version of the Midland Railway's

St Pancras terminal in London. After the station closed in 1966, its fate hung in the balance, but after it was listed in 1971 it was acquired by the council. It is currently leased by the Ethical Property Company.

Walk through the station and out through the old parcels office. Turn left across James Street West and continue up Charles Street. When you reach the corner of New King Street, cross at the pedestrian lights and continue uphill. At the top, cross and turn right along Monmouth Street. As you walk along, look how some of the buildings have steps leading up to their front doors, with their basements above ground level. As with the old gaol in Grove Street, it looks as through the street was originally intended to be higher.

Above: The Midland station today
Left: Cherub in Parsonage Lane
Below: Ironwork in Monmouth Street

It also looks as though No 29 has had a ground-floor extension added to conceal the fact. The ironwork above it, adorned with grapes and casks, dates from the mid-nineteenth century, when this was the Victoria Wine & Spirit Vaults. The mock-Georgian building next to it is modern, but the Griffin on the corner dates from when Monmouth Street was built in the 1730s.

Turn left by the Griffin and right into Beauford Square. Carry on into Trim Street, turn right at the end, cross Upper Borough Walls and head under the archway along Parsonage Lane. Near the end you will see an archway with black doors on the right. This was the entrance to a brewery which opened around 1810. A century later, it became the home of the *Bath Chronicle*. The Jacobean-style carvings to the left of the doors, however, are one of Bath's minor mysteries. No one seems to know where they came from, why they are here or how old they are; estimates of their age range from the seventeenth to the early twentieth century.

At the end of Parsonage Lane, turn left along Westgate Street, right into Stall Street and left into the Abbey Church Yard to return to the starting point.

14

THE GREEN ROOFS
Snow Hill & the London Road

Distance *2.5 miles*

Time *2-3 hours*

Accessibility *On pavements throughout; several flights of steps, with step-free alternatives available*

No public toilets

Starting point *Kingston Parade (outside Visitor Information Centre) – or at Walcot Buildings (opposite the bototm of Snow Hill) on the London Road*

> *Houses live and die: there is a time for building*
> *And a time for living and for generation*
> *And a time for wind to break the loosened pane.*
> TS Eliot, *East Coker*

Some silly people on the right nowadays wish the sixties hadn't happened because that was when people discovered sex and pot-smoking. I wish the sixties hadn't happened because that was when avarice and stupidity got to the wheel of the bulldozer. They called it enterprise and still do.
> Alan Bennett, 1994

Opposite: The Green Roofs of Snow Hill

This walk explores a part of the city most people only get to see while driving through it – or, as is more often the case, when stuck in a traffic jam while trying to drive through it. Unfortunately, this cocooned encounter rarely, if ever, awakens a desire for a more intimate acquaintance.

Yet Snow Hill and the first few hundred metres of the London Road are not only fascinating in themselves, but indicate how attitudes to conservation and heritage have changed since the mid-twentieth century, as well as raising the question of how those attitudes will evolve in the years to come. They also highlight how important a sense of community is if heritage is to denote anything beyond tourist trails and picture-postcard perversions of the past. On a lighter note, the walk will also introduce you to the seamier side of eighteenth-century high life.

Maps of the Snow Hill area in 1787 and 1800

The area explored in this walk remained largely undeveloped until the late 1780s. Comparing the map on the left, from 1787, when development was already under way, with the one below it, from 1800, shows just how rapidly buildings went up. Although some of them were lodging houses, the majority were terraced cottages for the construction workers who flocked to Bath as a result of the building boom across the river in Bathwick.

The lodging houses, built by Sir Peter Rivers Gay, failed to attract wealthy visitors and were soon converted to tenements and shops. Almost all the buildings survived, however, until the 1950s when the council declared large swathes of them unfit for human habitation – despite substantial evidence to the contrary – and they were bulldozed to make way for council flats.[1] It is a story that was repeated across the country, but is no less sad – or shocking – for that.

---

1 The map on the previous page indicates what Snow Hill looked like before the clearances of the 1950s.

To get to the starting point, **head north from the Visitor Information Centre, past the Abbey and along the High Street and Northgate Street. Continue along Walcot Street and London Street, cross the lights at Cleveland Bridge and carry on along the London Road for 150 metres, stopping opposite the bottom of Snow Hill.**

The photograph below shows what the view from here looked like a century ago. The imposing archway on the left originally led into the gardens of a large villa called Walcot House, built in the 1780s. It is believed

Looking up Snow Hill in the early twentieth century

to have been built as a manor house by the Rivers Gay family, who owned much of Snow Hill. When Walcot Buildings, which you are standing in front of, were built, Nos 8-11 had only two storeys, so as not to block the view of the river from Walcot House. By the time this photograph was taken, however, the glory days of Walcot House were over, and its gardens had been taken over by Tucker & Sons, hay & corn dealers and agricultural seed merchants, whose carts can be seen to the left of the blocked-up archway.

To the left of Snow Hill is Chelsea House, built in the 1950s, with the ground floor as a Co-op. Next to it, Domino's Pizzas occupies the former Longacre Tavern, built in the late 1960s and replacing a pub that had been there since the 1840s. It closed in 2010.

Although the two buildings across the alleyway from the old tavern may date from the eighteenth century, the building beyond them is nineteenth century. This was Vezey & Cos coach building factory, one of the largest and most prestigious companies in the city, whose clients

Longacre Hall

included Queen Victoria and the King of Sweden. The factory closed in 1908 after the rise of motor transport brought the coach-building trade to an end. The building became a Technical School until the late 1930s, when Henry King turned it into an 'art silk underwear' factory.

By 1961, it had been taken over by Sims & Co Motor Agents, later known as Longacre Motors. In 1978, the building, renamed Longacre Hall, became home to community groups and a Youth Training Project. There were carpentry and pottery workshops, a photographic gallery and opportunities for unemployed people to develop marketable skills. In 1985 a play garden was opened at the back of the building by Floella Benjamin. Sadly, Longacre Hall closed in the late 1990s after funding was withdrawn.

Turning our attention to this side of the road, Walcot Buildings was built as a row of lodging houses. As in Milsom Street, however, shopkeepers soon moved in. Grand doorways, such as that on No 16, survive as a reminder of what the ground floors of these buildings were originally

Walcot Buildings

like. As late as the 1960s, all the shops along here were still trading successfully.[1] Today, however, that vibrant shopping centre is but a distant memory, killed off by supermarkets. Many shopfronts are boarded up, signifying a reversion from retail to residential use. The problem is that, while a house converted to a shop looks like a shop, a shop converted to a house looks like an empty shop, with all the implications for the continued viability of the area that entails. Some shops have bucked the trend, however, and are now occupied by specialist traders, notably the Old Bank Antiques Centre, which has played a significant role in halting the downward trend along this part of the London Road.

Carry on along Walcot Buildings, past the top of Bedford Street, where the setts still survive. The old houses on the left once ran down to the river. In 1809, however, flash flooding caused by rapid melting of snow on the surrounding hills tore the houses nearest the river from their foundations, burying several of the inhabitants under the ruins.

Continue past the top of Weymouth Street to

Walcot Poor House

1 The retail history of this part of the London Road can be found in chapter 24 of *The Year of the Pageant*.

WALK 14: THE GREEN ROOFS

the end of **Walcot Buildings**, where you can see an old butcher's shop at No 29. From the massive pillar beside it an equally massive gate once hung; another gate hung from a pillar opposite to ensure that the inmates of the building in the yard beyond were not tempted to abscond. This was the Walcot Poor House, described as 'lately erected' in 1768. It was home to over 100 people who were cared for by the parish. It also housed a factory where 20 boys and girls were employed in the 'neat, useful, and meritorious occupation' of heading pins. The Tudor-style façade was added in 1828 and in 1848 the poor house became the Sutcliffe Industrial School, 'designed', according to its prospectus, 'to put down juvenile begging and vagrancy'. It has now been converted to apartments.

If you had stood here 60 years ago and looked across the road, you would have seen Dover Street running uphill, with the Traveller's Rest pub on the left-hand corner. This opened around 1841 and closed in 1956.

JW & EJ Fry's,
3 Dover Terrace

WJ Winckworth's,
6 Dover Terrace

The council paid just £1 to George's Brewery for the building, which was demolished two years later.

To the right of Dover Street was Dover Terrace, a row of four-storey Bath stone buildings dating from the late eighteenth century. There was a greengrocer's on the corner, with Bolwell's sweetshop – famous for its home-made humbugs – at No 2. At No 3 were JW & EJ Fry – carpenters, builders, decorators and general contractors. At No 5 was another butcher's, while another decorator, WJ Winckworth, was at No 6. Further along were a fruiterer's and Parker's cycle shop, with Billett's coal yard at the end.

Continue along the London Road to the Multiyork building,

Fry's Yard, 3 Dover Terrace

originally the Kensington Brewery, which opened some time before 1800. It was refronted in 1926 when Fortt, Hatt & Billings converted it to a furniture depository. The alleyway at the side led to a horse-tram depot in a yard at the back, which operated between 1880 and 1902. The building on the other side of the alleyway was the Porter Butt Inn, built in the late eighteenth century, extended in 1816 and closed in 2009. The Esso petrol station across the road stands on the site of another lost inn – the Pack Horse.

A couple of doors beyond the old Porter Butt is a high wall, with its two large windows blocked up. On the other side of the wall was a ballroom, decorated with plasterwork of the highest quality. Clearly, passers-by were not meant to see what went on inside. A few metres further on, you come to the entrance to a supermarket car park. Clark's Porter Brewery once stood in the open space here until it burnt down around 1817. So for a short period there were two large breweries almost side by side on this stretch of the London Road.

It is time, though, to turn our attention to York Villa, now renamed Norland College, where nannies and nursery nurses are trained. This charming building, the wall of whose ballroom you have just gazed at and whose gardens once extended down to the river, was built some time before 1787. There are two stories regarding its early history. The respectable version is that it was the Duke of York's Bath residence, and that he kept one of his mistresses here. The other, less respectable, version is that it was a high-class brothel. The evidence favours the latter.

When the Duke of York visited Bath for the first time in 1795, he took a long-term lease on the central house in the Royal Crescent. There is no record of any link between the Duke of York and this building, however. At the time he is supposed to have stayed here, it had a brewery in front and an inn at the back – not exactly the sort of place you would expect a member of the royal family to frequent. The internal layout of the building was odd as well; not only was there a ballroom, there were lots of little rooms on the upper floors. It followed, in fact, the design of high-class brothels in Georgian London. Bath was notorious for its brothels and, while those at the lower end of the market, in the Avon Street area, are well-recorded, information on those at the top end is virtually non-existent. This is hardly surprising. Women working in those at the lower end not only found themselves hauled before the magistrates on a regular basis but were also subject to scrutiny and condemnation by moral reformers. Women working in those at the top end, because of the social cachet of their clientele, operated with impunity behind a cloak of anonymity.

High-class prostitutes regularly travelled down to Bath from London to ply their trade. A French visitor called Briand Chantreau, writing about English prostitutes in 1792, claimed that 'there are in fact hardly any in London, except such as walk the streets, who have not been to Bath at least four or five times in their lives.' There are reports of entire bordellos moving to Bath for the season, and York Villa may have been one such seasonal establishment. It would have been ideally situated – well out of town, on the road from London, and next to an inn where horses could be stabled and servants lodged.[1]

Cross the London Road at the lights, turn left and then right up Brunswick Street, originally known as Cornwall Street. The houses on the left-hand side date from the late eighteenth century and are similar

Brunswick Street steps

to those in Church Street on Bathwick Hill, which were built around the same time. Today, they are very desirable properties, changing hands for nearly half a million pounds. In the 1950s, however, similar houses on Snow Hill were condemned as 'unfit for human habitation' and demolished. It is only because public opinion gradually turned against the wholesale clearance of old buildings that the houses on Brunswick Street did not share their fate.

Brunswick Street was intended to lead up to Hanover Square – another name borrowed from London. Instead, a flight of steps leads up to terraces built, like the east side of Brunswick Street, in the late nineteenth century.[2] **At the top of the steps, turn left and left again down Snow Hill for 25 metres, to stand opposite the road leading to Bennett's Lane and Dover Place.** Above you are some of the Georgian terraces that survived the devastation of the 1950s and 1960s. Below you, however – at the heart of a World Heritage city – nothing is more than 60 years old. Remarkably, given how badly other parts of Bath were hit, only one bomb fell in the Snow Hill area during the Bath Blitz of 1942. It landed in the road opposite where you are standing, destroying two houses on the left, where an archway now stands, and damaging several others.

1 While preparing this book for print, I was informed that the previous owners of No 10 Lambridge, an elegant villa further along the London Road, believed that their house, which dates from around the same time as York Villa, had originally been a high-class brothel. There is a high incidence of place names along the London Road taken from districts in London, such as Piccadilly, Grosvenor and Kensington. Larkhall took its name from the Larkhall Inn, which seems to have been named after the Lark Hall pleasure gardens in Vauxhall. These correspondences suggest that the London Road may have been regarded as 'Little London' in the eighteenth century, with all that that entailed.

2 To avoid the steps, head east along the London Road, take the second left up Upper East Hayes, turn left along Kensington Gardens and left downhill for 25 metres at the end.

The children's playground just below you stands on the site of the independent's burial ground. Next to it was the New Inn, which opened around 1850 and once had its own brewery.

Cross over and walk along the road opposite. Go past the turning to Bennett's Lane to reach

The New Inn survived until 1966 and was the last of Snow Hill's pubs to close.

Dover Place. Just beyond it is the old boys' school, built in 1882, which later became an infants' school before closing in 2005. It now houses a nursery run by the Norland Nannies. As you walk back towards Dover Place, notice that the end house has a lancet window at the back, along with ammonites and a gargoyle at the side.

Dover Place – the only part of the old Snow Hill to survive – is a good place to reflect on what happened to the rest of it. Most of the buildings on Snow Hill dated from the last decade of the eighteenth century; others were added in the early nineteenth century. Although the area came through the Second World War largely unscathed, five years after the war the council applied to the government for a compulsory purchase order. There had been slum clearance schemes in Bath before, but these were not slums. When a public meeting was held in September 1950, passions were running high. Surprisingly, the heritage issue was not even mentioned. What concerned the objectors was that almost all the buildings – while they might have benefited from a makeover – were well-built and provided perfectly adequate homes for hundreds of people. In all, 210 properties were scheduled for demolition. Eighty-two of the owners objected and were represented at the meeting by a lawyer called William Huntley, an ex-alderman of Bath. The council was represented by a lawyer called Herrick Collins.

'The city council,' Collins told the meeting, 'have considered the matter with great deliberation and they appreciate that hardship and inconvenience will be involved but they are merely carrying out the statutory procedure which has been laid down in the act.' With regard to compensation, he explained that, as the houses had been declared unfit for human habitation, 'it is part of the law of the land that the local authority shall pay the site value only of unfit houses … It is … not right that the ratepayers' money shall be paid out for houses which are worn out and are no longer fit for habitation … The houses are 120-150 years old and worn out … Homes are a wasting asset and do not last for ever.'

He was also critical of the design of Snow Hill. 'What a terrible layout has been instituted here,' he declared. 'Houses have been built with no consideration of access, which is often by way of unpaved paths or broken steps. Houses are built across the contours of the land and if one house is pulled down it places the rest of the row in jeopardy.' Sixty years on, the residents of Dover Place and Highbury Terrace, along with many other hidden corners of Georgian Bath, seem quite happy with the sort of inadequate access slated by Collins. As for his second point, pulling down one of the houses in a Georgian terrace, especially one on a steep hillside, is never a good idea, whether you are talking about two-storey townhouses or Palladian showpieces.

Alderman Huntley replied that none of the houses were unfit for human habitation. Architects and surveyors had inspected the properties and confirmed that they were essentially sound and fit to live in. A local doctor, called to give evidence, said that the incidence of illness in the area was no different to that in the rest of the city. Alderman Huntley went on to accuse the council of 'a cynical and dishonest attempt to avoid paying anything at all for the buildings they seek to acquire', claiming that they were 'guilty of a gross abuse of their powers'. He thought it iniquitous that the council would pay 'only a fraction of their market value, which is substantial … Some of these houses are occupied by their owners, but the majority are let to tenants, many of whom are in humble financial circumstances; the rentals are very low indeed. It is thought that few of these tenants would be willing to pay the much higher rentals in municipally provided houses, while many of them would be quite unable to do so and would suffer great hardship if compelled to move … This area, while far from ideal, is performing a useful function in a period of housing shortage; to demolish it would be criminally foolish.'

Mr Huntley's attack on the council achieved nothing, except the temporary reprieve of a few buildings in Dover Terrace on the London Road, and the bulldozers moved in.

Walk down the steps opposite Dover Place, turn left at the bottom and cross Snow Hill to where a telephone box is set back from the road.[1] This was the heart of the old Snow Hill, the point at which it was crossed by Dover Street. Directly below you was East Walcot Infants' School. Across the road was Adams' fish and chip shop; a little further up, on the other side of Dover Street, was Maynard's grocer's. Young's bakery was just around the corner. That was in 1952. Five years later, all had gone, along with most of the people that had patronised them.

In September 1957, when Berkeley House, the tower block opposite, was nearing completion, Alderman Sam Day declared that it 'showed the high class of architecture we have in Bath as well as the quality of building

---

1 To avoid the steps, walk back along the road to Snow Hill and turn right downhill.

which the city requires'. Referring to those who had labelled it a 'folly', a 'monstrosity' and a 'blot on the landscape', he claimed that 'when the scheme is complete it will be one of the best features in the city.'

Berkeley House was designed, along with the rest of Snow Hill, by Terry Snailum of Snailum, Huggins & Le Fevre.[1] He described it as 'a tall point block to provide a visual focus for the scheme of long terraces of flats and maisonettes along the contours of the hillside'. Copper roofs, which rapidly turned green, were one of his trademarks, and can also be found on the buildings he designed for King Edward's School on North Road.

The completion of Berkeley House on 31 December 1957 was reported by the *Bath Chronicle* in a style usually associated with old newsreel commentaries:

> The 100 feet high skyscraper block of flats, Bath's tallest modern building, rising for eleven storeys above the Snow Hill slopes at Walcot, was finished by the builders on the last day of the old year, the promised date. Eager prospective tenants, whose names are on the council housing list, climbed up and down its staircases, their paint still wet, choosing homes on the morning of New Year's Day. The electric lift with its automatic doors, which will carry up their furniture soon, was not in operation until this morning.

The report added that from the top floor, on a clear day, 'eastward it is possible to see as far as Atworth'.

Much of the area had yet to be developed, however. Most of it was waste land with odd houses still occupied between empty and derelict properties. The following August, councillors highlighted the plight of the people hanging on in these old properties 'with uncertain futures'. There were calls to build terraced houses instead of more flats, as they would cost less and rents would be lower.

Among the buildings still standing was a pub called the Berkeley Arms in Berkeley Street, which ran roughly where the row of flats below you stands today. When it opened in the 1790s it was known as the Half Moon and stood in Half Moon Street. The street was renamed around 1870 and the pub changed its name about 20 years later. When it closed in 1962, only one pub was left on Snow Hill – the New Inn, whose site you saw earlier. This survived – one of the last buildings of the old Snow Hill to be bulldozed – until 1966. On the last night, the loyal band of regulars presented the landlord, Frederick Kean-Lowe, with four brandy goblets as a memory of happier days.

Carry on down Snow Hill to where a side road branches off to the left. This is where Berkeley Street once ran. On the corner was another pub, whose name – the Coachmakers' Arms – suggests that workers from

---

1 In 1972, when the partnership had changed to Snailum, Le Fevre & Quick, it was responsible for the Beaufort Hotel – now the Hilton – in Walcot Street.

Vezey's factory were regular customers. To your right, Walcot House covers much of the site of Weymouth Square.

Walk to the bottom of Snow Hill and turn right along the London Road to the alleyway beside the old Longacre Tavern. This alleyway once led to a terrace known as Pleasant Place. Its current dereliction is an eloquent testimony to the changes this area has seen. It was here, in the early hours of New Year's Day 2007, that there was a fatal stabbing which shocked Bath and made the national headlines. This part of the city has had a lot to put with over the last 60 years or so: Georgian properties, which today would be highly sought after, demolished, their owners paid a pittance in compensation; people who had lived here all their lives uprooted and forced to move. More recently, the problems have been those familiar to many inner-city areas: shops closing as supermarkets leach trade from independent retailers, the deterioration of social housing stock, withdrawal of community facilities, pubs closing, lack of initiatives or investment to reverse decades of neglect. Not that there aren't plenty of local people who care deeeply about the area and are committed to making it a better place to live and work.

In the 1970s it seemed as though the Walcot Community Association in Longacre Hall would be the catalyst for the regeneration so vital to Snow Hill's future. Its closure in the late 1990s was a major setback, but after years of it lying empty a group called the Friends of Longacre Hall are now hoping to reopen it as a community hub.[1] The restoration of Longacre Hall would be a major step towards reviving some of the optimism which accompanied the completion of Berkeley House, and of restoring the sense of community that was so savagely destroyed in the clearances that preceded it.

To end this walk on a rather less reflective note, look across the road to a building whose Greek-Revival portico is surmounted by a bust of Aesculapius, God of Healing. Today, it is an undertaker's; the bust dates

from when it was an Ear & Eye Infirmary – if the light is right, the name of the infirmary can still be made out on the side wall. It only became an infirmary in 1837, however, and the presence of a cold bath underneath the floor indicates it was originally a bath house, with the portico added later. If that was the case, then Hawthorn House and Hawthorn Cottage could well have been ancillary buildings, like those at Larkhall Spa.

Carry on across the bottom of Thomas Street, past the superbly restored King William pub, cross at the traffic lights, turn right to cross the traffic lights at Cleveland Place and head on to Walcot Street to return to the city centre.

1 For more information see www.baka.co.uk/longacre/

15

WHERE EVERY PROSPECT PLEASES
With Jane Austen on Beechen Cliff
(or Whose Heritage is it Anyway?)

Distance *2.5 miles.*

Time *2-3 hours.*

Accessibility *This walk includes steps and footpaths which may be muddy*

Public toilets *Alexandra Park (on the west side of the park 75 metres south of the path along Beechen Cliff).*

Starting point *Kingston Parade (outside Visitor Information Centre).*

> *For the eye to distinguish the particular buildings of the city ... such as would view them more distinctly must ascend to the summit of Beaching Cliff, looking down from which, Bath will appear to them much the same that Virgil declares Carthage to have appeared to Aeneas.*
> John Wood, 1742

> *We shape our buildings, and afterwards our buildings shape us.*
> Winston Churchill, 1943

Our last walk is one that many may consider should have come first. A guidebook published just over a century ago advised visitors arriving in Bath by train to head straight for 'the famous Beechen Cliff view which has ever afforded delight and surprise to the stranger', adding that, 'from this precipitous brow the marvellous view of the city is brought within optical range with a suddenness that partakes of the dramatic'.

One reason it has been kept till last is that today the view from Beechen Cliff is dominated by late-twentieth and early twenty-first century buildings. Beechen Cliff itself, though visible from most parts of Bath, is a strange and surprisingly little-frequented place. It should be one of the most popular spots in the city, but more often than not it is deserted. Jane Austen, the tutelary deity of Bath's tourist industry, may be partly responsible for this, having made Catherine Morland, the heroine of *Northanger Abbey*, climb its slopes only to reject 'the whole city of Bath as unworthy to make part of a landscape'.

It has changed a bit since Miss Austen's day, of course. Until the late nineteenth century, the slopes of Beechen Cliff were grazed by horses and donkeys and much of it was treeless. About a century ago, it was acquired by the corporation, who set about smartening it up. Inspired by the cliff

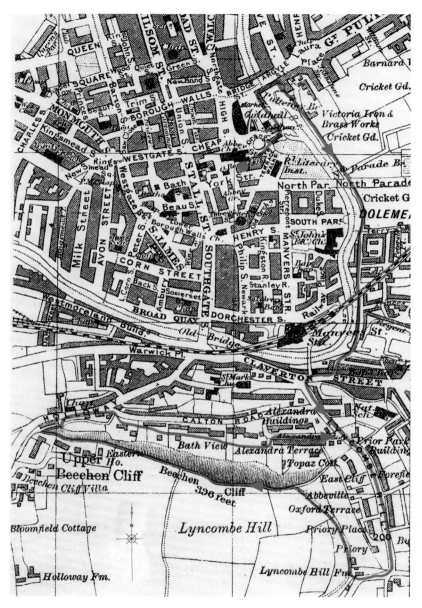

walks at Bournemouth, they planted pines and rhododendrons, created viewing platforms and even toyed with the idea of building a cliff railway.

Today, though, the slopes planted with such care a century ago are sadly neglected. Instead of pines and beeches, ash and sycamore predominate, with brambles filling the spaces in between, so that the views now are

A map of 1795 showing the riverside route Catherine Morland would have followed from Bathwick to Widcombe

The maze mosaic

largely hidden, while the steps Victorian visitors climbed to the summit get more uneven and dangerous every year. Twenty-first-century tourism seems to have left Beechen Cliff behind.

So let us turn to the past, to recreate that imaginary journey taken by Jane Austen's naïve young heroine one fine morning in 1797 or thereabouts. The only clue Jane Austen gives us as to the route Catherine – accompanied by Henry and Eleanor Tilney – took from Great Pulteney Street to Beechen Cliff is that they walked 'along the side of the river'. **From the Visitor Information Centre, head past the Abbey, across Orange Grove, along Grand Parade and across Pulteney Bridge, before turning right down the steps at the end of the bridge.** Catherine Morland would not have used these steps, which only become a through route in the twentieth century; she would probably have come through the tunnel from Grove Street.

Emerging from the tunnel, she would have seen Pulteney Bridge as well as the back of the buildings in Argyle Street and Laura Place. She would also have seen the building to the right of the Boater's beer garden, with rubble-stone foundations and a timber upper-storey. The beer garden itself was a yard – probably a timber yard. As she continued, she would have passed Spring Gardens, still open but a shadow of its former self. The development of Argyle and Johnstone Streets meant that it was next to a building site. Not only that, it had been open since 1735, was tired and unfashionable and had several rivals, notably the state-of-the-art Sydney Gardens, which so captivated Jane Austen. No trace of Spring Gardens survives, although a maze with a jolly mosaic at its centre now stands on part of the site.

Catherine would have passed a mill beside the weir, which looked across to another mill on the far bank. Beyond this there were no more buildings, nor any bridges. On the far bank she would have seen North and South Parades high above the river, with a flight of steps from South Parade down to a ferry. The ferry has long gone but its memory is kept alive, on this side of the river at least, by Ferry Lane, which you pass on the left.

Past South Parade, there were no buildings on the far bank either. Ralph Allen's tramway, which ran down to a wharf on the river a little further along, had been dismantled some 30 years earlier, but the wharf would probably have still been in operation. The canal which joins the river on the approach to Widcombe, however, had yet to be built.

Just past the canal, the way ahead is blocked by a busy road. Catherine Morland would have carried straight on – the road is less than 50 years old – to emerge onto Widcombe's main street. We, however, have to **turn right along the road, walk along to the pedestrian lights, cross the dual carriageway, turn right and then left up Lyncombe Hill.** Although you have now rejoined the route that Catherine Morland would have taken, this is where the problems begin. From here, there were – and still are – two ways to approach Beechen Cliff – from the west or from the east, and Jane Austen gave no indication which one Catherine Morland took.

Approaching it from the west would have involved walking up Holloway, one of Bath's less salubrious streets and hardly likely to have been frequented by the likes of Jane Austen or Catherine Morland. That leaves the eastern approach, but here too there are a couple of alternatives. The earliest guidebook giving precise directions to Beechen Cliff – *Rambles About Bath*, published in 1889 – informed visitors that 'the best way of reaching it is by the lane behind Pope's Villa, at the bottom of Lyncombe Hill'. This, of course, was almost a century after Catherine Morland's visit and much had changed. The lane referred to can be found on a map of 1852 but does not appear on earlier maps. The first part of it – between Calton and Alexandra Roads – has been closed off, but the rest of it – although no longer a lane – is still a right of way. When houses were built alongside it in the late nineteenth century, it was turned into a path with several flights of steps and acquired the name Jacob's Ladder. These steps are very steep in places and are now very uneven, making for a somewhat arduous climb.

If this route was not available to Jane Austen's heroine, she would have had to continue up Lyncombe Hill, and this leaves two possibilities. Lyncombe Hill was a long-established and well-frequented thoroughfare, leading to Lyncombe Spa and King James's Palace pleasure gardens. The houses that line it today had, for the most part, yet to appear in 1797, and there is a possibility that Catherine Morland would have taken a path that disappeared when the west side of the road was developed in the early nineteenth century. If you look at the map on the opposite page you

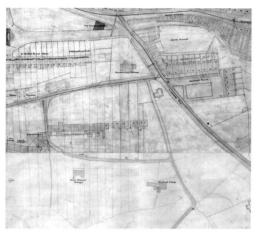
The lane to Beechen Cliff on a map of 1852

will see that the lane that became Jacob's Ladder makes a right-angled turn partway up. You will also see that a boundary wall continues the line of the lane eastward. This suggests that there may have been a way through here which was closed off and absorbed into a private garden. In the absence of documentary evidence, however, this must remain conjecture.

There is, however, another route which not only follows an old path, but leads through fields that have changed little since Jane Austen's day. **Carry on up Lyncombe Hill.** After passing Alexandra Road, there is a high retaining wall on the right, built when villas arose behind it in the early nineteenth century. If there was once a way through here it would have been roughly opposite the garage beyond No 37.

Carry on to the end of Lyncombe Hill, turn right along Greenway Lane for 75 metres and go through a kissing gate on the right. On your right – with a corrugated-iron roof substituted for the original thatch – is a barn which may date from Tudor times, making it one of the oldest buildings in the city. Walk up the path directly ahead. There are some splendid views across the valley from here, but gradually the trees close in and you are left with the illusion of being in the heart of the country, albeit with the racket of a twenty-first-century city for accompaniment.

The path curves slowly up to a kissing gate where you join the path from Jacob's Ladder. Turn left and carry on uphill to Alexandra Park, named after Edward VII's queen and opened in 1902. It was originally going to be covered with houses – part of the Poet's Corner estate – until the council bought it for £4,000.

From the viewing platform on your right the city lies spread out below you. This is the view dismissed so peremptorily by Catherine Morland – a dismissal that requires a little explanation. Long before reaching Beechen Cliff, she tells Henry Tilney that she never looks at it 'without thinking of the south of France.'

When he expresses surprise that she has been abroad – Britain had, after all, been at war with France since 1793 – she replies that her knowledge of France is based on the descriptions in *The Mysteries of Udolpho*, a popular Gothic novel. This sparks a debate on the respective merits of novels and historical writing which leads to a discussion of notions of the Picturesque. Although the Tilneys both seem well informed on the subject, Catherine is not:

> They were viewing the country with the eyes of persons accustomed to drawing, and decided on its capability of being formed into pictures, with all the eagerness of real taste. Here Catherine was quite lost. She knew nothing of drawing – nothing of taste: and she listened to them with an attention which brought her little profit, for they talked in phrases which conveyed scarcely any idea to her. The little which she could understand, however, appeared to contradict the very few notions she had entertained on the matter before. It seemed as if a good view were no longer to be taken from the top of an high hill, and that a clear blue sky was no longer a proof of a fine day. She was heartily ashamed of her ignorance.

Under Henry's tutelage, however, she becomes a willing pupil:

> She confessed and lamented her want of knowledge, declared that she would give anything in the world to be able to draw; and a lecture on the picturesque immediately followed, in which his instructions were so clear that she soon began to see beauty in everything admired by him, and her attention was so earnest that he became perfectly satisfied of her having a great deal of natural taste. He talked of foregrounds, distances, and second distances – side-screens and perspectives – lights and shades; and Catherine was so hopeful a scholar that when they gained the top of Beechen Cliff, she voluntarily rejected the whole city of Bath as unworthy to make part of a landscape. Delighted with her progress, and fearful of wearying her with too much wisdom at once, Henry suffered the subject to decline, and by an easy transition from a piece of rocky fragment and the withered oak which he had placed near its summit, to oaks in general, to forests, the enclosure of them, waste lands, crown lands and government, he shortly found himself arrived at politics; and from politics, it was an easy step to silence.

Henry's opinions, which Catherine is so eager to concur with, are drawn from one of the most influential aesthetic theorists of the age, Uvedale Price. He too had little time for Georgian Bath:

> I remember my disappointment the first time I approached Bath, notwithstanding the beauty of the stone with which it is built, and of many of the parts on a nearer view. Whoever considers what are the forms of the summits, how little the buildings are made to yield to the ground, and how few trees are mixed with them, will account for my disappointment, and probably lament the cause of it.

It was Price and people like him who made the city of eighteenth-century Palladian terraces unfashionable, spurned by those whose aesthetic judgements were often no more soundly based than Catherine Morland's. The nineteenth century would see the hills around Bath developed along lines laid down by the pioneers of the Picturesque movement – leafy suburbs with secluded villas embowered in trees.

Although Jane Austen leaves us in no doubt as to the naïveté of Catherine's dismissal of the view from Beechen Cliff, she herself echoed

Price's remarks in a letter to her sister in May 1801: 'The first view of Bath in fine weather does not answer my expectations; I think I see more distinctly through rain. The sun was got behind everything, and the appearance of the place from the top of Kingsdown was all vapour, shadow, smoke, and confusion.' This suggests that her well-known antipathy to the city was due at least in part to an espousal of the picturesque.

The view dismissed by Catherine Morland was very different to the one you see today, however, with the foreground dominated by something that would probably have given Henry Tilney apoplexy – the new Southgate shopping centre. Apart from the Abbey, it is difficult to find many points of contact between then and now. The tower of St James's church in Stall Street, which would have dominated the foreground, was demolished in 1957, while the spires of St Michael's and St John's, so prominent today, were not built until well into the nineteenth century.

Looking beyond the old city, Catherine Morland would have seen the Paragon curving away, and behind it Camden Crescent, still with the ruins of its eastern end isolated on a bleak promontory. She would also have seen the Circus – now identifiable chiefly from the enormous trees in the centre – as well as the Royal Crescent and Lansdown Crescent. To the east, Great Pulteney Street, in all its shining newness, would have stretched to Sydney Gardens, but beyond that there would have been little, apart from some sporadic development along the London Road, except woods and fields.

Today the view to the east is dominated by the green roofs of Snow Hill, while to the west, beyond the CD drum of the bus station, are more monolithic blocks, punctuated by ranks of parked cars. But as you look, the shock of the new recedes as you begin to take in the wider picture. The colour of Bath stone predominates as it did over two centuries ago. The surrounding hills are as verdant as ever and the Georgian terraces and crescents still seem to stand on the edge of the country.

When Nash, Allen and Wood arrived in Bath, the city lay behind high walls, skirted by green fields. By the end of the eighteenth century, they – and those inspired by them – had transformed it beyond all recognition, but, although much of the Georgian city has survived, any continuity between the view Catherine Morland would have seen and the view you see today is tenuous at best, and the noise of trains, planes and automobiles is a constant backdrop.

Bath from Beechen Cliff in 1724

The distant hills may not have changed much, nor the lines of Georgian buildings, but what you see before you is emphatically a modern city.

If you **walk along past the viewing platform** and look down to the right, you will see one of the finest panoramas of the city, with the railway

Looking eastward

Faced with the new Southgate, how many of today's visitors to Beechen Cliff feel inclined to reject 'the whole city of Bath as unworthy to make part of a landscape"?

crossing the river in the foreground, the spire of St John's to the left and, in the distance, Bathwick, Larkhall and the hills around Batheaston. A little further along, a gap in the trees gives an unrivalled view of the new Southgate – a shopping centre like so many others, with the same shops, except that here it has been encased in a gossamer-thin veneer of what passes for Bath stone. Panned for being neo-, mock- or – in Alan Bennett's telling phrase – Kentucky-Fried Georgian, from here, you can see that Southgate is nothing of the sort. It harks back to a far more recent architectural tradition, developed in the late nineteenth century by the builders of seaside piers. The twin towers on the central building, in particular, look as though they were modelled on the entrance to the Garden Pier – no longer with us – in Atlantic City, New Jersey.

Costive neoclassicism – like Jane Austen re-imagined by Barbara Cartland – has laid a heavy hand on the city and still seems to hold it in thrall. After all the technological advances of the past two centuries, with all the new materials that have been developed, all the architects that have transformed our relationship to buildings, we fall back on aping the Georgians and not doing it very well.

That is not to say that drawing inspiration from the past is a bad thing. John Wood and his contemporaries looked back to Palladio and what they believed to be the origins of architecture; the Victorians were more

The view from Beechen Cliff a century ago. Virtually all the buildings in the foreground and middle distance have gone.

eclectic, looking back to the Gothic, to the Italian, to anything that took their fancy. And Edwin Lutyens, regarded by many as Britain's greatest architect, developed a style rooted in a reinterpretation of the vernacular. None of which justifies, however, the lazy application of second- or third-hand ideas.

If architecture is, as Goethe claimed, frozen music, we can perhaps extend the analogy – with the Circus thawed out as Handel's *Zadok the Priest*, the Royal Crescent as the finale of Mozart's *Jupiter Symphony*, Lansdown Crescent as Rossini's overture to *The Barber of Seville*, Cavendish Place as the slow movement of Schubert's *Death and the Maiden Quartet*, Beckford's Tower as Liszt's *Années de pèlerinage* ... and the new Southgate as Richard Clayderman plays Andrew Lloyd Webber.

As you **carry on along the path**, you come to a toposcope, installed in the 1930s. Many of the buildings marked on it have gone, lost to bombs or bulldozers, many more are now hidden by trees. To the west, you won't see Prospect Stile or Kelston Round Hill; to the east not only is Sham Castle hidden from view, but you cannot see St John's church, Sydney Gardens or the Parades. You will also look in vain for St James's church, the old Avon Street, Holy Trinity or St Andrew's – all long gone, while the LMS station, although it survives, saw its last train pull out in 1966.

Much of what catches the eye from here does not feature on the toposcope. Directly below and leading steeply downhill are St Mary's Buildings. Beyond them is Camden Mill and the red-brick Bayer Corset Factory. Beyond that, on the far side of the river, modernity predominates in the form of Kingsmead Flats, the City of Bath College, Kingsmead House and a soon-to-be-demolished telephone exchange. On the northern slopes, however, are some of Bath's most iconic buildings – Camden Crescent, Gay Street leading to the clump of trees at the heart of the Circus, the Royal Crescent, Cavendish Crescent and Lansdown Crescent, flanked by Lansdown Place East and West, half hidden by trees. Beyond are the encircling hills, thick with trees, the essential part of the composition.

As you carry on along the path, lined with houses enjoying some of the most stunning views in Bath, you can observe a curious reversal of architectural history. In the early eighteenth century, gables gave way to parapets; here you can see how, a century and a half later, parapets were ousted by gables.

After passing another viewing platform with its view obliterated by tall trees (not to mention a vigorous buddleia), the path swings to the right down a flight of steps. A second flight of steps leads to the entrance to Magdalen Gardens, one of Bath's

Magdalen Gardens on a 1920s postcard

most profoundly forgotten corners. When it was laid out a century ago, its views were celebrated, its flowerbeds tended and children played on its manicured lawns. Today, a solitary and rarely-occupied bench looks across scrubby grass to where banks of laurel blot out the view in this little-known, abandoned park.

Carry on down the path to emerge on Holloway, the ancient road into Bath from the south. 'Or ever I came to the bridge of Bath that is over Avon,' wrote John Leland in 1530, 'I came down by a rocky hill full of fair springs of water: and on this rocky hill is set a long street as a suburb to the city of Bath; and in this street is a chapel of St Mary Magdalen.' To find the chapel, **turn right past a recently-restored horse trough and walk downhill.** It once served a leper hospital founded in the eleventh century. After falling into ruin, the hospital was demolished in 1761 and replaced by Magdalen Cottage, originally a home for the mentally handicapped. The chapel dates from the

The chapel of St Mary Magdalen

late fifteenth century, but, after being altered and extended several times, was partly destroyed by bombing in 1942 and had to be rebuilt.

Next to Magdalen Cottage is Paradise House, built in the mid-eighteenth century and distinguished by two splendid Venetian windows, as well as a polychromatic Victorian extension and modern attic storey.

Below Paradise House lay one of the most vibrant, labyrinthine and architecturally eclectic bits of Bath – a bit run-down in parts, but with buildings dating back to the seventeenth century if not earlier. Although German bombers managed to knock out one or two chunks, it survived more or less intact until the late 1960s when the whole lot was razed to the ground and what we see today arose in its place. One of the few reminders of the old Holloway can be seen opposite Paradise House – a gap in the wall where a couple of steps led up to a cottage destroyed by bombing in 1942.

Just past this **turn right through a row of concrete bollards, right up a flight of steps by a litter bin, and then left along a path leading to another flight of steps. At the top of the flight, carry on, and, when you reach the bottom of the next long flight of steps, turn left along a path through the woods.** This takes you past the site of ruined cottages, with fragments of walls and piles of

Holloway decorated for George V's Silver Jubilee in 1935

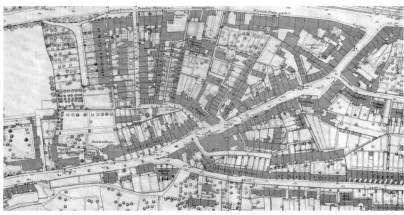

Holloway, identified on this Ordnance Survey map from the 1880s as the Fosse Way. The buildings shaded green are the only ones to survive today.

stones and bricks in the undergrowth. After about 60 metres you come to a clearing where a long, low wall has been brightly spray-painted. If you look up to the right you will see another ruined wall at right angles to the

hillside. Above it, half hidden in the undergrowth, is a far more extraordinary survival – the skeletal remains of an Anderson shelter.[1] Named after Sir John Anderson, who was in charge of Air Raid Precautions in the Second World War, these were distributed free to poorer households; families with a weekly income of more than £5 could buy one for £7. They consisted of six curved sheets of metal bolted together with steel plates at either end and could accommodate up to six people. When this one was assembled here in the dark days of World War Two, the walls that now stand ruinous formed part of cottages. The spray-painted one was Bryne's Terrace, a row of four with carefully-tended gardens front and back. A little farther along was a row of three called Beautiful View – as it would have been, for there were few trees to get in the way. These cottages survived the Bath Blitz, only to fall victim to the bulldozer. It is astonishing to think how decisively nature has reclaimed this bit of suburban Bath in less than 50 years.

> Dust in the air suspended
> Marks the place where a story ended.
> Dust inbreathed was a house –
> The wall, the wainscot and the mouse.

Our difficulties in imagining what Catherine Morland would have seen from the top of Beechen Cliff are nothing to the difficulty of imagining what it must have like on those two nights in April 1942 when the residents of long-forgotten cottages crouched in their Anderson shelters as the ground shook with the impact of bombs and the sky shone bright with unfriendly fire. There is little now to recall those two nights 70 years ago – a few Bath stone walls pockmarked with shrapnel, lines of graves, names on a memorial ... This Anderson shelter is one of the more potent reminders, yet it is deteriorating more rapidly with every passing year. Soon there will be nothing left to see on this remote and little-frequented way through the woods. Yet the Bath Blitz is as much a part of the city's heritage as Jane Austen or John Wood. The reasons Bath was targeted will probably never be fully known – there was plenty of industry and

---

1 If you are tempted to scramble up for a closer look, be aware that the route can be treacherous, especially after rain, and the way down is trickier than the way up.

important war work going on in the city, as well as three major railway lines. Yet many believe these were 'Baedeker Raids' – carried out with the sole purpose of destroying Bath's heritage – which would have been a terrible price to pay for something so intangible.

Whatever the motives behind the raids of 1942, it remains true that if something is worth preserving it is also worth destroying, if only to discompose those who wish to preserve it. Sadly, it is not just Britain's enemies who have targeted Bath's buildings; since the Second World War they have come under attack many times – from developers, councillors, speculators and those obsessed with clearing away the detritus of the past in order to begin afresh. Too often they have got their way.

A city without history is a city without a future. Just as individuals learn from their experiences and the precepts handed down to them, so communities cohere and grow on the basis of common heritage and shared experience. Those that do not, disintegrate – or, to use current terminology, become dysfunctional.

Bath's heritage is under attack on two fronts: from those who seek to expunge the past – on the grounds that it is holding the city back – and those who want to turn the city into a theme park or a gallimaufry of photo opportunities for tourists. Which poses a greater threat is difficult to say, for often they seem to be working in tandem. Creating fantasy worlds from a selective distortion of an imagined past is perhaps a more insidious threat because of the difficulty of perceiving it as a threat. Heritage is a living, breathing and constantly redefined dialogue between past, present and future or it is nothing. And if it is a rose-tinted simulacrum, a shadow of an illusion decked out in frills and furbelows and wallowing in misperceived imaginings, it is less than nothing.

Paul Farley and Michael Symmons Roberts, in *Edgelands*, their illuminating contribution to our literature of place, claim that 'the heritage industry tends to rely on a kind of freeze-framing of time in order to present the tourist and visitor with a reordered, partial, tidied-up account of what happened at a particular site.' By contrast, edgeland sites like this, where the graffiti-covered walls of forgotten houses stand beside a disintegrating Anderson shelter, 'contain a collage of time … Encountering the decay and abandonment of these places is to be made more aware than ever that we are only passing through; that there is something much bigger than us.'

Continue along the track – a woodland walk through lost gardens, past the ruins of old cottages – with the noises of the invisible city echoing through the trees. **When the path forks, take the left-hand, more-travelled path – where you may have to negotiate a fallen tree – to emerge on a patch of grass by a children's playground. Turn right along Alexandra Road, past the bottom of Jacob's Ladder, and turn left down Lyncombe Hill to retrace your steps one last time to the starting point.**

ACKNOWLEDGEMENTS

First and foremost, thanks must go to my wife, Kirsten Elliott, who first opened my eyes to the beauty of Bath and was the inspiration behind these walks. On a more practical note, she undertook the task of proof reading and made many valuable suggestions, as well as taking several of the photographs.

Thanks must also go to Colin Johnston and the staff at the Bath Record Office who not only helped me track down much of the information but also allowed me to reproduce the old maps on pages 11, 12, 21, 31, 46, 51, 62, 107, 116, 117, 134, 151, 152, 175, 183, 189, 252 (bottom), 265, 267. Thanks also to the Somerset Record Office for permission to reproduce the top map on page 252; to Mary Warne for information on old businesses along the London Road, to Margaret Burrows for information on 10 Lambridge; to Roger Holly for information on the Larkhall Inn; and to many others, too numerous to mention, who provided me with information and ideas which have found their way into the walks.

Shorter versions of some of the walks first appeared in *The Bath Magazine*, and I am grateful for permission to reproduce them here.

As for the illustrations, thanks to Geoffrey Hiscocks for the photo of the Scala on p245; Stuart Burroughs of the Museum of Bath at Work for the photos of Avon Street on p74 and Longacre Hall on p257; Mr & Mrs EJ Fry for the photos of 3 Dover Terrace on p257; Mary Warne for the photo of 6 Dover Terrace on p257; Bruce Crofts for the old photos of St James's Square on p84 and Pulteney Bridge on p153; Sam Farr for the photos on p98; Nick Cudworth and photographer Peter Stone for the picture of the Corn Market on p100; Dr Karen Francis for the photo of the Walcot Street dartboard on p106; Steve Lord for the photo of Axford's Buildings on p113; Colin Johnston of Bath Record Office for the photos of Fielding's Lodge on p205, the old prison on p247 and Snow Hill on p253; Paul De'Ath for the photo of Twerton Lower Mills on p210; and Christopher Wheeler for the photo of Brougham Hayes on p204. The rest of the illustrations are from the Akeman Press Archive.

FURTHER READING

Hundreds of books have been written about Bath and the recommendations that follow represent only a tiny fraction of them. The best introduction to the city and its history is *Bath* by Kirsten Elliott, with photographs by Neil Menneer, published by Frances Lincoln in 2004. For an introduction to the city's architecture, the *Pevsner Architectural Guide to Bath* by Michael Forsyth, published by Yale University Press in 2003, is indispensable. Both books combine scholarship and an in-depth knowledge of the city with a readable, approachable style and should be on the shelves of anyone even remotely interested in the city. Of the many other excellent books, these are a few that I have found especially useful:

General Books on Bath

Christopher Pound, *Genius of Bath: The City and its Landscape*, Bath, 1986

Barry Cunliffe, *The City of Bath*, Gloucester, 1986

Peter Borsay, *The Image of Georgian Bath 1700-2000*, Oxford, 2000

Andrew Swift & Kirsten Elliott, *Awash with Ale: 2000 Years of Imbibing in Bath*, Bath, 2004

Graham Davis & Penny Bonsall, *A History of Bath: Image and Reality*, Lancaster, 2006

Architecture

Mowbray A Green, *The Eighteenth Century Architecture of Bath*, Bath, 1904

Bryan Little, *The Buildings of Bath*, London, 1947

Walter Ison, *The Georgian Buildings of Bath*, London, 1948

Charles Robertson, *Bath: An Architectural Guide*, London, 1975

James Stevens Curl, *Georgian Architecture*, Newton Abbot, 1993

Neil Jackson, *Nineteenth Century Bath: Architects and Architecture*, Bath, 1991

Kirsten Elliott, *The Mythmaker: John Wood, 1704-1754*, Bath, 2004

Elizabeth Devon, John Parkins & David Workman, *Bath in Stone: A Guide to the City's Building Stones*, Kingston Bagpuize, 2001

Jonathan Holt, *Somerset Follies*, Bath, 2007

Eighteenth Century Social Life

RS Neale, *Bath: A Social History, 1680-1850: or A Valley of Pleasure yet a Sink of Iniquity*, London, 1981

Rev John Penrose (edited by Brigitte Mitchell & Hubert Penrose), *Letters from Bath, 1766-1767*, Gloucester, 1983

Mark Girouard, *The English Town*, New Haven & London, 1990

Trevor Fawcett, *Voices of Georgian Bath*, Bath, 1995

Books on other historical periods

Barry Cunliffe, *Roman Bath Discovered*, London, 1971

Peter Davenport, *Medieval Bath Uncovered*, Stroud, 2002

John Wroughton, *Tudor Bath: Life and Strife in the Little City*, Bath, 2006

John Wroughton, *Stuart Bath: Life in the Forgotten City, 1603-1714*, Bath, 2004

John Wroughton, *A Community at War: The Civil War in Bath and North Somerset, 1642-1650*, Bath, 1992

Andrew Swift & Kirsten Elliott, *The Year of the Pageant*, Bath, 2009

Andrew Swift, *All Roads Lead to France: Bath and the Great War*, Bath, 2005

Pauline Forrest, *Childhood Memories: Growing Up in Kingsmead and Weston*, Bath, 2008

Niall Rothnie, *The Bombing of Bath*, Bath, 1983

David & Jonathan Falconer, *Bath at War: The Home Front, 1939-1945*, Stroud, 2001

Adam Ferguson, *The Sack of Bath*, London, 1973, republished with a new preface, 2010

Books on specific areas
The Old City:

Mike Chapman & Elizabeth Holland, *The Spa Quarter of Bath: A History in Maps*, Bath, 2006

Bathwick:

Bathwick: A Forgotten Village, Bathwick Local History Society, Bath, 2004

Bathwick: Echoes of the Past, Bathwick Local History Society, Bath, 2008

Combe Down & Prior Park:

Combe Down History, Combe Down Townswomen's Guild, Bath, 1965

Keith Dallimore, *Exploring Combe Down*, Bath, 1988

Peter Addison, *Around Combe Down*, Bath, 1998

Derek Hawkins, *Subterranean Britain: Bath Stone Quarries*, Monkton Farleigh, 2011

Gillian Clarke, *Prior Park: A Compleat Landscape*, Bath, 1987

Lyncombe & Widcombe:

Maurice Scott, *Discovering Widcombe & Lyncombe*, Bath, 1993

Walcot & Larkhall:

A History of the Parish and Manor of Walcot, Walcot/Larkhall Townswomen's Guild, 1987

A History of the Parish and Manor of Walcot, Book 2, Walcot/Larkhall Townswomen's Guild, 1989

Weston:
A Weston Miscellany, Weston Townswomen's Guild, Bath, 1999
Weston Village Journal, Weston Local History Society, Bath 1998

Other aspects of the city:
Duncan Harper, *Bath at Work*, Bath, 1989
R Gilding, *Historic Public Parks: Bath*, Bristol, 1997
RA Buchanan, *The Industrial Archaeology of Bath*, Bath, 1969
Ken Andrews & Stuart Burroughs, *Stothert & Pitt: Cranemakers to the World*, Stroud, 2003
Kirsten Elliott, *Queen of Waters: A Journey in Time Along the Kennet & Avon Canal*, Bath, 2010
Andrew Swift, *The Ringing Grooves of Change: Brunel and the Coming of the Railway to Bath*, Bath, 2006
Colin G Maggs, *The Mangotsfield to Bath Line, including the Story of Green Park Station*, Usk, 2005
John Owen, *Life on the Railway*, Bath, 1989
Duncan Harper, *The Somerset & Dorset Railway: Opening of the Bath Extension, 1874*, Bath, 1998
Andrew Swift & Kirsten Elliott, *The Lost Pubs of Bath*, Bath, 2005

Bookshops
Bath is well supplied with bookshops, all of which stock a range of local titles. Apart from a branch of Waterstones in Milsom Street, the other bookshops are independent and can be found at the following locations:

Good Buy Books, North Parade (High-quality discounted titles plus an excellent range of local books)
Mr B's Emporium of Reading Delights, John Street (Independent Bookshop of the Year, 2008 & 2011)
Oldfield Park Bookshop (Popular bookshop in Moorland Road with a large range of local titles)
The Titfield Thunderbolt, Lambridge Street, Larkhall (Specialising in local books and transport titles).
Topping & Co, The Paragon (Enormous range of titles with a section devoted to local books)

There are also two excellent second-hand bookshops: Bath Old Books in Margaret's Buildings and George Bayntun in Manvers Street.

ALSO FROM AKEMAN PRESS

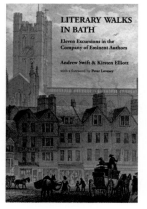

Few cities have been so celebrated in print as Bath – from Smollett to Jane Austen, from Dickens to Fanny Burney, and from Sheridan to Georgette Heyer. Many other famous writers have passed through as well – Mary Shelley wrote *Frankenstein* in a house in the Abbey Church Yard, Coleridge met his wife in the city, and in the twentieth century John Betjeman championed its architectural heritage. Even Shakespeare – or so it is believed – turned up to take a dip in the hot springs. These eleven walks look at Bath through their eyes, creating a vivid social history of the city over the last 300 years and bringing the past alive with unparalleled immediacy.

The Bath Pageant of 1909 was only one highlight of a momentous year. 1909 saw the birth of the welfare state and the dawn of mass motoring. Political crisis at Westminster was accompanied by a deep and growing recession, with millions of men thrown out of work. Over all hung the threat of German invasion and an escalating arms race. Closer to home, the battle to save Bath Street marked the birth of the Bath preservation movement, while the pageant marked the beginnings of Bath's transformation from faded health resort to heritage tourist destination. With chapters on shopping, employment, housing, suffragettes, transport, the media, street life, the Abode of Love and much more, this fascinating book records Bath's struggle to redefine its identity at the dawn of the modern age.

£15 each from Akeman Press
For a full list of titles visit *www.akemanpress.com*